Rutherford Studies in Historical Theology

Editors

DAVID F. WRIGHT
Senior Lecturer in Ecclesiastical History,
New College, University of Edinburgh

DONALD MACLEOD
Professor of Systematic Theology,
Free Church College, Edinburgh

Tertullian's Theology of Divine Power

RUTHERFORD STUDIES IN HISTORICAL THEOLOGY
RUTHERFORD STUDIES IN CONTEMPORARY THEOLOGY

A full listing of titles in these series appears at the end of this book.

Tertullian's Theology of Divine Power

Roy Kearsley

Published for Rutherford House

by

paternoster press

Typeset by Rutherford House, Edinburgh
and Printed by
Alpha Graphics, Nottingham

Dedication

To Jan

without whose encouragement there
would have been no author and no book

Contents

Preface

This book began life as a doctoral thesis in the University of Glasgow. The research for it originally yielded a work rather longer and thesis-looking than that which follows. An extensive re-draft has slimmed down the presentation by the editing of some sections and a summarising of many quotations particularly the longer ones and those not in English. On the other hand a more analytical summary has linked the work to concerns in theology today.

Tertullian's writings covered many subjects which are alive, well and commanding high intellectual endeavour in our times. These include topics treated today under such headings as authority, baptism, contextualisation, pluralism, nature, discipleship, charismatic gifts and Christianity's engagement with politics and culture. Some of his work, naturally, is dated. Much of it, however, is as trenchant, defiant and as engaging as the day it was written. His texts still receive attention in the departments of classicists and philosophers. This book intends only to make a small contribution to attempts to anchor modern theological discussions in the often neglected insights of the early Christian authors. Perhaps such attempts may remind a sometimes superior generation that there are few problems which are entirely without ancestry.

Acknowledgements

It is a special pleasure to record thanks to friends and colleagues who contributed so much to reducing the flaws in this book. My supervisor at the thesis stage, Professor John Zizioulas, not only tested and stretched my scholarship but kept me alert to the profound insights of Greek Orthodox theology. David Wright, former Dean of New College, Edinburgh, displayed superhuman patience with the unforgiving flow of proof flaws in several drafts. He was death to sloppy expression and typographical error. I am also indebted to my colleagues Rose Dowsett, David Graham, Rick Hess and Eddie Adams for highly professional proof-reading when college duties were at a demanding high.

The many flaws that remain are my very own work! For these and all other inadequacies I take full responsibility.

CHAPTER 1

Introduction: Tertullian Today

Most teachers in the field of early Christianity, its thought or life, recognise the importance of Tertullian in their work. Many devote as much class-time to him as to, say, Origen or Athanasius. Yet the last British book dedicated to the theological 'system' of Tertullian appeared seventy years ago,[1] the previous one four years before that.[2] Given the extensive research on Tertullian since then, an attempt to search for some roots of Tertullian's theological system seems almost innovative. There is another reason for turning back to him today. Some conservative Christian theologies are reeling from repeated and assorted allegations of religious imperialism and other forms of oppression. Not just feminist theology but also other concerned political theologies have turned in revulsion not only from church structures of power but also from the suspected real villain, namely the early teaching on God. According to these views, that science of God which projects upon the deity the absolute ambitions of state politics lies behind disreputable ecclesiologies now out of joint with the age of democrats and equals. Luther's *theologia crucis*, championed by him against a *theologia gloriae*, has germinated far beyond anything he imagined. And the blame for villainy now reaches right back to the notion of God as creator in the traditional sense and the absolutism believed to flow from it. Menacing questions now arise. How far do we blame the theology of early Christian writers for our being so far from home today in the way both churches and theologians handle the question of power? Did the doctrine of creation erode 'true' Christian roots? Did something else do

---

[1] R.E. Roberts, *The Theology of Tertullian*, London, J.A. Sharp, 1924.
[2] J. Morgan, *The Importance of Tertullian in the Development of Christian Dogma*, London, Kegan Paul, 1928.

so? Did any of the early writers take much interest in this subject anyway?

Tertullian is a perfect quarry for the hunt. The product and watcher of empire, he both brandished the doctrine of 'creation from nothing' (*creatio ex nihilo*) and expounded an uncompromising theology of divine power (*potestas*). The study which follows traces Tertullian's handling of power into most of his major themes. Power emerges as pervasive to the foundations and development of his thought, even on several occasions linking one doctrine to another and sometimes providing a kind of rationale within a doctrine. But tensions and uneasy connections appear, questioning the absolute determining character of the power-concept as a key, yet disclosing some information about the role played by the early Christian doctrine of the creator.

The evidence will show that the emergence of a firmed-up doctrine of creation in Tertullian stems from the seriousness with which he took the potential threat to Christian belief, as he saw it, in dualistic cosmologies. It will also show that this issue can stand clear of that handling of the divine power which betrays the influence of, and reaction to, ancient empire. Here, imbalances begin to appear in the apologist, exposing the inadequacy of power to provide a comprehensive theological model, even though he exploits the theme to the full, sometimes to unimpeachable ends with surprising success.

Some may follow Tertullian's fate at the hands of this research out of interest in the early Church's contribution to a classical Christianity on trial today. They will want to know how representative he really was of the tradition he claimed to defend. Each chapter will therefore place him in the process which includes the preceding Greek apologetic tradition. This should produce in some measure not just a study of Tertullian but also a study of some early Christian forms of power-theology.

Even this breadth will not be enough. Edwin Hatch's 1888 Hibbert lectures[3] ensured that no one could again offer an account of early Christian writers without reference to the impact of Hellenism. In the case of Tertullian, whatever his disclaimers, this influence of philosophy has been significant in certain parts of his theology. A full account of the role of philosophy in Tertullian's thought, however, would be the product of a lifetime's labour. J.H. Waszink found that a survey of Tertullian's *De Anima* was enough to furnish a major work.[4] Hence, my discussion of the role of contemporary philosophy in Tertullian's conception of divine power will focus on selected significant texts

---

[3]E. Hatch, *The Influence of Greek Ideas and Usages upon the Christian Church*, London, Williams and Norgate, 1901.

[4]J.H. Waszink, *De Anima, Edited with Commentary*, Amsterdam, J.M. Meulenhoff, 1947.

illustrating its impact. For the rest, the chief aim is the discovery and discussion of all relevant passages in Tertullian on the divine power, with the result of reinforcing, challenging, or further illuminating received wisdom. I shall use secondary sources extensively but the main work will be scrutiny of relevant texts in Tertullian's apologetic and doctrinal agenda. I hope the results will service the proper contemporary concerns of today's theological writers and contribute towards disentangling early Christian faith from whatever elements may have skewed it.

CHAPTER 2

The Making of Tertullian

A traditional favourite game amongst researchers of Tertullian has been the scanning of his writings for intellectual fragments from earlier Christian writers. The practice has left its mark on the textbooks. Undoubtedly ancient eclecticism gave us Tertullianism. Some influences bear more responsibility than others,[1] but no single influence may claim complete blame or credit. J. Daniélou assembles an impressive list of antecedents, most, or all, of which merit further investigation. Naturally, Justin and Irenaeus occupy a dominant position,[2] as Tertullian himself confesses in *Adv Val* 5. He allegedly seems indebted also to traditional testimonia which the Greek authors merely handed down.[3] Long ago Tertullian scholars detected a debt to Justin and Irenaeus in Tertullian's Logos theology,[4] his economic Trinity,[5] and his description of Christ as Spirit.[6]

Occasionally, scholars find echoes of many lesser Greek authors, even Gnostic ones[7] and the likes of Melito and Papias.[8] Such affinities can

[1] J. Daniélou, *A History of Early Christian Doctrine*, Vol. III: *The Origins of Latin Christianity*, London, Darton Longman & Todd, 1977. Compare the critique in G.L. Bray, *Holiness and the Will of God. Perspectives on the Theology of Tertullian*, London, Marshall, Morgan & Scott, 1979, especially p. 39 where he thinks the theory that North African Christianity sprang directly from Jewish roots is unproven, at least from Tertullian's writings.
[2] J. Daniélou, op. cit. xiii.
[3] Ibid. 272, for just one example.
[4] R.E. Roberts, *The Theology of Tertullian*, London, J.A. Sharp, 1924, 113.
[5] Ibid.
[6] Ibid. 164.
[7] J. Daniélou, op. cit. xiv.
[8] Ibid. 13.

betray the widespread preference amongst early writers for the Gospel of John.[9] We have known for a long time of the affinities with Greek apologists in Tertullian's language about Christ as Head, Master, Enlightener, Logos, Word, Reason, and Power, as well as in his imagery of sun and ray for the Father–Son relationship and in an apparent subordinationism.[10] Antecedent Latin works making an appearance include *Passio Perpetuae*, *Adv Judaeos*, *De aleatoribus*, *V Esdras*[11] whilst contemporaneous writings stretch detectably to *De centesima* and *De montibus Sina et Sion*.[12] Views conflict on the question of which came first, the *Octavius* of Minucius Felix,[13] or the *Apologeticum* of Tertullian.[14]

Tertullian's repeated doctrinal 'Rule of Faith' (*regula fidei*), in *De praes* 13, 36, *De virg vel* 2 and *Adv Prax* 2, makes contact with similar statements in the earlier work of Irenaeus (*Adv haer* I 10.1 and *Dem* 6). There does seem to be substantial agreement of content[15] between the two apologists and R.F. Refoulé agrees with E. Flesseman Van Leer that it points to what the early writers saw as a normative doctrinal tradition,[16] one which includes belief in an almighty creator, the coming of the Son of God in the flesh and the resurrection of the flesh (*De praes* 36). Given Tertullian's access to such a legacy, it occasions no surprise to hear the claim that even by AD 197 the *Apologeticum* had some of his major lines of theological thought in place.[17]

[9]Ibid.

[10]Roberts, op. cit. 100.

[11]J. Daniélou, op. cit. xiv.

[12]Ibid.

[13]Ibid. xv.

[14]T.D. Barnes, *Tertullian, A Historical and Literary Study*, Oxford, Clarendon Press, 1971, 194.

[15]E.J. Fortman, *The Triune God: A Historical Study of the Doctrine of the Trinity*, London, Hutchinson, 1972, 109. A. Hamman also sees more or less a consistency: 'Résurrection du Christ', *Revue des Sciences Religieuses* 50 (1956) 1–24 (p. 6).

[16]R.F. Refoulé, *Tertullien. Traité de la prescription contre les hérétiques. Introduction, texte critique, et notes*, Paris, Éditions du Cerf, 1957, 53.

[17]R.F. Evans, 'On the Problem of Church and Empire in Tertullian's Apologeticum', E.A. Livingstone, ed., *Studia Patristica*, Vol. XIV, Berlin, Akademie-Verlag, 1976, 21–36 (p. 29). Evans contends that *Apologeticum* presents a consensus, rather than an idiosyncratic, view of the faith. This squares with the theory of P. Keresztes that in the work Tertullian aims indirectly at winning the goodwill of the ruling emperor, the only person kindly handled, for the Christian population. See his 'Tertullian's Apologeticum: A Historical and Literary Study', *Latomus: Revue des Études Latines* 25 (1966) 124–133 (p. 133).

Besides these convergent pressures on Tertullian's thought rank two other great contributions. The first is the Jewish. Tertullian emerges as both indebted to the Jewish tradition and moving in response to it.[18] The Jewish agenda finds shape in manner of quotation,[19] apocalyptic imagery,[20] angelology,[21] millenarianism,[22] parables,[23] and, perhaps, Christology,[24] and Trinity.[25] Tertullian may even be opening fire on a distinctively Latin form of Jewish-informed theology.[26] Other Jewish elements appear in the shape of the *Shepherd of Hermas*,[27] apocryphal literature,[28] Jewish monotheism[29] and anthropology[30] and Jewish Gnostic-esoteric traditions.[31] In terms of theology, Von Campenhausen concludes Tertullian to be almost a Jew.[32]

The second great influence upon Tertullian is classical culture, especially philosophy. His disclaimer that Jerusalem and Athens do not belong together is well known, but the identity of the Athens so sweepingly disparaged remains less certain. He seems sometimes to condemn Greek thought root and branch but, in other occasional diversions, recognises the affinity of Christianity with the best in philosophy[33] as well as sharing the common Christian assumption of his time that the philosophers directly or indirectly drew upon the Old Testament.[34] Many modern commentators recognise that the apparatus of philosophy always lies at Tertullian's disposal and he invariably musters it in the heat of the battle. He uses his philosophical education in easily discernible language and ideas, leaning on such technical vocabulary as *ratio, natura, substantia,* and *status.*[35] Moreover, examples of philosophical technique remain embedded in Tertullian's

[18]J. Daniélou, op. cit. 139.
[19]Ibid. 140ff.
[20]Ibid. 142.
[21]Ibid. 143–144.
[22]Ibid. 144–145.
[23]Ibid. 145–146.
[24]Ibid. 149.
[25]Ibid. 149–150.
[26]Ibid. 152.
[27]Ibid. 154.
[28]Ibid. 154–155.
[29]Ibid. 157–159.
[30]Ibid. 159–161.
[31]Ibid. 176, 182, 187–188.
[32]H. Von Campenhausen, *The Fathers of the Latin Church*, London, A. & C. Black, 1964, 35.
[33]J. Daniélou, op. cit. 209.
[34]J. Daniélou, ibid.
[35]Von Campenhausen, op. cit. 18.

methodological principles, dialectical distinctions and presuppositions of proof.[36] He would have scorned the attempts of Justin and Origen to contextualisation and accommodation but put what he knew of pagan learning to very good use.[37]

This approach may indeed have been behind his claim that to don the pallium of the philosopher implies for consistency's sake embracing the Christian faith.[38] But this is certainly not the whole story, especially if one accepts that the Athens which is despised stands merely for Gnostic 'heretical' or idolatrous features in the philosophy of Tertullian's day. Rather, antagonism to philosophy finds genuine expression in various ways,[39] but especially where it seems to support heresy, sharing with it an 'insatiable curiosity and conceit' (De anima 1; 2).[40] It may be true that whereas the Greek apologists stressed the affinities of philosophy with Christian thought, Tertullian 'sees only the differences.'[41] What affinities there may be, where not from Judaism, are according to Tertullian, 'the sensus communes (traced) to the elements of reasonable insight in which everybody participates by nature.'[42] Hence such insights confirm Christianity rather than philosophy.

Some find Tertullian's vehemence against philosophy puzzling.[43] One answer has explained the antagonism not only by the alliance of heretics with Greek thought but also by such factors as the alliance of philosophy with pagan religion, sheer apologetic habit, and the tendency of philosophical restatement to dilute the rigorous pristine Christian faith.[44] Since Tertullian freely accepted both method and content from philosophy when it suited him, it seems perhaps a little generous to summarise the matter by saying that all Tertullian wished was 'an appropriate limitation of the intellectual hubris of man according to the criterion of God's Word.'[45]

M.L. Colish in a fine review has helpfully charted the modern story of attempts to unravel Tertullian's apparent love–hate relationship with

---

[36]Ibid.
[37]Barnes, op. cit. 120.
[38]Ibid. 230–231.
[39]For a useful summary, see Bray, op. cit. 35–37.
[40]Von Campenhausen, op. cit. 21.
[41]Ibid. 17.
[42]Ibid. 18.
[43]Ibid. 16–20.
[44]T.R. Glover, The Conflict of Religions in the Early Roman Empire, London, Methuen, 1909, 336–338.
[45]Von Campenhausen, op. cit. 19.

philosophy.[46] At least four groups of commentators emerge: (1) those who see the negative attitudes in Tertullian as authoritative and explain the positive responses as an apologetic convenience; (2) those who detect the real Tertullian in his pro-philosophy stance and write off his aggressive moments as a mere rhetorical flourish; (3) those who take both stances to be exaggerations, deliberate oratorical practice, common in Tertullian's day, of using current thought as either Aunt Sally or ally according to the needs of the moment; (4) those, finally, who see the tension in Tertullian as part of a process of the conversion of Classicism. These approaches carry varying degrees of merit, but it seems to me that Tertullian reviled philosophy precisely because he took it so seriously, whether menaced or emboldened by it. We cannot therefore treat references to philosophy in him casually.

On the other hand, in Tertullian's interaction with philosophy we do face a very complex and probably non-recoverable process. Platonist-related thought could have reached him through so many different sources: standard collections of quotations from the philosophers, the writings of their antagonists, the usual curriculum of schools of rhetoric, Jewish recasts, as in Philo (and even then perhaps transmitted only indirectly through a popular tradition) and the fertile eclectic contortions of Gnosticism, a 'parody of Platonism'.[47] In addition, Tertullian thought he understood something of the Platonists from the attempts of 'Christian' authors to integrate selected classical themes with the religion of the New Testament and, as we shall see later, launched himself at a target he thought was Plato. A. Kenny's observation applies even to the second-century apologist: '"Platonism" is an unhelpful word. "Platonism" in philosophy, like "Fascism" in politics, is a word whose evaluative meaning has eroded its descriptive meaning.'[48]

Any one of the channels just mentioned contained great potential for distortion. It becomes almost impossible to say with confidence that Tertullian enjoyed a direct mastery of the works of the most imposing thinkers of the Platonist tradition. And this tradition itself is far from uniform, in many respects straying quite cheerfully from the master. Certain themes, however, could not disappear from a truly Platonist agenda of that time. Of these the relationship of a 'One' to the 'many' occupied a foundational position. The One usually enjoyed a marked transcendence over the many, the sphere of all variegated reality. This

---

[46]M.L. Colish, *The Stoic Tradition From Antiquity To The Early Middle Ages*, II: *Stoicism in Christian Latin Thought Through the Sixth Century*, Leiden, E.J. Brill, 1985, 11–15.

[47]J. Dillon, *The Middle Platonists. A Study of Platonism 80 BC to AD 220*, London, Duckworth, 1977, 387.

[48]A. Kenny, *The God of the Philosophers*, Oxford, Clarendon Press, 1979, 16.

relationship nearly always implied at least one mediating principle between the One and the many. Middle Platonism, the most dominant form of the tradition at the time of Tertullian, partook not only of Plato and Aristotle but also of Stoicism. It increasingly became committed to a transcendent supreme principle and a non-material world above and beyond this one which stood as a paradigm for it.[49] This issue made secondary, for Platonists, the question of an actual creation of things. They could differ on whether or not Plato's description of creation in *Timaeus* applied literally as taking place in time or simply should be regarded as a model for instructional purposes.[50] Most Middle Platonists followed the view of Speusippus and Xenocrates that the process described by Plato in the *Timaeus* was timeless and eternal,[51] a sort of translation of 'the order of ontological and causal dependence in a chronological tale.'[52] On the other side, Aristotle claimed to be the first to uphold the eternity of the ordered universe[53] and Plutarch and Atticus held to a literal view of *Timaeus* in support of their dualistic tendencies.[54] The relationship of the transcendent One to the varied world of the many, involving all the insecurities and evils of life, and the order and harmony involved, took centre stage. Christians like Tertullian, committed to a belief in an essential divine control over a linear history, were sure to be troubled by the Platonist perspective, especially when they did not appreciate by direct contact its subtleties and deep questioning.

Tertullian sometimes used, and sometimes discarded, ideas associated with both Middle Platonism and more distinct Stoic thought, but his sympathies lay more with the latter. Hostility to Platonist traditions can surge brutally into the text. He vigorously attacks its inspiration of Gnostic doctrines (*De anima* 23).[55] He sometimes singles out those themes which surround metempsychosis and the world of Ideas. He shares with Gregory of Nyssa a common resistance to the Middle Platonist Albinus on the strength of a shared Stoic stock of ideas.[56] Tertullian does not receive Stoicism as a package.[57] Specifically, he roots

[49]Dillon, op. cit. 51.

[50]Ibid. 33.

[51]Ibid. 7. Plutarch and Atticus took the *Timaeus* account more literally.

[52]J. Mansfeld, *Studies in Later Greek Philosophy and Gnosticism*, London, Variorum Reprints, 1989, I, 129–188 (p. I 140).

[53]Ibid.

[54]Dillon, op. cit. 7.

[55]J. Daniélou, op. cit. 224.

[56]Ibid. 227–229. The direct influence of Albinus is far from certain. I raise the issue again in chapter 4 below.

[57]Ibid. 403. Compare P. Hinchliff's observation that Tertullian uses Stoicism when it is convenient but accepts no other authority than revelation, in a review

out aspects of the Stoic concept of corporeity[58] and its monism that takes Christ's soul to be fleshly rather than rational.[59] He also rejects its attachment to the permanence of natures which he fears as an obstacle to the doctrine of the incarnation.[60] On the other hand, to one trained in Latin rhetoric where legal principles permeated, Stoicism remained very attractive with its universal harmony and Spermatikos Logos ordering all things.[61] Specific traits bearing the stamp of Stoic thought, according to some, include the vintage theme of patience;[62] method of argumentation; universal corporeity;[63] realism;[64] the self-perception of the soul;[65] natural law and the testimony of the soul.[66] R.F. Evans sees Tertullian as drawing upon the Stoic doctrine of natural law to unite his affirmation of life and his revolutionary fervour in a world illegally occupied by demonic powers.[67]

The ambivalent relationship to Stoicism, typical of Tertullian's handling of philosophy in general, becomes rational according to Colish,[68] with the help of a distinction. On the one hand the attacks on Stoicism focused upon narrow, selected themes (not integrated in Tertullian's treatment) such as the condition of the human soul and the nature of God. He even misconstrues the Stoics as believing that God manipulates the world from outside. On the other hand when he reaches out for Stoic ideas to unseat the heretics, especially Marcion and the Gnostics, he displays a direct knowledge of individual authors, particularly Seneca, marshalling the arguments for God's existence, the natural knowledge of God and even a sort of corporality of all beings. This simply underlines the apologist's intention to make philosophy work for his own ends.

Amongst the Latin non-Christian authors exploited by Tertullian, Cicero and Seneca[69] take chief place, particularly the latter with his

---

of Daniélou's *Origins of Latin Christianity*, in *Journal of Theological Studies*, NS 29 (1978) 222–224 (p. 224).

[58]J. Daniélou, op. cit. 218.

[59]Ibid. 385–390.

[60]Ibid. 218–219.

[61]Ibid. Glover, op. cit. 314.

[62]J. Daniélou, op. cit. 324.

[63]Ibid. 215.

[64]Ibid. 127.

[65]Ibid. 387.

[66]Glover, op. cit. 315.

[67]R.F. Evans, *One and Holy. The Church in Latin Patristic Thought*, London, SPCK, 1972, 21.

[68]Colish, op. cit. 15–19. Most of the authorities cited by Colish crop up during my later analysis of Tertullian.

[69]Glover, op. cit. 314.

explicit Stoicism. Indeed, the claim reaches us that Stoicism came to Tertullian through the Latin Stoa, especially Pliny the Elder (who follows Posidonius, author of the Middle Stoa) and Varro,[70] and Tertullian became one of the great representatives of Latin Stoic teaching.[71] Tertullian must have steeped himself in the antiquarian researches of Varro.[72] In *Apologeticum* quotations appear, perhaps through a fallible memory,[73] from 30 or more pagan authors.[74] Glover calls Tertullian a master of great Roman literature,[75] but sees his education as typical of a tendency to manual and 'cyclopaedia'.[76]

The Latin method found in Tertullian and his Christian sources probably counts for as much as the literature used by him. For some scholars it accounts for a stress on biblical theology, the typology of primitive Christianity, and a theology of history.[77] In Tertullian these issue in a coherent theological synthesis, a vision of various orders of reality, and a classifying of these orders.[78] The distinctively Latin spirit, in contrast to the Greek, focused his thought on social matters, on the Church as a political society and on the elements of will, standards and discipline.[79] A practical orientation dominated[80] and has much to do with the theology of divine power which permeates so much of Tertullian's work. In Tertullian the doctrine of the Church becomes an important concern as it does with succeeding Latin Fathers in general.[81] Accordingly the Latin vocabulary seems to be non-technical. Words like *census, status, gradus* and *substantia* display a wide range of meaning arising from their common and widespread use.[82] It all points in the direction of a practical and alive style with a certain independence from the early Greek agenda,[83] though not all scholars subscribe to the theory of Tertullian's rugged originality of thought.[84]

---

[70]Ibid. 231 and 309.

[71]Ibid. 231.

[72]T.D. Barnes, 'Tertullian the Antiquarian', E.A. Livingstone, ed., *Studia Patristica*, Vol. XIV, Berlin, Akademie-Verlag, 1976, 3–20 (p. 9).

[73]Ibid.

[74]Ibid.

[75]Ibid.

[76]Ibid. 308–309.

[77]J. Daniélou, op. cit. xv–xvi.

[78]Ibid. xv.

[79]Von Campenhausen, op. cit. 35.

[80]Ibid.

[81]R.F. Evans, *One and Holy*, 1.

[82]J. Daniélou, op. cit. 354–360.

[83]Glover, op. cit. 342.

[84]For a stress on Tertullian's indebtedness see E.P. Meijering, *Tertullian contra Marcion. Gotteslehre in der Polemik Adversus Marcionem* I–III, Leiden, E.J.

Whilst the traditional assumption of Tertullian's occupation as a lawyer still remains under the cloud of T.D. Barnes' challenge,[85] it still seems fairly clear that the apologist's thought was at home in the atmosphere of law.[86] Peculiarly Stoic themes of harmony and order underline the legal tone. Assessments of Roman rhetoric in Tertullian have pointed to an advocate's training.[87] R.D. Sider has, however, gone further and credited the rhetoric with actually shaping Tertullian's thought.[88] On this account Tertullian becomes the 'sophist of the churches.'[89]

To all this one must add the imperial backdrop of Tertullian's Latin heritage. Says R.F. Evans,

> the Church is an outpost of that kingdom (of God)... Christ is the 'imperial commander' to whom the Christian soldier now owes the complete obedience proper to his baptismal oath of allegiance.[90]

The resultant 'shadow empire'[91] is made all the more central by the strategic cosmic and ruling role normally accorded the emperor.[92] This theme will resurface when we come to a survey of the 'power' motif in Tertullian.

Many commentators identify Tertullian's own spirit and temper behind his work. This approach notes his moral rigorism,[93] together with his severity and discipline possibly arising out of the influence of the martyrs in his pre-conversion experience.[94] In his later work it has to contend with the growth of Christianity amongst upper classes. This occurred between the writing of *Apologeticum* and *Ad Scapulam* and

---

Brill, 1977. See also the conclusion drawn about Tertullian's originality in a review of Meijering by A.H. Armstrong, *Journal of Theological Studies*, NS 29 (1978) 556–557.

[85]See T.D. Barnes, *Tertullian*, chapter 4.

[86]Glover, op. cit. 332. See also Von Campenhausen, op. cit. 29, 31, 34. A full treatment of the question appears in I.L.S. Balfour, *The Relationship of Man to God. From Conception to Conversion in the Writings of Tertullian*, PhD thesis, Edinburgh, 1980.

[87]Evans, *One and Holy*, 21, Glover, op. cit. 309–310, Von Campenhausen, op. cit. 5.

[88]R.D. Sider, *Ancient Rhetoric and the Art of Tertullian*, Oxford, University Press, 1971, 127, T.D. Barnes, 'Tertullian the Antiquarian', 6.

[89]Barnes, op. cit. 6.

[90]R.F. Evans, *One and Holy*, 9.

[91]Ibid. 19.

[92]Ibid. 7.

[93]Ibid. 5–6.

[94]Ibid. 5.

produced a Church 'forced to struggle with the meaning of social prominence and wealth for Christians.'[95]

Finally, Von Campenhausen sees in Tertullian an African expression of the Latin religion:

> It is a characteristically African form of the Roman spirit which tends to combine discipline with criticism and a state of order with scorn and passion and which prefers self-sufficiency even to the point of rebellion, rather than blindly to follow and obey.[96]

[95]D.E. Groh, 'Upper-Class Christians in Tertullian's Africa', E.A. Livingstone, ed., *Studia Patristica*, Vol. XIV, Berlin, Akademie-Verlag, 1976, 41–47 (p. 47).

[96]Von Campenhausen, op. cit. 5.

CHAPTER 3

The Classification of Divine Power

A.C. McGiffert argued that Tertullian concerned himself with the world of individual human beings more than with the physical world of nature.[1] In other words, Tertullian reflected the western tradition of pursuing practical rather than metaphysical interests. This meant a preoccupation with God as personal ruler more than with a metaphysical absolute.[2] Tertullian sought to 'conserve the divine independence and omnipotence.'[3]

There is much that is true here. But a complicating factor arises all the same, in Tertullian's absorption with the question of creation and God's consequent control over nature. This must rest on a traditional doctrine of God stemming from familiar biblical material. Yet both the absoluteness of the divine power and its comparability to the Roman imperial sovereignty leave a mark everywhere upon his theology. Tracing every reference to power in Tertullian's work to either its biblical or cultural source seems impracticable. Rather we need to monitor the impact of the power-motif upon the theology that takes shape. This requires at least a rudimentary nailing of the categories in which Tertullian conceived divine power, and a natural first step will consist in examining his vocabulary. The occurrences in the English translations of the word 'power' represent, of course, several Latin words, each with its own nuance. We always need, however, to have a sharp eye for disparity

---

[1]A.C. McGiffert, *A History of Christian Thought*, Vol. 1: *The West from Tertullian to Erasmus*, London, Scribner, 1933, 14.
[2]Ibid. 12.
[3]Ibid. 13.

between strict etymology and the habit of usage adopted by any writer.[4] I want, then, to begin with a brief résumé of modern influential word studies of Tertullian and, with these findings to hand, move on to categorise some major conceptions of the divine power in his thought. The range of words employed by Tertullian to designate divine power has become fairly manageable thanks to the pioneering work of such authors as R. Braun. We do not need to review every single word underlying the English translations but those listed below form the main terms for power found in Tertullian.

Potestas

According to Braun, *potestas* in Tertullian translates both the biblical words *exousia* and *dynamis*.[5] It therefore includes the idea of sovereign authority, though normally quite distinct from *auctoritas* which very occasionally functions as a synonym for it.[6] *Auctoritas*, as T.G. Ring points out, is a rational decree or command along the lines of the imperial decree.[7] It particularly focuses on the ethical relationship and only occasionally receives the English rendering 'power'. *Potestas*, on the other hand, more generally marks the properties or faculties characteristic of a being[8] (though in rare cases a word like *posse* comes into play as in *Adv Prax* 10, discussed later in this section). It can also express the absoluteness of God's power, what Braun calls the absolute freedom of will, the absolute possibility of an act.[9] He argues for an underlying tradition which speaks of 'the sovereign liberty of the creator'.[10] A connection with the biblical *dynamis* seems likely in the sense of a strength or power either as a quality of its possessor or as

---

[4]Gerald Bray's caution about the shortcomings of the *Sondersprache* school of interpretation deserves consideration (Bray, op. cit. 28). He is right to warn that fixed meanings in isolation can be misleading in determining theology and that linguistic precision did not exist much before Nicea.

[5]R. Braun, *Deus Christianorum. Recherches sur le vocabulaire doctrinal de Tertullien*, Paris, Publications de la Faculté des Lettres et Sciences Humaines d'Alger, 41 (1962) 106 and 110.

[6]T.G. Ring, *Auctoritas bei Tertullien, Cyprian und Ambrosius*, Cassiciacum, Band XXIX, Würzburg, Augustinus, 1975, 62. See also A. Beck, *Römisches Recht bei Tertullien und Cyprian. Eine Studie zur Frühen Kirchenrechtsgeschichte*, Halle, Max Niemeyer, 1930, 166.

[7]Ring, op. cit. 62.

[8]Braun, op. cit. 110.

[9]Ibid. 111.

[10]Ibid. 111.

exercised by him.[11] That rootedness of Tertullian in the biblical expression appears central to his thought on God.[12]

Potentia / Potens

Potentia seems often enough to be a synonym for *potestas* and may sometimes displace it only for reasons of symmetry.[13] *De bapt* 2 describes God as wise and powerful (*sapiens* and *potens*) even though he works in foolishness and incapability, the opposites of wisdom and power. Here wisdom and power make up intrinsic and permanent *qualities* or *attributes* which in turn qualify God for *operations* of power.[14]

Dominus

Tertullian's *dominus* is equivalent to *kyrios* in the NT. As such, it probably carries the idea of sovereign power, of the absolute authority of God over the human creature.[15] It had equally served to translate *despotes* in spite of the unfortunate political overtones,[16] but Tertullian employs it mainly, if not exclusively, for expressing the divine lordship, the absolute power and discretion of God over the creature.

Omnipotens

The word occasionally appears in parallel with *dominus*[17] (*Adv Prax* 1; 21). In Theophilus its Greek equivalent (*pantokrator*) can even function as a title for God.[18] Thus *omnipotens* is reckoned to be more than a mere adjective, expressing rather the very idea of God.[19] So its synonym *omnia*

---

[11]E. Evans, 'Tertullian's Theological Terminology', *Church Quarterly Review* 139 (1944) 56–77 (p. 74).

[12]Braun, op. cit. 32. According to Braun, Tertullian's understanding of God takes its inspiration from the Judaeo-Christian concept, not that of philosophical monotheism.

[13]Ibid. 113.

[14]In the Latin Bible *potentia* can translate the Greek *kratos* in a pejorative sense of domination: Braun, op. cit. 113.

[15]Ibid. 92. Compare P.G. Van der Nat, 'Tertullianea', Part I, *Vigiliae Christianae* 18 (1964) 14–31 (p. 23), where he sees in Tertullian a view of the Christian life as both service to a Lord (*dominus*) and a complete freedom towards the world.

[16]Braun, op. cit. 92.

[17]Ibid. 101.

[18]Ibid. 98.

[19]Ibid. 100.

potens crops up with *Deus* or *divinitas*[20] and can state the potency of God, his ability to do anything.[21]

Omnipotens, as later work will show, shades off also into supernatural power and sheer potency in certain particulars, especially creation.[22]

Virtus

Of the words used by Tertullian for power, *virtus* often expresses the most vividly the biblical notion of divine *dynamis*.[23] Moreover it almost always appears in Tertullian's biblical quotations,[24] being the natural translation of *dynamis*.[25] According to Braun *virtus* signals in Tertullian not so much an attribute as the very form or identity of God,[26] and through its use for 'miracle' reveals the deity of Christ.[27] *Potestas* also, however, can translate *dynamis* as concrete instances of efficient power in action[28] (*Adv Hermog* 34, *Adv Marc* IV 35, *De fuga* 5), and so occupies some of the space typical of *virtus*.[29]

Maiestas

H. Drexler holds that a religious perspective marks *maiestas*[30] whilst Braun finds in it a definition of deity.[31] It can indeed serve as a synonym for deity[32] (*Apol* 15, *Adv Prax* 30), and ties up with power in, for instance, the expression 'majesty of divine power' (*De paen* 4). Political supremacy also lies to hand in the Roman usage.[33]

---

[20] Ibid. 100–101.

[21] Ibid.

[22] Ibid. 101.

[23] Ibid.

[24] Ibid.

[25] Cf. A.J.B. Higgins, 'The Latin Text of Luke in Marcion and Tertullian', *Vigiliae Christianae* 5 (1951) 1–42 where he maintains that *virtus* is the usual word for *dynamis* in both Marcion and Tertullian.

[26] Braun, ibid. 108.

[27] Ibid.

[28] Ibid. 110.

[29] Ibid. 106, 109–110.

[30] H. Drexler, 'Maiestas', *Aevum* 30 (1956) 195–212 (p. 210).

[31] R. Braun, op. cit. 40, where he sees in Tertullian's conception of God a divine majesty contrasted with human ordinariness.

[32] Ibid. 45. Cf. also Drexler, op. cit. 210–11. A religious perspective, in his view, is essential to an understanding of *maiestas*. In a ruler it never came without might and precluded admission by an emperor that an enemy was dangerous.

[33] Drexler, op. cit. 210–211.

Some Preliminary Conclusions

An analysis of Tertullian's language for power has exposed a wider nuance of meaning than simply *operations* of power. At least three other ways of talking about God's power emerge. In the first place, divine power can mean for Tertullian an infinite *potentiality* or *potency* residing in God and quite inseparable from one's definition of him, whether it issues in any particular concrete exercise of power or not. Secondly, divine power can so distinguish God in Tertullian's writing from all that is 'not-God', that it functions as a title for deity and from time to time highlights in Tertullian's theology the divine honour and dignity itself. Thirdly, divine power sometimes serves to describe God in active relation to 'not-God' realities. Whereas the power of God's *dignity* sets him infinitely apart from all else, the power of his *rank* establishes him in a supreme position over the hierarchy of powers. All power is his. All other powers derive their power from him, and the contradiction this produces in the case of the gods, the powers of the pantheons, leads logically to the conclusion that they are really an illusion.

For the meantime I want only to illustrate these categories and establish them towards later thematic theological analysis and to do so without being pinned down to earlier lexical material alone. It is mainly Tertullian's apologetic work which forms the backdrop for this analysis. Moreover, many of Tertullian's major *doctrinal* affirmations make an embryonic or even mature, appearance in the early work, *Apologeticum*. As F.J. Cardman points out, for Tertullian, 'Doctrinal and apologetic concerns intertwine.'[34] Here, then, are some further comments on these three forms of divine power in Tertullian.

Power as potency

As we have seen, Tertullian sometimes conceived power as an intrinsic capacity or potential, underlying acts of power. In his work against Hermogenes (analysed in depth later) it assumes a central position. There, the doctrine of 'creation from nothing' not only demonstrates God's output of power but also the infinite potentiality which supports such operations. To be creator, for Tertullian, means more than creating or being the cause of creation. It denotes the possession of the unique capacity of omnipotence, marking God off from the creature. It spells 'creatorhood' as opposed to 'creatureliness'. The idea of unlimited potentiality surfaces too in the work against Marcion, particularly *Adv Marc* II 7:

---

[34]F.J. Cardman, *Tertullian on the Resurrection* (Dissertation, Yale University) New Haven, Connecticut, 1974 (microfilm), 144. Cardman is particularly discussing *De res* 14–17.

God keeps all his attributes and potentialities[35] unimpaired – his distinguishing attribute of goodness, and the rationality of his creative act, as well as his unlimited foreknowledge and power (*et natura bonitatis et ratio dispositionis et praescientiae et potentiae copia*)....

However, divine goodness also conditions the actual exercise or operations of power, as does rationality and foreknowledge. Later in the chapter Tertullian speaks of both foreknowledge and a 'fore-power' (*praescientiam et praepotentiam*) which form the basis for any divine intervention. The power of God emerges as a freedom or omnicompetence which characterises God-in-himself and by which he *can* do anything he considers appropriate.

But all this naturally leads to the question of the will of God. The power of God, in Tertullian, answers to the complete freedom and efficiency of his will. Tertullian captures this in his characteristic rhetoric with a phrase as follows: 'his power, which is identical with his will (*eadem virtute et voluntate*)' (*Adv Hermog* 15). This seems not to be an occasional quirk but occurs also at *Adv Prax* 10:

> For God's power (*posse*) is his will (*velle*) and his inability (*non posse*) is his absence of will (*nolle*): and what his will was, that was in his power (*quod autem voluit, et potuit*).

We have here, of course, an early form of the conventional assertion that omnipotence denotes not God's power to do literally *anything* but merely his power to do what he *wills*. Hence in *Adv Prax* 10:

> On this reckoning there will be something difficult for God, that, in fact, which he has refrained from doing, not because he could not but because he would not.

On this occasion the apologist was unseating the monarchians' appeal to God's omnipotence by which they supported their unlikely notion of a God who was his own Son. A little lesson on logic, focusing upon the meaning-value of such an idea, should have sufficed but Tertullian prefers to use the opportunity for a lesson on divine omnipotence. It is too difficult for God since God does not *will* to do it. Although quite the wrong answer, it assists us by underlining the rational base in Tertullian for divine power and also Tertullian's commitment to omnipotence.

When, therefore, Tertullian tackles the question of a divine power which measures up to the *creatio ex nihilo* he is willing to raise the stakes very high indeed in *Adv Hermog* 14. The priority of goodness mentioned

---

[35] A justifiable rendering by E. Evans, *Tertullian Adversus Marcionem*, Oxford, Clarendon Press, 1972, 105.

earlier seems now to disappear, and Tertullian prefers God as the author of evil to a God not capable of doing what he wills:

> It was more appropriate to him to make (the things that are) of his own will than of necessity – in other words, out of nothing rather than out of matter. It is more becoming to believe that God, even as the author of evil, is free than that he is subservient: power, of whatever kind it be, is more appropriate to him than infirmity.

Tertullian will in any case clear God of the charge, but now power as the *freedom* of God arises as the guardian of God's goodness, rather than the other way round, simply because it does not make any practical difference whether it was by weakness or by his own will that the Lord became the author of evil (*Adv Hermog* 15). Power as freedom, as liberty to resist evil imposed from elsewhere, both guarantees good and is more appropriate to God than goodness combined with impotence (*Adv Hermog* 16).

Liberty, freedom and power function here as synonyms, just as infirmity, necessity and weakness form an opposing trio. It should occasion no surprise, then, to find Tertullian closely linking *potentia*, *potestas* and *licentia* (freedom)[36] in the early work *De res* 11. In *De praescriptione haereticorum* 1, Tertullian argues that, 'When it has been determined that a thing must by all means be... this secures the power through which it exists.' There can be no will without its effective and powerful execution, the two being simultaneous and indivisible where the will concerned belongs to God. Tertullian deploys the priority of such a will against Marcion's dualism, as E.C. Blackman has observed,[37] and makes use there of the language of providence: *dispositum, dispositio, praedicatio*. Theologically, this rests upon the priority of the divine will in creation and contrasts sharply with the approach of some of his chief opponents.[38]

Does Tertullian derive his understanding of the omnipotent will from ideas of fate in Stoicism? Certainly the first Stoic interpretation of the

---

[36]E. Evans understands *potentia* as God's inherent power, *potestas* as his control over creation, and *licentia* as his moral right to exercise control (Tertullian's *Treatise on the Resurrection. The Text, Edited with an Introduction, Translation and Commentary*, London, SPCK, 1970, 225).

[37]E.C. Blackman, *Marcion and His Influence*, London, SPCK, 1948.

[38]E.P. Meijering, 'God, Cosmos, History. Christian and Neo-Platonic Views on Divine Revelation', *Vigiliae Christianae* 28 (1974) 248–276 (p. 249) reports the view that Christians especially objected to Gnostics and Platonists because they denied that the world was created by the divine free will.

universe issued in the verdict, 'whatever will be, will be',[39] and the dictum that all things happen by necessity, that is, by fate,[40] in a thoroughly deterministic sense.[41] 'Fate', however, is not the same thing as 'God'. In the Latin expression of Stoicism *providentia* is supposed to be 'a bodily presentment of deity',[42] but, according to one authority, necessity encircled deity.[43] If anything, then, Tertullian overturns the current notion of fate by asserting the priority of the personal divine freedom of will and power, unquenchable by necessity of any kind. As A.C. McGiffert can claim, 'This insistence upon the freedom of God was common among the Fathers.'[44] He cites Irenaeus as saying, 'It is not seemly to say... of... God... free and independent, that he was slave to necessity.... Otherwise, necessity will be made greater and more controlling than God.'

Tertullian, therefore, draws more upon the common teaching of the apologists for his outspoken defence of God's power and freedom, than directly upon Stoic ideas of providence, whatever Stoic elements nevertheless crop up in his work. At any rate, power as a feature of the unconditioned freedom of God in creation and providence, focuses up sharply the notion of intrinsic potency. Tertullian did not, then, altogether box down the power-motif to the active 'economy', the works of God. Power characterised God-in-himself. In God lay an infinite and invisible potency ready to be unleashed upon evil. To be God was to be power.

Power as glory

The term *maiestas*, wedded to the idea of divine power in Tertullian as shown later, also highlights the divine dignity or unique glory and grandeur of God, marking him out as alone worthy of worship. Tertullian's use of the word bears out Braun's suggestion of its function as a synonym for deity. *Maiestas* was native to the language of religion and served to describe a variety of deities. Of actors in his time Tertullian wrote, 'they overturn the honour of deity (*honorem*

[39]E.V. Arnold, *Roman Stoicism*, Cambridge, University Press, 1911 (re-issued, London, Routledge & Kegan Paul, 1958) 200.

[40]Ibid. 199.

[41]Ibid.

[42]Ibid. 204.

[43]Ibid. 208. He finds the Stoics having to admit that providence is limited by an all-encircling necessity. See also J. Mansfeld, 'Providence and the Destruction of the Universe', *Studies in Later Greek Philosophy and Gnosticism*, 131–133, 179–180.

[44]A.C. McGiffert, *The God of the Early Christians*, Edinburgh, T. & T. Clark, 1924, 166.

divinitatis), and blot out every trace of majesty (*maiestatis vestigia*)' (*Apol* 15; cf. also the phrase in *Ad nat* I 10). If there were really a plurality of gods, he remarks, demons would be afraid to behave as gods and so 'misuse a majesty beyond doubt above them (*maiestate superiore*), the majesty of *powers* they feared' (*Apol* 23). To Marcion, Tertullian speaks of the alleged 'high estate of majesty' of Marcion's 'higher' God laid aside in a docetic human appearance. When the Christians pay homage to another besides the gods, they fall foul of the label, 'religion of a second majesty' (*Apol* 35). In some places, a grading of *maiestas* in pagan thought appears, each divine status carrying its own rewards (*Apol* 11, 13, 35).

It is against this background that Tertullian offers a supreme *maiestas* in the Christian's God, one which regulates and controls all others including Caesar's (*Apol* 33). Caesar enjoys political power with great *maiestas*, but even so, the form of God's *maiestas* is so superior that it justifies worship being offered to it.

The fullness of this divine *maiestas* explains the Father's invisibility (*Adv Prax* 14). This is true of the Son also before the incarnation, just as in his return Christ will be, 'in the majesty of Deity displayed' (*Apol* 21) and, equally, as the Holy Spirit emerges, 'the third sequence of majesty (*tertium gradum maiestatis*)' (*Adv Prax* 30). An apparently different approach[45] to the Son in *Adv Prax* 14 means merely that although the Son is included in the fullness of divine majesty he now also is visible:

> We must acknowledge the Son as visible because of the manner of his derivation (*pro modulo derivationis*).

The sun and its lightbeams illustrate this point. The sun represents the fullness of majesty and invisibility. But that full majesty discloses itself in the lightbeam which shares in the majesty of its source.

Acts of power, such as floods and fire, disclose 'his avenging majesty' (*Apol* 18). Providential power, feeding Israel in the wilderness and the crowds with Christ, displays the divine *maiestas* (*Adv Marc* IV 21). Homage to the *maiestas* of a deity springs not so much from pure reflective reason as from 'regard for power (*potestas*) that can act on the instant' (*Apol* 28). *Maiestas*, then, containing as it does natural overtones of religious dignity commanding homage, implied also the presence of impressive power. In the case of the Christian's God this was infinite power. No text expresses it better than one in Tertullian's earliest work:

---

[45]E. Evans, *Tertullian's Treatise Against Praxeas. The Text Edited, with an Introduction, Translation and Commentary*, London, SPCK, 1948, 275.

You concede… that there is a god, more sublime and more potent (*potentiorem*), Emperor as it were of the universe, of absolute power and majesty (*perfectae potentiae et maiestatis*). (*Apol* 24)

The Son enjoys divine dignity 'of his own right' precisely as 'almighty' (*omnipotens*), invisible and in receipt of 'power (*potestas*) over all' (*Adv Prax* 16). The supreme greatness of God comes down to 'form and reason and might (*vis*) and power (*potestas*)' (*Adv Marc* I 3).

The impulse to worship of the Christian's God springs from a recognition rooted in the concept of power, as *Apol* 17 puts it:

What we worship is the one God (*Deus unus*[46]) who made this whole fabric… who by… word… by… reason… by the might wherewith he could do it (*virtute qua potuit*), fashioned it out of nothing, to the glory of his majesty.

The *qua potuit* points up divine potency, what God is *able* to do, not just the concrete exercise of power. Works of power give testimony as evidences of an infinite potency (*virtutis et potestatis*) 'excellent in glory and power' (*Adv Marc* IV 35). So glory, honour, splendour and grandeur connect with the divine *potestas* (*Ad ux* 1,[47] *De fuga* 12). These appear in the true Christian God, in crushing contrast to Marcion's manufactured 'lower' god (*Adv Marc* V 11). Involvement with creation enhances, rather than compromises, the Christian God's unique glory (*gloria*). Marcion's unfortunate lofty god seems to revel in feebleness (*infirmitas*) and so dishonour (*dedecus*). In Tertullian's opinion this was the fate of most pagan gods with their compensating pomp and ceremony.[48] Acts of power in the concrete world of the creation bear the hallmark of divine dignity.

Power as rank: 'positional' power

J. Daniélou has reminded us that Tertullian is far less concerned with the inner reality of things than with 'placing them in the correct mutual relation'.[49] He gives the Latin *status* as a useful illustration. It indicates a

---

[46]J. Daniélou, op. cit. 193, comments that Tertullian follows the same theme as that found in Minucius Felix who, in Stoic tradition, regards names as natural. Hence *deus* is the name 'which points to God in his absolutely unique and incommunicable character.'

[47]Braun, op. cit. 45, sees both *gloria* and *claritas* as translations of *doxa*. (W.P. Le Saint traces Tertullian's words to the New Testament doxologies: *Tertullian, Treatises on Marriage and Remarriage*, London, Longmans, Green & Co., 1951, 114).

[48]E. Evans, *Tertullian's Homily on Baptism. The Text edited, with an Introduction, Translation and Commentary*, London, SPCK, 1964, 7.

[49]J. Daniélou, op. cit. 356.

factual state or nature but Tertullian concerns himself with detecting various types of *status* and placing each within a hierarchy of realities and determining its 'order' and its relation to other 'orders'.

Tertullian often enters this world of hierarchical orders via the power theme. It is admittedly difficult to distinguish the divine honour or *maiestas* of God from the rank or *position* of power which God holds relative to other powers. Mainly, however, the dignity of God as signalled by infinite and absolute potentiality, sets God apart and emphasises his distance, or 'otherness', rather like the concept of holiness in the Old Testament. The model of a power-rank, on the other hand, is a device for informing God's working relationship with the various realities. He has possession and power over them, and they are subject to his will in much the same way as the effective emperor can do what he wants with his people and lands. Tertullian makes both points in *Adv Marc* III 2. God and Christ attract worship but more specifically as 'established above all the eminences of forces and powers' (plurals of *virtus* and *potestas*). Worthiness of worship is one thing, rank and position another, but the two relate intimately. Yet, God is not only worshipped at a distance in a purely religious way, but he is also established at the top of a fixed order of 'powers' or 'ranks'.

Tertullian opts to focus up positional power by the use of the Latin title *dominus* which in *Adv Hermog* 3 he distinguishes from the eternal name *Deus*, since 'Lord is the name not of a substance, but of a power (*potestas*) ' and it became God's when things began to exist upon which the power of the Lord could operate. The power of the '*dominus*' even inspires human fear of a kind for *potestas* implies this (*Adv Marc* I 27). Nothing, however, stirs up appeal to the divine position of power in Tertullian more than the rivalry offered to it in paganism. The demons, as God's rivals, steal his divinations (*Apol* 22) and Christians must, by God's power, trample them down and expel them (*De spect* 29).

Power over the demons, of course, only discloses a more profound superiority. In *Apol* 24 Tertullian hypothetically concedes the existence of the gods in order to show their inferior standing to the God of the Christians. If they did exist they would have to recognise that God is loftier and mightier (*sublimius* and *potentius*). As 'foremost' (*princeps*), a synonym for emperor (*imperator*), he holds the highest rank of power commanding 'perfect power and majesty (*potentia* and *maiestas*).' All three types of power, *potency*, *dignity* and *position*, appear here. Comment on what he sees as the more menacing threats to the Christian faith brings out in Tertullian the more aggressive (if because defensive) statement of the divine power. For instance, exorcism, according to *Apol* 23, demonstrates well the divine power:

All this sovereignty and power (*dominatio et potestas*) that we have over them derives its force (*valet*) only from the naming of Christ, and the reminder of what they expect... from God.

The same subservience defines the fate of the gods, as *Apol* 24 tried to show. In fact, Tertullian reserves the right to pray to *that* God on the emperor's behalf rather than to the petty gods who can only owe their power to the God over all. It looks like an innocuous appeal for freedom of worship but before he has finished with the chapter Tertullian is calling his God the true God because God over all. To possess in reality all power among other claimants to independent power, as the *true* God does, is to eliminate them from the arena altogether and to expose their illusory character. The all-powerful supremacy of God implicitly destroys the viability of the polytheistic system. The only justification for the existence of the gods might be that the supreme God might require their assistance (*Apol* 11). However, this hardly seems credible to Tertullian, since God holds a perfect rank of power and an infinite potency. What started as an alternative source of help by prayer for the emperor now strangles its rivals. According to *Apol* 29, impotent gods like these actually fall under Caesar's protection, owing their origins to his mines, their security to his patrolled temples and their safety in transit to the legions of the highways. Yet the pagans seek Caesar's safety from gods without the power to give it and 'pass by the one whose power (*potestas*) it is'.

By the same token the gods cannot take credit for Caesar's military victories. They do not confer empire. It springs from the great times and fortunes of the nations, and they owe *their* direction to the Great Being 'who dispenses kingdoms, and has now put the supremacy of them into the hands of the Romans...' (*Ad nat* II 17). Latin thought had transformed the otherwise discredited classical pantheon into guardians of the pluralistic empire.[50] For Tertullian, however, only one guiding hand governed events, his to whom the world, its story and its emperor belonged (*Apol* 26). The troubles of the empire found their explanation in punishment by the mighty God (*Apol* 40, 41) and only underlined the great offence to the divine majesty involved in recognising the gods as valid powers (*De idol* 21).

The positional supremacy of God enjoys yet deeper grounds in his uniqueness and power as creator, a doctrine which emerges with such force primarily out of Tertullian's, and Christianity's, struggle against

---

[50]L.G. Patterson, *God and History in Early Christian Thought. A Study of Themes from Justin Martyr to Gregory the Great*, London, A. & C. Black, 1967, 20 and R. MacMullen, 'Tertullian and the "National" Gods', *Journal of Theological Studies*, NS 26 (1975) 405–410 (p. 457).

polytheistic religion in the empire. All the powers assumed by the gods were really nothing more than the powers of the natural universe (*Apol* 11) which derived *their* existence only from the power and rank of the one who is the mighty creator. How absurd to imagine that God would create inferior ranks of deity to help him create the natural world upon which their own powers in turn are modelled (*Ad nat* II 5)! The pagan system dies in any case from a bad attack of self-contradiction, since gods of such an order cannot logically exist: they cannot be both the fashioners and the imitations of the elements. Tertullian's anxiety, along with other early Christian writers, to argue the *creatio ex nihilo* stems from the presence of conflict and threat, including this showdown with the popular gods, more than from some bare philosophical fight which he is picking with Greek thought. It has to do with God's powerful position:

> He is no longer almighty, if his might did not extend to this also to produce all things out of nothing. (*Adv Hermog* 8)

The viability of pagan gods, then, founders upon the divine power and position, which in turn springs from an almightiness implied by the *creatio ex nihilo*. We return to this subject later.

The position and status of the Christian God over against the emperor together form another crucial area by which to illustrate rank as a category of power. For Tertullian, the emperor receives his power from God. Sometimes, Tertullian wishes to state this in the most sympathetic manner, as in *Apologeticum* where the welfare of the emperor and of the empire rests upon the eminently desirable *status quo*. So the notion of divine omnipotence, in some of its aspects, nestles comfortably in the atmosphere of the Roman imperial destiny.

On the other hand, this kindly approach later turns to antagonism, and other conclusions for the empire emerge but from the same imperial model. The basic subjection of the emperor gains prominence. The one omnipotent God 'is also the Emperor's Lord' (*Apol* 34). Tertullian speaks of God's ordaining, 'in whose hand the king's heart is, of kingdoms and empires' (*De fuga* 12), and states acutely the distinction between divine and imperial ranks in *Ad Scap* 2, where the emperor is

> the human being next to God, who from God has received all his power, and is less than God alone.

Here we have to consider what at first sight seems a divergence of opinion on the existence of precedents for extending the imperial model into religion. One view holds that in the Roman world, efficiency in matters of secular organisation 'did not as a rule extend into the religious sphere'[51] and that there was no concept of divine right.[52]

Another view maintains that the idea of power became a major concern of metaphysics because of the concentration of political power in Rome,[53] and so in the system of Posidonius there is nothing which God cannot do,[54] a line pursued also by one of Tertullian's guiding lights, Seneca. However, the first view is saying only that no developed theological system sprouted from the notion of imperial power. For the Romans the secular base of imperial majesty produced in its religious aspect only a symbolic cult promoting political loyalty. Divine omnipotence in Tertullian supports a system of theology which actually regulates the relationship of God to creation and especially to humanity including the emperor. According to Tertullian, the rank of the real supreme 'emperor' totally overshadowed the imperial power in Rome and would finally emerge visibly as the ruling power to bring a new and noble empire.[55] An initially sympathetic view of the emperor in *Apologeticum*, resting upon a *status quo* helpful to Christian expansion, had given way to antagonism. Even in *Apol* 34 Tertullian announced God omnipotent as 'also the Emperor's Lord', echoed in *De fuga* 12, mentioned above. R.D. Sider concludes from *De spectaculis* that, for Tertullian, Rome led by her emperor was 'a paradigm of human perversion'[56] which the divine rule would finally destroy. Not merely the inequality but the incompatibility of the two rules led Tertullian to oppose the military oath to the emperor (*De cor* 11, 12). In a passage which properly scandalises modern Christian thought, Tertullian just too rhetorically and too gleefully celebrated the ultimate downfall of the Roman imperial might under the power of divine avenging omnipotence (*De spect* 30). The model of sovereignty, which had not altogether unfaithfully reflected the Jewish concept of Jahweh and the New Testament theme of God's kingdom, began to mirror also the most unchristian and worldly features of the worst Roman leaders.

This later harsher expression of divine omnipotence sprang, of course, from a growing sense that the emperor was more an enemy than a friend. Ultimately he was a demonic tool of rebellion against God's rule, whilst

[51]Bray op. cit. 95.
[52]Ibid.
[53]R.M. Grant, *Miracle and Natural Law in Graeco-Roman and Early Christian Thought*, Amsterdam, North-Holland Publishing Co., 1952, 128.
[54]Ibid.
[55]Bray, op. cit. 133.
[56]R.D. Sider, 'Tertullian on the Shows', *Journal of Theological Studies*, NS 29 (1978) 339–365 (p. 349).

the Roman judges had also failed despite their lofty position.[57] Persecution especially made visible the nature of the struggle, which came down to opposition between human powers and the power of God.[58] The emperor's reputation for playing a role in governing the cosmos and protecting humanity[59] conflicted with a divine prerogative, one which in Tertullian's time led to acute choices of allegiance.[60] A revived sense of being in the last times underscored opposition to what Tertullian saw as Roman pretensions.[61] Perhaps, as someone has suggested, a revolutionary tinge found its way into the apologist's thought.[62] Military images certainly penetrated his language[63] suggesting that the uniting of political and military power in the earthly emperor became projected on to God. So divine omnipotence, where driven by the imperial model, took an oppressive and monarchical ring. Modern complaints against the traditional model of God and his relation to the world has correctly detected this disquieting development, at least as it is found in Tertullian. However, divine omnipotence had other roots too and to one of the most important of these we now turn.

[57]On this aspect of *Apologeticum* see R.D. Sider, 'On Symmetrical Composition in Tertullian', *Journal of Theological Studies*, NS 24 (1973) 405–423 (particularly p. 409).

[58]J.-M. Hornus, 'Etude sur la pensée politique de Tertullien', *Revue d'Histoire et de Philosophie Religieuses* 38 (1958) 1–38 (p. 30).

[59]R.F. Evans, *One and Holy*, 7.

[60]Ibid. 5.

[61]W.H.C. Frend, Review of J.-C. Fredouille's *Tertullien et la conversion de la culture antique*, in *Journal of Theological Studies*, NS 24 (1973) 249–251 (p. 251).

[62]Ibid.

[63]T.P. O' Malley, *Tertullian and the Bible. Language–Imagery–Exegesis*, Utrecht, Van de Vegt N.V., 1967, 110.

CHAPTER 4

Creation and Omnipotence

Influences upon Tertullian's doctrine of creation

Even in the confused world of the second century, Christianity was not
the only system to speak of a creator. However, Tertullian champions, in
his *regula fidei* (Rule of Faith), a God who creates the universe through
the Word (*verbum*). R.F. Refoulé is clear that Tertullian means to
describe a 'creator in the Christian sense of the word'.[1] This observation
only raises the question of what distinguished the Christian concept
from its contemporary counterparts in the non-Christian world.

The major alternative approaches to cosmology in ancient times
rested with variations upon Stoicism and Platonism,[2] if we leave out the
more colourful cosmologies of pagan mythology and Gnosticism.[3] In

[1]R.F. Refoulé, op. cit. 106. Refoulé, however, bases his judgement on two
authorities in lexical studies, W.J. Teeuwen: *Sprachlicher Bedeutungswandel bei
Tertullian*, Paderborn, 1926, 129 and C. Mohrmann: *Die Altchristliche
Sondersprache in den Sermones des hl. Augustinus*, Nijmegen, 1920, 173.

[2]R. Cantalamessa believes he can find two responses in Hellenism to the need
for a God who is near to take part in human affairs: one is the Stoic nature-god
who is supreme but not personal (in the words of Cleanthes, the 'law and
destiny of all things') and the other is the panoply of intermediate deities,
personal but not supreme; Raniero Cantalamessa, 'The Development of the
Concept of a Personal God in Christian Spirituality', *Concilium* 103 (1977) 57–
66 (p. 58).

[3]Gnosticism sometimes receives serious treatment as a type of philosophy. P.
Perkins maintains that some of its works question the Platonist doctrine of the
eternity of the universe and the Stoic notion of cyclic worlds as well as modifying

Tertullian's time, synthesising forces in Middle Platonism produced what is sometimes called a Platonised Stoicism. Roman forms of Stoicism had traditionally opted for a cyclic succession of worlds,[4] a view surprisingly favoured by Origen even though the doctrine of *creatio ex nihilo* was well established by his time.[5] Tertullian's rejection of such schemes even before the time of Origen does not just anticipate the Church's later concern for the uniqueness of the Christ event.[6] It also cultivates belief in God's capacity to terminate evil and finally establish the human destiny in a resurrected body and a renewed cosmos.[7] Obviously for him this embraces also the redemptive events of the career of Jesus. This particular conflict between Christian and Greek approaches comes down to the question of the character and operation of a personal power behind the cosmos.[8]

Tertullian was not without sympathy for Stoicism in itself. When in his famed negative pronouncements he denounced philosophy, it was Platonist-inspired systems more than Stoicism which he had in mind, particularly mutations of Middle Platonism often mutilated at the hands of writers with a Christian background.[9] Roman Stoicism, after all, believed in providence and in a supreme deity with boundless power and kindly purpose.[10] According to J.-C. Fredouille, in *De bapt* 1 Tertullian actually bases his argument on the Stoic doctrine of divine omnipotence,[11] although he buttresses his case from biblical texts. Just how much the idea of omnipotence featured in Stoic thought generally, however, seems less secure.[12] Christian thought confronted Stoicism with

the severity of fate and demonic domination, 'On the Origin of the World (CG II 5): A Gnostic Physics', *Vigiliae Christianae* 34 (1980) 36–46 (p. 45).

[4] Olaf Pederson, 'The God of Space and Time', *Concilium* 166 (1983) 14–20 (p. 15).

[5] Ibid. 15.

[6] Ibid.

[7] R.M. Grant in *Miracle and Natural Law*, 24, notes that in the *Octavius* (II.1) of Minucius Felix a Stoic-influenced opponent of Christian eschatology argues for the indestructibility of nature, its laws and its elements.

[8] C.N. Cochrane, *Christianity and the Classical Tradition, A Study of Thought and Action from Augustus to Augustine*, Oxford, University Press, 1957, 500–501.

[9] Although, for Tertullian, Platonism was far too recognisable in Gnosticism. See the comments of Steinmann, *Tertullien*, Paris, Chalet, 1967, 78.

[10] E.V. Arnold, *Roman Stoicism*, 17.

[11] J.-C. Fredouille, *Tertullien et la conversion de la culture antique*, Paris, Études Augustiniennes, 1972, 329.

[12] R.M. Grant, for instance, reports that, 'the Roman Stoic Seneca accepts divine omnipotence – probably reflecting the thought of Posidonius – but is aware that it is a highly debatable question' (*Miracle and Natural Law*, 129).

the demand for belief in an omnipotence already exercised in the free
origination of all things. It was a hard bargain for a cosmology that
conceived God as inseparable from nature[13] and that espoused a creative
principle which was not the master of its medium.[14] For Tertullian those
Stoic doctrines meant that the 'creator' would not be almighty in
directing the destiny of the world since he was not almighty in
producing it.[15] Many of his complaints against the dualism of
Hermogenes strike Roman Stoicism too.[16] The alleged presence of
fatalism[17] in Stoicism would also yield a God nowhere near personal
enough for Tertullian. By contrast Tertullian's view is simple enough.
He speaks of a personal God with will and intervention, whose great,
primal, creative act puts him in possession of the world. This inspires the
allegiance and worship of its human occupants whilst his prior potency
guarantees their personal bodily survival.

Where, however, Stoicism does triumph in Tertullian is in the Logos
idea. The distinction between *logos endiathetos* (immanent Logos) and
logos prophorikos (the Logos expressed or 'spoken out') seems to have
emerged in the third century BC at the hands of the Stoic Chrysippus,[18]
but passed into general philosophical terminology and featured strongly
in Philo.[19] Justin and Tatian welcomed it for its binitarian ring but
Irenaeus suspected it for its anthropomorphisms.[20] Theophilus first
explicitly developed the scheme in a Christian context, fully embracing
its language,[21] and it is very possible that Tertullian's Logos development

[13]Cf. Grant, ibid. 8: 'among the Stoics the term "nature" is used very loosely.
It is the whole of existence, it is God, it is Zeus, it is the rational principle of the
universe, it is the first cause, it is providence, it is a spirit or a fire.'

[14]Arnold, op. cit. 202. Compare Meijering who connects in Stoic thought the
true and the real with that which is active power and final cause, 'Bermerkungen
zu Tertullians Polemik gegen Marcion (*Adversus Marcionem* 1.1–25)', *Vigiliae
Christianae* 30 (1976) 81–108 (p. 95). This way of thinking, maintains
Meijering, underlies Adv Marc I 9–11 and has a precedent in Seneca *Ep.* 65, 12
(according to Zeller) and in Irenaeus, *Adv haer* III 12.14 and II 46.2–4
(according to A. Bill).

[15]Arnold maintains that for the Stoics God is indeed the universe but not in a
pantheistic sense of being evenly diffused throughout all things (op. cit. 219). At
the same time they accepted a first principle of living and creative fire, the deity,
which contains the germ of the whole creation (ibid. p. 17).

[16]Ibid. 194.

[17]Ibid. 199–209.

[18]R.M. Grant, 'Theophilus of Antioch to Autolycus', *Harvard Theological
Review* 40 (1947) 227–256 (p. 245).

[19]Ibid. 246.

[20]Ibid.

[21]Ibid. 247.

stemmed either from Stoicism indirectly through Theophilus, and possibly Justin, or more directly from the Stoic schools or general philosophical terminology. At any rate we have here a Stoic source. It bears upon Tertullian's use of divine omnipotence, precisely because both he and Theophilus trace the emergence of the Logos to the work of creation.[22] As such, the Logos in Tertullian does not surface as a 'soul' of the universe, but rather reflects God's transcendence over the universe as a kind of spoken *creatio ex nihilo*.

But what of Platonism? Certainly Tertullian's predecessors betray unmistakable marks of its influence. Justin plundered the text of Plato himself.[23] Even Irenaeus seems occasionally indebted,[24] even though he so formidably wrecked Gnosticism, that wayward stepchild of Platonism. Yet whatever legacy passed from Justin and Irenaeus to Tertullian, the classic Christian teaching on creation remained perfectly intact in the hands of all three early Christian writers. It may be true that Tertullian, like Hermogenes, reworks a basically Platonist scheme for creation which involves three principles, namely *God*, the *Forms* and *Matter*.[25] But this would not be typical friendliness to Plato. Usually, Tertullian treated Plato with more suspicion than he did any of the philosophers.[26] This has been put down to Plato's willingness to recognise in matter a 'principle of limitation'[27] though perhaps not the actual source of evil. Plato receives a special mention in *Adv Marc* I 13 where he bears the greatest blame for superstitious elements which deify the natural elements. It results, says Tertullian, in philosophers recoiling from the idea of a beginning and end of everything in case they cast doubt upon the divine status of the natural elements. Here is the eye of the storm created by Greek and Christian cosmologies in conflict. Tertullian bombards Greek-inspired theories at this very point. He blames Plato for

---

[22]On Theophilus cf. Grant, 'Theophilus of Antioch', 247, citing *Ad Autol* II 22, where he sees Theophilus formulating his Logos doctrine from Scripture but in terms derived from Stoic-Philonic psychology. Similarly, see him on *Ad Autol* I 4 (ibid. p. 230).

[23]Thus Grant says, 'As a Christian he could use whatever weapons were to be found in his old philosophical arsenal: in the *Timaeus* he could still find a fairly reliable account of creation.' (R.M. Grant, *Augustus to Constantine*, 136).

[24]H. Chadwick, 'Freedom and Necessity in Early Christian Thought about God', *Concilium* 166 (1983) 8–13 (p. 11) and E.P. Meijering, 'Wie Platonisierten Christen? Zur Grenzziehung zwischen Platonismus Kirchlichem Credo und Patristischer Theologie', *Vigiliae Christianae* 28 (1974) 15–28 (p. 24).

[25]J.H. Waszink, 'Observations on Tertullian's Treatise Against Hermogenes', *Vigiliae Christianae* 9 (1955) 129–147 (p. 141).

[26]Refoulé, *De Praescriptione*, 96.

[27]Cochrane, op. cit. 79.

Hermogenes' falling prey to belief in the co-equality of matter with God (*Adv Hermog* 8). Equally the Gnostic systems come from Plato's school (*De praes* 7). Although in this same passage he discusses Marcion's concept of God as an offspring of Stoicism, the denunciation is not so philosophically fundamental,[28] and it probably aims at defence of the resurrection idea.[29]

Tertullian's resources in philosophy often came to him welded to contemporary Jewish thought. The exposition of Genesis 1:1 in *Adv Hermog* 19–20 points in this direction[30] where the equating of principium with wisdom has antecedents in the Jewish commentaries. Theophilus, an influence upon Tertullian, in turn contains Jewish sources.[31] The chief traces of this dependence have been found in Tertullian's praise of creation,[32] his description of the fall into sin,[33] and his use of the Old Testament.[34] Admittedly, however, it is not always easy to see where we are in the presence of a particularly Jewish source rather than a previous Christian one.

The Christian precedents for Tertullian's handling of power themes do not simply teach us that he borrowed shamelessly from his predecessors. They also show us that his motif of power did not leap arbitrarily into a doctrinal vacuum. Tertullian did not invent the notion of divine free omnipotence in creation.

G.T. Armstrong, like many commentators, sees in Tertullian's work the culmination of earlier controversial and apologetic writings.[35] R.M. Grant, following C. Becker,[36] agrees, and, moreover, believes he can find

[28]T.R. Glover, *Tertullian, Apology, De Spectaculis*, London, Heinemann, 1960, xv.

[29]Refoulé, op. cit. 96. On alleged sarcasm in Tertullian at this point see J.G. Gager, 'Marcion and Philosophy', *Vigiliae Christianae* 26 (1972) 53–59 (p. 54).

[30]On the significance of Jewish Wisdom concepts in Tertullian, see especially G.T. Armstrong, *Genesis in die Alten Kirche, Beitrage zur Geschichte der Biblischen Hermeneutik 4*, Tübingen, 1962, 103.

[31]R.M. Grant, 'Theophilus To Autolycus', 254. This gains further significance if one accepts the Antiochene identity of Theophilus as does D.S. Wallace-Hadrill in *Christian Antioch. A Study of Early Christian Thought in the East*, Cambridge, University Press, 1982, 43–45.

[32]Cf. Grant, op. cit. 231.

[33]Ibid. 239–242.

[34]Ibid.

[35]Armstrong emphatically places Tertullian in this tradition: *Die Genesis in die Alten Kirche*, 93–94.

[36]Grant cites C. Becker, *Tertullians Apologeticum*, Munich, 1954, 71–88 (publisher not given), in support of the judgement that Tertullian appropriated and re-worked an earlier shared apologetic tradition which was most adequately

evidence for use of a distinct body of apologetic writings.[37] Hence Tertullian drew not only on the more obvious Justin and Tatian, but also on Theophilus, Athenagoras and Melito.[38] To these we may add, on Tertullian's own account in *Adv Val* 5, the names of Miltiades, Irenaeus and Proclus. For his views on creation, however, Tertullian depended most heavily on Irenaeus and Theophilus. They especially display knowledge of some Rule of Faith. For Tertullian this Rule of Faith begins with the words in *De praes* 13: 'there is only one God, nor is there any other besides the creator of the world, who from nothing produced everything through his Word, who was before all else sent out (*Unum omnino Deum esse nec alium praeter mundi conditorem qui universa de nihilo produxerit per verbum suum primo omnium emissum*)'.[39]

Theophilus too begins his brief survey of Christian principles in *Ad Autolycum* III 15 with the doctrine of a creator God, 'the God and fashioner of the whole creation.' In *Ad Autolycum* III 9 equally he stresses the Christian belief in one God, creator and maker and fashioner of the whole universe,[40] if not always echoing earlier Church teaching.[41] Irenaeus is closer to Tertullian's *regula fidei* although not an exact template for it.[42] In *Adv haer* I 22.1 he says,

There is one God almighty, who created all things by his Word, and adapted them, and made them all out of not being to be.

expressed in Irenaeus, R.M. Grant, 'The Chronology of the Greek Apologists', *Vigiliae Christianae* 9 (1959) 25–33 (p. 32).

[37] R.M. Grant, 'Review of Carl Becker's "Apologeticum"', *Vigiliae Christianae* 9 (1959) 254–256 (p. 255).

[38] Ibid.

[39] It is significant that Tertullian thought this to be the faith of the apostles. Refoulé (*De Praes.*, 53) sees the *regula* as a condensation and formulation of the apostolic tradition.

[40] See J. Bentivegna, 'A Christianity without Christ by Theophilus of Antioch', E.A. Livingstone, ed., *Studia Patristica*, Vol. XIII, Berlin, Akademie-Verlag, 1975, 107–30 (p. 116).

[41] Grant says of *Ad Autolycum Book* II that it lacks the firm grasp on the apostolic tradition to be found in Justin, Irenaeus, Melito of Sardis and even Athenagoras (R.M. Grant, 'Theophilus to Autolycus', 242).

[42] B. Lohse reminds us that scholars have failed to establish a fixed wording of the creed in Irenaeus and Tertullian, but the process of formation of the creed was all the same well advanced by the end of the second century (*A Short History of Christian Doctrine*, Philadelphia, Fortress Press, 1966, 33).

In the Latin translation the terminology of the opening title is the same as Tertullian's *unus Deus omnipotens*.[43] Tertullian, then, does not invent the connection of *creatio ex nihilo* with the free omnipotence of God, but rather picks it up as a primary datum of the Church tradition. Irenaeus' precise words for creation from nothing, when appearing in Latin, differ slightly from Tertullian's terminology (*quod non erat* for Tertullian's *ex nihilo*). However, both find the agency of the *creatio ex nihilo* in the Word.

Irenaeus goes on to develop the rule in words which include the following:

> The Father made all by him, whether visible or invisible, sensible or intelligible, temporal with a view to some economy, or everlasting and eternal: not by angels, nor by any powers severed from his own mind – for the God of all has need of nothing but both by his Word and his Spirit making and ordering and guiding and giving being to all.

Tertullian does not say all this in his 'Rule of Faith' but it breaks through in other ways for other ends elsewhere. Whereas Irenaeus intends 'not by angels, nor by powers' to silence Gnosticism, Tertullian marshals that same conviction against Hermogenes to defend the divine omnipotence against challenge from unborn matter. He also wishes to eliminate the Roman deities from discussion on the basis of their redundancy to the divine work of creation. 'Severed from his own mind' in Irenaeus qualifies and strengthens the anti-Gnostic turn of phrase but it also recalls Tertullian's words in *Adv Hermog* 18:

> A substance such as God could have needed, needing what was his rather than alien property.

Both apologists instinctively reserve the *creatio ex nihilo* exclusively for God. Aeons and matter are, in different ways, extrinsic to God. The Word, or wisdom, is not. This principle will eventually furnish Tertullian with a power-rationale for unity between God and his Logos . Irenaeus himself had already approached the matter in terms of the *freedom* of God in *Adv haer* II 1.1:

> But of his own mind he freely made all things (*sed sua sententia et libere fecit omnia*)... being the only God... Lord... and creator... alone upholding all things... giving to all things their existence.[44]

---

[43]From J.T. Nielsen, *Irenaeus of Lyons Versus Contemporary Gnosticism – A Selection From Books I and II of Adversus Haereses*, Leiden, E.J. Brill, 1977, ad loc.

[44]Ibid.

Equally in *Adv haer* IV 20.1,2 he discounted the creative contribution of lower powers by insisting, as did Tertullian, that God had no need of assistance but made all things freely and voluntarily. Irenaeus then finished with the familiar appeal to creation from nothing (*fecit ex eo quod non erat ut essent omnia*). As with Tertullian, the freedom of God shielded the assurance that nothing extrinsic to God dictated the shape of the creation.

In *Adv haer* II 5.3 Irenaeus argued that locating evil in defective emanations and angels could not free God from guilt, just as Tertullian was later to argue that no inferior creator-God could clear God of complicity in the existence of evil. Both stood by God's freedom from necessity and saw the direct or indirect implication of some weakness in God as too high a price to pay for his defence. Irenaeus foreshadows Tertullian with the protest:

> They will make necessity greater and more absolute than God, since what has more power is before all in dignity.

Irenaeus, though counted as a 'Greek' apologist certainly has divine omnipotence as action in mind with these pronouncements. Certain phrases unmistakably make this clear: 'he did of himself and by his own power freely make... the only almighty... founding and making by the Word of his power' (*Adv haer* II 30.9); 'to ascribe the substance of the things which are made to the power and will of him who is God of all, is credible... the things which are impossible with men are possible with God' (*Adv haer* II 10.4).

So already in Irenaeus three themes merge: freedom, omnipotence and the creation from nothing (with a prominent creative role for Word and wisdom,[45] as later in Tertullian). Tertullian clearly takes his lead in these keynotes from Irenaeus and, by implication, from an established Church tradition. This tradition builds a foundation for Church doctrine in omnipotent creation of all things from nothing by the one God. The very standing and worthiness of this God as an object of worship, and as a saviour, depended in early writers upon these ideas.

Creation, dignity and power

Previous discussion has shown that divine power fixed, for Tertullian, God's unique dignity and honour. The notion of creatorhood also belongs in just this sphere of thought. In *Adv Marc* V 11 mentioned earlier, Tertullian backs a creator-God whose creative power provides the vessels for divine grace and glory, securing divine dignity (*eminentia*)

---

[45]See *Adv haer* II 11.1, II 27.2, III 8.3, IV 20.2–4, IV 32.1.

uniquely for him. Power-associated language rooted in creatorhood then abounds:

> The glory is the creator's, and it is his vessels that savour of the excellency of the power (*virtus*) of God, and the power (*virtus*) too is his because these things were entrusted to earthen containers... that his eminence (*eminentia*) might receive recognition.

Marcion, argues Tertullian, must take the whole package. Power, divine majesty and creatorhood go together. Marcion misses the whole point by dissociating power and glory from the mundane, the very things which placard God's status. The conflict with Marcion did not, however, trigger here a response novel to Christian faith. Tertullian had said it earlier:

> God is supreme greatness (*summum magnum*) in both form and reason and might and power (*et forma et ratione et vi et potestate*). (*Adv Marc* I 3)

We may be looking at standard philosophical terminology but the purpose to which Tertullian bends it can claim to be Christian, since he soon identifies the *summum magnum* with the creator *who sends Christ*. An ancient philosophical argument for divine oneness from divine greatness may or may not lurk in the background,[46] but Tertullian certainly makes philosophy the carrier of Christian ideas.[47] The mention of *forma* and *ratione* recalls the cosmogony inherited and developed by him elsewhere. They highlighted God's complete and solitary freedom in creation. The way the patristic writers normally distinguished God from the creation usually implied that 'uncreated' also entailed 'freely creating', an idea at its sharpest in the *creatio ex nihilo*. So an earlier part of *Adv Marc* I 3 sets down a ground principle that as *uncreated* and before time, without beginning or end, 'God is the supremely great (*deum summum esse magnum*).' The absolute potency to create everything defined the *summum magnum* or absolute greatness.

These themes do not form mere embroidery for the further humiliation of Marcion, but function as *foundations* of Tertullian's theology. Moreover, they stick firmly to Trinitarian forms far from innovative. Tertullian musters not some smart new defence of the Christian God, manufactured for Marcion's benefit, but the very idea of God which he instinctively appropriates from the second-century doctrinal legacy. Two early works confirm this. In *De test* 2 Tertullian wants to show that the human soul testifies not to the existence of pantheons and lesser deities, but to the uniquely pre-eminent God.

---

[46]E.P. Meijering, *Gotteslehre in Der Polemik*, 16.
[47]Ibid.

There can only be *one* with such dignity and the soul's testimony corroborates his claim. But the soul's evidence points more specifically to that one: the God 'from whom all things come'. Even the non-Christian, by prayers and oaths, testifies to God's creatorhood and the resulting ownership and administration. Even more significantly, *Apol* 17 argues,

> What we worship is the one God (*deus unus*),[48] who shaped this whole fabric... who by the word (*verbo*) with which he commanded, by the reason (*ratione*) with which he ordered it, by the might with which he could do it (*virtute qua potuit*), shaped it out of nothing, to the honour of his majesty (*de nihilo expressit in ornamentum maiestatis suae*).

The interlacing of creation, dignity and power had in fact cropped up already in *Apol* 11. As we saw in the previous chapter, Tertullian tolerated hypothetically the assumption that God's creative operation even embraced alleged nature gods in the pagan world (though even the pagans had to admit a God who is the true owner[49] of deity). All the same such deities were really superfluous. The natural laws and functions projected on to the gods existed independently of them and exposed them as surplus and unreal.

This polemic persists into the work against Marcion even in the thick of more sophisticated controversies. In *Adv Marc* I 6 the apologist explains the kind of dignity suitable to possession of the 'whole content of divinity' (*totum statum... divinitatis*). This can belong only to the supremely great (*summum magnum*). Tertullian, of course, immediately plays on the impossibility of two of this kind. Who then claims the crown? His own choice in *Adv Marc* I 7 is predictably clear. The *summum magnum* takes his description from being 'unbegotten, and uncreated, uniquely eternal, the creator of the universe'. No particular 'power-language' appears here but the quotation does fasten upon one particular operation of power, namely creation, to secure supreme greatness and dignity exclusively for Tertullian's God alone. Moreover,

---

[48]J. Daniélou remarks that for both Tertullian and Minucius Felix, names are regarded as natural (*physei*), not as conventional (*thesei*), so '*Deus* is the name which points to God in his absolutely unique and incommunicable character' (op. cit. 193). A question hangs over the first part of the assertion in the light of *Adv Marc* I 7 where Tertullian recognises that name and nature may sometimes not coincide though he identifies name and substance on that occasion.

[49]This is the quite valid choice of Glover in translating *mancipem*. This rather than 'dealer in', 'seller in', is preferred on contextual grounds, notwithstanding the fact that the latter sense better fits *Ad nat* I 9 (*sub eodem mancipe erroris*) which refers to the devil as the instigator of error. In *Ad nat* II 13 (*mancipem quendam divinitas*), the same choice faces the translator.

Tertullian often instinctively states the divine creatorhood in terms of power. Hence the unique dignity of the creator rests on a recognised exercise of power (*Adv Marc* I 1). Creation itself conjures up the power-theme, according to *De resurrectione mortuorum*, especially chapter 5:

> The whole universe of things, being servants, came into existence by the request and command (*imperio*) and by the sole power of the voice (*sola vocali potestate*)....

So, if the divine *potestas* in Tertullian's language points to a status of dignity, it is often more than just a casual reference to divine dynamic.

In preparing the ground for his analysis of Tertullian's Trinitarianism, J. Moingt observes that the word *potestas* usually indicated a *dynamis* intrinsic to the divine nature but that the idea of *active* power belonging to creation and providence took priority.[50] It is not always easy to detect in Tertullian's writings whether we are looking at power as an essential attribute and potency of the divine nature or merely at a status or even at an operation of power such as the work of creation or of providence. At any rate creatorhood and divine power come to us intimately related to each other. For Tertullian this very touchstone spells doom for Marcion's 'higher' god suitably tucked away from the squalid associations of creation and matter. Tertullian gloats in *Adv Marc* I 11,

> No-one has the right to believe the godhead of that other who has created nothing: unless... either... he had no wish to create anything or... he had no power.... But to have no power is unworthy of a god (*sed non potuisse indignum deo est*).

Here, creativity merely externalises something much deeper: God actually defined as power. Divine status consists precisely in both having power and exercising it, albeit upon a world considered unworthy by Marcion.

Although the theme of divine power is not unique to Tertullian, he takes his stand upon it more instinctively than any of his predecessors.[51] His near idiosyncratic treatment of baptism illustrates this. He traces a

---

[50]J. Moingt, *Théologie Trinitaire de Tertullien*, Vol. 1, *Histoire, Doctrine, Méthodes*, Paris, Aubier, 44. He cites as supporting authorities, Braun, op. cit. 112, Evans, *Tertullian's Treatise Against Praxeas*, 55–56, and K. Woelfl, *Das Heilswirken Gottes durch den Sohn nach Tertullian* (Analecta Gregoriana Vol. 112), Roma, 1960, 64–67.

[51]Cf. the observation of Meijering: 'Irenaeus stresses the divine plan or will before the world, because only this makes it clear that the creator is not a limited, inferior and weak being.' (*God, Cosmos, History*, 251).

line straight from the miraculous power of the baptismal water to the wisdom and power of God in creation:

> If God is wise and powerful (*potens*) as even those who pass him by are prepared to admit, quite justifiably has he established the materials he works with in foolishness and incapability, the opposites of wisdom and power (*potentia*). (*De bapt* 2)

Tertullian here celebrates not just the miraculous power at work in baptism but also that power in the primal work of creation which establishes water as the mysterious element it always is. The very weakness and simplicity of water means that its dignity and centrality in creation depend upon a converse almightiness and freedom in God its maker. Here he exploits a whole sweep of ideas involving divine sovereignty and freedom, miracles and resurrection/restoration.[52] Further examples of creation as power crop up repeatedly, for example, in *Adv Hermog* 19 where Tertullian interprets Genesis 1:1 as a reference to the 'pre-eminence (*principatus*) and power (*potestas*)' through which God made heaven and earth; and *Adv Marc* IV 9 where he speaks of that *potestas* of the creator which by a mere word produced the universe. References like these make it clear that the *chief* characteristic of the creative work, in Tertullian's mind, was the presence of a truly divine power.

It has, however, to be admitted that in two important accounts of creation, Tertullian gives an equal place to wisdom or reason. Thus in *Apol* 17 the commanding word (*verbo*), and the ordering reason (*ratione*), not simply the power (*virtute qua potuit*), lie behind the *creatio ex nihilo*. Then again in *Apol* 21 we read,

> God devised the whole universe by word (*verbo*), by reason, (*ratione*), by might (*virtute*).... We, too, to that word (*sermoni*), reason (*rationi*) and power (*virtuti*) (by which we said God devised all things) would ascribe spirit... and in spirit giving utterance we should find word; with spirit ordering and disposing all things, reason; and over spirit, achieving all things, power (*virtus*).

At first sight it seems that the *virtus* enjoys no special standing. It looks as though the three qualities, word, reason and power, whether facets or stages of the operation or even various names for the Logos,[53] each enjoy

---

[52] T.G. Ring, *Auctoritas bei Tertullian*, 56.

[53] Crucial words follow: 'This, we have been taught, proceeds from God... called Son of God.... This ray of God... entered into a certain virgin....' The first word of the sentence is in fact Glover's non-committal translation of *Hunc*. There seems little doubt, however, that 'he' correctly renders it and that word, or reason, or power could equally be substituted.

an equal eminence in the work of creation. It would be a typical second-century sentiment. That, however, is our key. Tertullian does not in this chapter explore the nature of God as he later does against Marcion and Hermogenes. Rather he is establishing the status and role of the Logos in order to pave the way for his doctrine of the incarnation, and to achieve this he simply marshals the standard Logos expectations of his era. He wishes only to show that he includes the Logos in the powerful work of creation, no more no less. All the same, he does say that power is over (virtus praesit) all things. Glover's translation even has 'power over Spirit', where the latter indicates the divine nature. Virtus is the animating quality of the divine nature in which Logos participates for creation.

A similar team of ideas appears in *Adv Hermog* 44, 45 but in quite a different context. Tertullian is attacking the view which, by a partial theory of 'spontaneous' creation, relieves God of active responsibility for evil in the creation. Hermogenes maintains that matter simply turned into creation spontaneously in the presence of an approaching God. Tertullian however offers a creation involving the actual labour of God, because 'the greater is his glory if he really laboured'. The universe exists by an operation of God. Evidence for this arises from the role of wisdom (*sophia*) and the word (*sermo*). Wisdom is 'the beginning of his ways for his works', and the word is, 'God's right hand... by which he worked and built the universe.' So God actively created by his own powers:

These are his powers (*Haec sunt vires eius*) by which he worked and created this universe.

We may safely assume that *haec* refers to wisdom and word[54] as God's conscious and determining faculties. By quotation from Jeremiah another feature has crept into the discussion:

God has made the earth by his power, he has prepared the world by his wisdom and has stretched out the heavens by his understanding.[55]

Modern biblical exegesis would, of course, recognise here some Hebrew parallelism, but it would be anachronistic to expect this approach in Tertullian. It seems therefore at least possible that for Tertullian the first clause stands on its own as an overall characterisation of the operation of creation, whilst the following clause mentions wisdom and understanding as the faculties through which this power operates. We

---

[54]Waszink holds that *Haec* may be treated as either a *feminine* or *neuter* plural (J.H. Waszink, *Tertullian, The Treatise Against Hermogenes, Translated and Annotated*, London, Longmans Green & Co., 1956, 169).

[55]For a full discussion of complete textual difficulties in this passage, J.H. Waszink, op. cit. ad loc.

should then be driven back, after all, to the earlier impression that it is really 'power' which predominates.

One problem with this approach intervenes from another part of the chapter:

> The universe exists by the operation of God (*operatione dei*)... who... applied... his mind, his wisdom, his power, his understanding, his word, his spirit, his might.

Does power, after all, form only one more faculty amongst others in the work of creation? We should weigh certain factors. First, for Tertullian, *any* activity of the divine understanding and the word invariably involved some conscious exercise of the divine will and therefore of the divine power. It would be surprising if 'power' did not come rolling in behind the noetic functions in this list. Tertullian mentions 'power', the underlying potency of the operation, not to slot it in beside understanding and word but because as the primary character of the work, he cannot *not* mention it. Secondly, just here there comes a not untypical explosion of Tertullian's rhetoric as he realises that in these closing sentences he must make clear the conscious involvement of God in the production of the world, as opposed to the 'spontaneous creation' theory of Hermogenes. He therefore throws together indiscriminately any and all the features to hand which reinforce that particular point. The active power of God proves indispensable to this end. Thirdly, the earlier line of argument against Hermogenes has taken as its main shaft divine power as an indispensable mark of an authentic God. It is unlikely that, whatever Tertullian's interest just here, he now intends to shift power from its foundational position. Even here, where by reference to the noetic faculties he means to stress the conscious creative activity of God, the divine power almost presses right into the foreground.

De praes 1, although not about creation, enshrines something of the priority of divine power in creation and recalls what we saw earlier about the identity of power with will:

> When it has been determined that a thing must by all means be, it receives the (final) cause for which it has its being. This secures the power through which it exists, in such a way that it is impossible for it not to have existence.

It may be that Tertullian is here following a pattern of thought found in Tatian, as Alasdair Heron suggests about *Adv Prax* 5–7,[56] which describes creation through word, reason and discourse. Tatian speaks of

---

[56]A. Heron, '"Logos, Image, Son": Some Models and Paradigms in Early Christology', R.W.A. McKinney, ed., *Creation, Christ and Culture: Studies in Honour of T.F. Torrance*, Edinburgh, T. & T. Clark, 1976, 43–62 (p. 57).

God's 'aloneness' which includes within itself the potential, or *dynamis*, of everything else that will be, and labels the 'power of the Logos', or 'rational power', the very rational capacity of God himself.[57] The idea recurs in Tatian:

> The beginning is the power (*dynamis*) of the Logos.... In so far... as he himself was all power (*dynamis*)... everything was with him. With him also, through his rational power there came to be the Logos.[58]

Some of this finds an echo in Tertullian and reflects divine omnipotence. For God, merely to will a thing is to secure its existence. In himself he is a commanding *dynamis* and thereby contains within himself all possibilities, all *potentia*. For that reason 'rational power' probably means more than simply 'rational capacity', or 'rational faculty'. Rather it points to unlimited power which nevertheless can only ever remain divinely rational, that is, coinciding with the divine will. The stress falls upon the *dynamis* ('In so far... as he himself was all power') and the *logike* ('rational') stamps that power as volitional. It is just this kind of power of which *De praes* 1 speaks. Here, of course, the apologist recognises divine providence at work even in the uncomfortable fact of heresy. It is the same rational will and power which calls creation out of nothing and recalls the dead to life:

> Why could you not again come out of nothing into being, by the will of the very same author whose will brought you into being out of nothing?... Your doubts... will be about the power (*vis*)[59] of God... who set together the universe. (*Apol* 48)

Tertullian answers the question whether a power adequate to a resurrection exists by appeal to the first creation, but the idea he stresses is the divine will (*voluntas*).

Hence, in a number of key texts which address the subject of divine creation, *potestas* or *vis* dominate even where noetic and volitional ideas enter (doubtless under the influence of Logos speculation in earlier writers). The *creatio ex nihilo* at last confronts us.

Power and the *creatio ex nihilo*

With the doctrine of 'creation from nothing' Tertullian simply returns to a tradition as early as Clement of Rome.[60] It had later germinated in

---

[57]Ibid. 56.

[58]Tatian, *Ad Graecos* 5, in Heron, op. cit. 56.

[59]*Vis* is unusual in Tertullian for the divine power, but here nevertheless suitable in view of the idea of renewed life and strength.

[60]J.N.D. Kelly, *Early Christian Doctrines*, London, A. & C. Black, 1973, 83.

Irenaeus.[61] Another of Tertullian's sources, Theophilus, spearheads rational argument for its necessity.[62] Through the creation from nothing 'God's greatness can be known and apprehended'[63] and the 'power of God is shown by this, that he makes whatever he wants out of nothing.'[64] The appearance of such thinking in the Jewish-influenced Theophilus strengthens the impression that the roots of belief in a free divine production of all things from non-existence are to be found in Jewish,[65] and therefore Old Testament, teaching. So the confrontation between creationism and dualism did not form a peripheral battle precipitated unexpectedly by Tertullian. It sprang not only from Jewish monotheism but also from the work and concerns of the early apologists. In them too the doctrine of creation neutralised the threat posed to the whole Christian system of thought by dualism. This struggle spanned the earliest era in clashes with the remote deity of Gnosticism, with Marcion's higher 'good' god, or with the system of Hermogenes where matter existed co-eternally with the creator. Only with Theophilus of Antioch, however, did a sustained defence first take shape for the one doctrine that totally forestalls dualism, namely the *creatio ex nihilo*.[66] For Theophilus the divine monarchy hung on the thread of that doctrine over against what he called the Platonist teaching of an unborn universe alongside an unborn Father and creator.[67] Although Plato seemed to talk of a beginning of the creation in time, standard tradition understood this to be purely an instructional device not to be taken literally.[68] Possibly Theophilus was especially familiar with contemporary ideas[69] and his interest in them may have generated discussion of the doctrine of creation in Christian theology. However, the foundations already stood in place from the work of Irenaeus.

It is difficult to say just how much Tertullian derived his emphasis on the fully developed doctrine of creation from Theophilus. Other factors are to hand. It seems that the whole preceding history of the discussion

---

[61] See Irenaeus, *Adv haer* II 10.4.

[62] J.H. Waszink, *Treatise Against Hermogenes*, 11; O. Pederson, *The God of Space and Time*, 15.

[63] The paraphrase of *Ad Autol* II 4, offered by J. Bentivegna, op. cit. 110.

[64] *Ad Autol* II 4, as rendered by Waszink, op. cit. 10, Bentivegna op. cit. 109, Grant, *Theophilus of Antioch to Autolycus*, 223, 241.

[65] Theophilus is found to be more in sympathy with Jewish thought than the Church fathers generally.

[66] J.H. Waszink, *The Treatise Against Hermogenes*, 11.

[67] *Ad Autol* II 4, as rendered by Waszink, ibid.

[68] On the question of how literally Plato intended his account of creation in *Timaeus* see my earlier summary of Tertullian's use of philosophical sources.

[69] See Nicole Zeegers-Vander Vorst, 'La création de l'homme (Gn 1.26) chez Théophile d'Antioch', *Vigiliae Christianae* 30 (1976) 258–267 (pp. 264–265).

came to be summed up and thrown together in Tertullian's unsorted and encyclopaedic style. By then the Christian teaching had come to stand defiantly on the *creatio ex nihilo*. Contemporary dualism of course aimed to contain the problem of evil without overthrowing metaphysics altogether and the breathtaking stand of the Christians committed them to an engagement with theodicy whether they wished it or not.[70]

It has to be admitted that Tertullian's impatience with the questions of philosophy rendered him ill-equipped fully to appreciate the issues involved in such an engagement. But he too attempted to vindicate the creator's universal goodness and the resulting conception of nature as a divine gift to humanity.[71] The precedent for arriving at this point appears already in Irenaeus, whose 'insistence on the *creatio ex nihilo* implies that he cannot speak disparagingly about the world'.[72] Similarly the world, for Irenaeus, deserves not destruction but consummation.[73] In Irenaeus, then, the *creatio ex nihilo* ensures the essential goodness of the world[74] and supports the reliability of God to deliver what he has promised for it. Against Gnosticism, Irenaeus sees in the world an intrinsic worth, justifying its consummation rather than its destruction. Moreover, the world, for Irenaeus, presents itself to the creator as a suitable medium of revelation, one by which the Logos may initiate new relationships between God and humanity. Through the world, through the human creature formed by the creator and through the word made visible, the Father is displayed (*Adv haer* IV 6.6).

Hence the *creatio ex nihilo* became the cornerstone of Tertullian's theology of divine power. For him it did not distance God from the human beings but supported his relationship with them. Nothing was more important in Patristic thought than the knowledge of God. For Tertullian this could only come through recognition of the divine power. The *creatio ex nihilo*, he held, stimulated such a recognition, one which would never be learnt from the philosophers[75] but was a standard belief among the various Christian schools. This latter claim concerning

[70]F.M. Young, 'Atonement and Theodicy: Some Explorations', E.A. Livingstone, ed., *Studia Patristica*, Vol. XIII, Berlin, Akademie-Verlag (1975) 330–333 (p. 330).

[71]H.B. Timothy, *The Early Christian Apologists and Greek Philosophy*, Assen, Van Gorcum and Co., 1973, 56. He has *De spect* 2 in mind.

[72]E.P. Meijering, *God, Cosmos, History*, 262.

[73]Ibid. 262–263.

[74]*De an* 10; *De res* 26; *Adv Marc* I 1 and 14; *De pat* 2 et al. J.-M. Hornus finds some political connotations in this perspective, *Étude sur la pensée politique de Tertullien*, 6.

[75]Most writers incline to the view that in this matter at least Tertullian did not primarily lean upon the philosophers though there is affinity with Philo as well as Irenaeus. See G.T. Armstrong, *Die Genesis in der Alten Kirche*, 103.

standard belief is significant, though how much it means to allege that the *creatio ex nihilo* enjoyed a standard credal status, we cannot say. What we can say is that the doctrine constituted a clash with such writers as Marcion and Hermogenes who owed much to contemporary thought. On the outcome there hung, for Tertullian, every major tenet of the *regula fidei*. Cochrane suggests that bound up in the affirmation of *creatio ex nihilo* is the faith itself untrammelled by the observable or visible,[76] a root confession for Christian faith affecting the whole basis of a person's relationship to God.

Tertullian saw, in his opponents' systems of thought, primarily a prejudice against God's directing the whole physical world to a beneficent end. How much or little this prejudice owed to the pagan schools of the time is not the main point. Tertullian was attacking the disparagement of nature in the form it occurred in Marcion and the Gnostics. His own strategy meant equating the 'Good' God with the omnipotent creator. He opts for a similar approach against Hermogenes, but with a more abstract tone. According to Cochrane, traditional Christianity sets its face against any views committed 'to a cosmos which is doomed to irremediable imperfection or evil'.[77] The Christian view usually saw nature as neither self-generating nor self-fulfilling but absolutely dependent for its destiny upon God.[78] It did not, in other words, enjoy a status to rival God's but rather fell under his sphere of influence. Only the intervention of divine action 'free from all compulsion or limitation, internal or external'[79] could resolve the apparently remorseless flowering of evil. This placed the doctrine of bodily resurrection amongst the chief doctrinal themes. In *De Resurrectione* 11 (as in *Apol* 48), Tertullian defends the resurrection of the flesh (the most practical conceivable form of evil's overthrow), on the strength of the *creatio ex nihilo*:

> Trust therefore that he has brought forth this everything out of nothing, and you will at once know God by trusting that God has so much power (*valeo*).[80]

Evans is ready to say that Tertullian's programme of writing was indeed working its way towards this supreme interest although weightier problems, such as the incarnation, constituted intermediate stages.[81] To

---

[76]C.A. Cochrane, *Christianity and Classical Culture*, 238.

[77]Ibid. 239.

[78]Ibid.

[79]Ibid.

[80]*Valeo* is, like *vis* in n. 59 above, an unusual choice, but perhaps selected for the same reason as the choice of *vis* since the context is identical.

[81]E. Evans, *Treatise on the Resurrection*, x–xi.

say anything rejuvenating at all to the metaphysic of its time, Christian teaching had to place evil under a higher power, whether it was evil in the world or in the Christian.[82] In the teeth of attractive alternatives from Marcion and Hermogenes, Tertullian opted for a higher power of an absolute order who called all things into being from total non-existence. Such a God displayed a capacity to deliver what the prophets, Christ and apostles promised.

Tertullian did not, however, work from a base of *naked* power. Key words like 'reason', 'wisdom' and 'understanding' hover around Tertullian's use of *potestas* and his notion of *creatio ex nihilo*. Whatever their philosophical provenance, they serve to guard the divine power from any idea of internal compulsion, that is, from arbitrariness, blind irrationality or cold domination.

The issue came down to this. The idea of a pre-existent material in creation presented grave difficulties for both Jews and Christians since it put limitations upon God.[83] In his tract against Hermogenes Tertullian reflects and develops this concern. Very early on, his biting irony tackles Hermogenes' foisting of a co-eternal matter upon God:

> Matter is clearly superior, since it provided (God) with the material for his work; and... God is evidently inferior to matter, since he needed its substance.... Great indeed is the service which matter rendered to God, that today he can have something through which he may be known as God and be called the Almighty (*omnipotens*), except that he is no longer almighty if his might (*potens*) did not extend to this also – to produce all things out of nothing.[84] (*Adv Hermog* 8)

It is only an introduction but his convictions are immediately plain. God's omnipotence comes attached to the *creatio ex nihilo* and defies negotiation, or else nothing remains of the Christian hope. In the next chapter he erects God's Lordship on the same platform. Without the *creatio ex nihilo* God finds himself at the mercy of an evil, or at least alien, substance,

> under the constraint (*necessitas*) of his weakness which made him unable to draw his resources from nothing, and (therefore) not from his power (*potestas*).

[82]Cf. J. Steinmann, *Tertullien*, 138.

[83]McGiffert thinks the doctrine of *creatio ex nihilo* was inevitable in both Christianity and Judaism, *God of the Early Christians*, 168. *Adv Hermog* 17 demonstrates the dependence, in Tertullian's mind, of monotheism upon the *creatio ex nihilo* but equally, *Adv Hermog* 20 betrays Tertullian's lack of ideas on the scriptural basis for it.

[84]The text as suggested by Waszink, *Treatise Against Hermogenes*, 117.

Tertullian tolerates no middle ground between dualism and the *creatio ex nihilo*.[85] It is the same in *Adv Hermog* 14 when discussing creation from nothing:

> It is more becoming to believe that God, even as author of evil, is free[86] than that he is subservient: power (*potestas*), of whatever kind, is more appropriate to him than weakness.

In chapter 16 Tertullian even lurches into dangerous territory. Since freedom (*libertas*) is more appropriate to God than necessity, Tertullian would rather have it 'that God wanted to create evil things out of himself than that he was unable to *prevent* their creation.'

We can salvage something of the apologist's reputation from this reckless statement. In the first place it is hypothetical and therefore not to be taken too seriously. His serious position was a kind of early freewill theodicy. Moreover he admits that no complete answer to the problem of evil lies to hand and that no God can be spared the predicament which evil presents (*Adv Hermog* 10). He would, in reality, never resort to postulating that God produced evil out of himself. But if he *had* to choose between the two unpalatable options, he would prefer a God capable of producing evil from within himself to one incapable of preventing it. This can only be because it at least denies the sheer necessity of evil. What free, unlimited power generates, it may also extinguish, especially if it operates through reason and wisdom. All the same, Tertullian would have been better not to make the statement, since it leaves the impression that active divine power and freedom is an end in itself and to be evaluated positively quite apart from the moral character of God. By contrast, the Christian tradition has usually seen the divine action as taking its direction from the divine moral character.

However, Tertullian does have a legitimate point he wishes to make. The power and freedom of God reflected in the *creatio ex nihilo*, with all its problems, ensures that evil does not exist necessarily and that one word from God will erase it from all existence. Any attempt, inspired by Greek ideas, to relieve God from responsibility for evil by distancing him from the creation and its evil undermines the very omnipotence by which evil may at last be destroyed. In *Adv Hermog* 19 he presses an alternative to Hermogenes' interpretation of 'in the beginning' of Genesis 1:1. Hermogenes translates the Greek *arche* as material substance. Tertullian argues that, instead, it indicates primacy in order and power, and that 'beginning' (*principium*) 'can be used for both "sovereignty" (*principatus*) and "power" (*potestas*)'. Why? 'For it was in

---

[85]Tertullian repeats his proscription of the middle ground in *Adv Hermog* 17.

[86]McGiffert, op. cit. 166, draws attention to Irenaeus, *Adv haer* II 5.4, II 30.9 and Theophilus, *Ad Autol* II 4.

his sovereignty and power that God made heaven and earth.' This is not a rare link in his work.[87] It places divine omnipotence near the centre of Tertullian's theology because he saw the doctrine of creation as fundamental to the survival of the Christian faith. According to *Adv Prax* 1, when the devil pretends to defend the truth,

> He is champion of the one Lord, the almighty, the creator of the world (*omnipotentem mundi conditorem*), so that he may make a heresy out of the unity.

Against heretical views the Paraclete 'will bear witness to the selfsame Christ... and to the whole design of God's creation' (*De monog* 2). Failure to grasp the idea of God as creator will lead to hopeless confusion about his work of grace amongst people. The Holy Spirit, however, will lead people back to a proper conception of God through Christ. Dosing out withering comments to heresies in *De praes* 40, he concludes either that they set up a rival deity to the creator or else they craft a creator of a different kind. Whether it be Marcion's promotion of a higher 'good' god, or the demeaning reconstruction by Hermogenes, heresy strikes at the idea of a divine status whose definition involves unique potency leading to creation from nothing.

Behind all this is a desire to speak of the intrinsic value of the cosmos and of the essential goodness displayed in it.[88] Being the creator brought God near as the concerned possessor of all things. The world, and especially humanity, thus enjoyed a particular value. A special relationship between them and their creator follows. This is clear from the tract *De paenitentia* which begins with an explanation of the reason for repentance. It can only come from God himself, the 'Author' or 'Creator' of reason which itself accounts for people's revulsion at their own evil deeds. True repentance can only spring from the 'Maker' and a person knows what sin is when found by that One (*De paen* 3). These sins may spring from either spirit or flesh since God created both.

Tertullian's concern really centres on the relationship of people to God which, for him, stems from the *creatio ex nihilo*. Hence in *Adv Hermog* 13 he observes, on the strength of his opponent's own presuppositions, that if matter is eternal and contains both good and evil potential, then both good and evil originate from it. But then, he complains,

---

[87]Braun, op. cit. 101. He cites as examples *Adv Marc* I 4, II 2, II 21, *Adv Prax* 1, *De virg vel* 1. See also *De test* 2.

[88]Of this passage T.A. Burkill concludes, 'The creator is the Supreme Lawgiver, and it is the proper function of the human creature to obey the commands of his Maker.' (*The Evolution of Christian Thought*, Ithaca, Cornell University Press, 1971, 59.)

we shall owe to God neither gratitude for good things nor resentment for evil things… he has been the servant of matter.

The more Platonised types of Christianity shared the legitimate Greek concern over the problem of evil. But Tertullian was concerned about the problem of the *good*. The good rested upon humanity's relationship with God, constituted by the powerful act of creation. Without that, Tertullian detected no foundation for the practice of Christian religion with its claimed support of everything considered good for humanity. It alone guaranteed that God could be an involved party made known to his human world. A deity may only set up a relationship with people by revealing himself in the creation. This is the sort of being that the human world appropriately honours[89] rather than Marcion's lofty and remote nominee, who enjoys no such organ of self-disclosure.

Only a creator, a kind of 'begetter', can assume the title of 'Father', according to *Adv Marc* IV 26. To make everything is to own everything as its Lord and to have the power to dispose by goodness. It can only be the creator who commands the spirits (a stinging strike since Marcion has jealously guarded the spiritual kingdom for his own non-creating deity), possesses the bread and holds in his hand the highest rulers. Marcion's god does not even possess a scorpion, let alone bread, to withhold from those who ask for it as Jesus commanded. In order to command a rescuer, God needed a status as creator:

> That supremely good god of yours, coming without being asked, to grant gifts to the man who is not his own, could not have demanded of him either toil or persistence.

The name not only of 'Father' but of 'God' belongs only to the one 'from whom all things come, and who is the Lord of the universe' (*De test* 2), the one 'to whom everything belongs, as did even the beginning, and from whom also are the times' (*Adv Marc* V 17). The 'everything' includes both beginning itself and time itself because they emanate from the creator, the one who 'grasps the whole world in his hand like a nest' (*Adv Marc* II 25).

Why then has Tertullian's type of religion drawn such fierce criticism in modern thought? For God to be creator, argued Tertullian, is for him to be the Lawmaker before whom there can be no questioning. Obedience finds its rationale in the 'majesty of the divine power (*maiestas divinae potestatis*), the authority of the one who commands' (*De paen* 4). The irreducible principle of authority which governs the Christian religion, both in morals and worship, is rooted in the fact that

---

[89]Cf. E.P. Meijering on *Adv Marc* I 12, *Bermerkungen zu Tertullians Polemik gegen Marcion*, 95.

it is with the creator of everything-from-nothing that the Christian has to deal. If asked to say what his religion was, Tertullian would have answered in the words with which he opens his defence of Christianity in *Ad Scap* 2:

> We are worshippers of one God, of whose existence and character nature teaches all men; at whose lightnings and thunders you tremble, whose benefits minister to your happiness.

This passage settles what kind of God may uniquely receive worship but he seems at best like a loud headmaster and at worst like the human emperor in bad form. Hence, the Roman emperor himself has received his power from this God, and any sacrificing on his behalf must consist in personal prayer, since the 'creator of the universe has no need of odours or of blood.'

Evidently Tertullian, as ever, was looking over his shoulder at the emperor, the only rival universal deity. As a result, he has allowed himself to corrupt the biblical God, even the law-giving God, into the *alter ego* of a human ruler, with some of the less worthy tones which that conveys. Fortunately he does not always regress this far. The religious concern in his offensive against Marcion simply attacks self-confident human blurring of the lines between creator and creature, as well as scything down Marcion's hostility to a God who comes in a human fleshly life.[90]

In summary, this possession which God enjoys over the spirit world, physical nature and humanity, stemming from the free unconditioned creation of them, governs the whole creator–creature relationship.[91] Without this sovereignty Tertullian perceives no way of working out his own great themes, especially in the area of morals and religion. Some of these seem worthy even to many modern critical readers, especially the worthiness of nature and the close involvement of God in the concerns of human beings. Others understandably arouse hostility: omnipotence as absolute power over human affairs; legalism in soteriology and ethics;

[90]H. Von Campenhausen, *Fathers of the Latin Church*, 21. A. Heron argues that before Nicea the radical qualitative difference between God and not-God was obscured by the hierarchical pattern of thought ('"Logos, Image, Son": Some Models', 53). This is certainly true of the *Logos*, the major interest of Heron's article, though Tertullian is breaking that mould in *Adversus Praxean* and the Nicean breakthrough grows from roots in Irenaeus, Theophilus and Tertullian with their radical doctrine of creation which distinguishes, by means of the *creatio ex nihilo*, the not-God character of everything which is nature. Origen is of course more ambiguous on this matter.

[91]Cf. the words of another part of *Adv Marc* IV 26: 'Who is it has anything to give to him that asks, except him whose are all things, whose also am I who am asking.'

the perceived paternalism of cosmic ownership. These problems and others will receive further attention in due course.

Before this survey closes, an apparently anomalous use of *omnipotens* in *Adv Marc* II 5 warrants some comment. In a crucial passage Tertullian has been countering a problem posed by Marcion, one which still forms a formidable objection to the Christian faith, namely that in a world of evil it is impossible to maintain simultaneously the goodness, prescience and *omnipotence* of God the creator. The creator's works, Tertullian replies,

> are great just because they are good: and God is powerful just because all things are his (*vel sic deus potens, dum omnia ipsius*), and for that reason he is omnipotent (*unde et omnipotens*).

Earlier I traced the evidence for seeing in the description '*omnipotens*' an infinite potentiality out of which all things came into being. In this quotation, however, Tertullian seems to argue that God's present possession of all things causes him to be *omnipotens*. It is possible that the translation given should simply stand as a rare example of an unusual, functional, or concrete, connotation in *omnipotens*. It would, in other words, connote the acts of providence and redemption rather than an all-embracing potency lying behind those works. Yet this would leave us with an unlikely and narrow sense for Tertullian, who treated the exalted title with some reverence. Moreover the matter as a whole is not so simple. The immediately preceding passage describes the creator's 'works' as good, of his power, and as *made out of nothing*. Evidently then, Tertullian's mind focuses here not at all on the divine *acts* in space–time history at all but on the *materials* in space–time history, the *products* of the *creatio ex nihilo*.

I offer a solution for the Latinists to sit in judgement upon. We might give *unde* not a causal sense, 'whence he is omnipotent', (that is, 'he is omnipotent because he has all things') but rather a *logical* sense: 'whence the *conclusion* that he is omnipotent'. The case is stronger than first apparent since the sentence looks like a word-play (*potens* + *omnia* = *omnipotens*). It also forms the climax of Tertullian's discussion of omnipotence. So we have here a fitting dénouement: 'whence we deduce his omnipotence' or, 'and for that reason, *we infer that* he is omnipotent'.

Tertullian starts with the human relationship to God which sprang out of the divine proprietorship of the universe. Only from here, he held, could one reach a proper understanding of the whole *regula fidei*, both its inner logic and its practical outcome. Only the creator's absolute possession of the whole world explains the divine commitment to humanity involved in the incarnation. Moreover, the divine *power or ability actually to achieve entry* into the human sphere seems to Tertullian more credible on such an account. It highlights not only human subjection to the Father of creation but also the Word's own assumption of this relation on the human side. The Word accepts the relationship of God to created humanity and sets a kind of seal upon it as the very condition in which he reveals God and redeems humanity.

Tertullian's defence of the creation as a medium of God's goodness seems a fair reply to Marcion's disparagement of it, but is it secure as a theodicy? His opponents have taken the high ground, treating goodness and kindness as the non-negotiable properties of any self-respecting God from Christian quarters. Tertullian has succeeded in showing this to be no more than a theoretical gain if the same God finds himself trapped in necessity and weakness. But he has not taken the high ground itself. The agendas of Marcion and Hermogenes have dictated the stress and rhythm of the apologist's theology. Dignity and power, easy enough to justify from the tradition, have assumed *too* pivotal and foundational a position so that goodness will have to find and follow them. Omnipotence lurks everywhere, shadowing and haunting every tendency to speak of the goodness of God. It conveys the impression not that power is of the essence of God but that it is the quintessence. Even repeated references to the rationality in that power, and to redemption, providence and the incarnation itself, seem only to give resonance to the theme of divine power born out of persecution, apologetics, and a clash of metaphysics. Yet Tertullian surprises us with how committedly he dedicates himself to retrieving the goodness of God from the unpromising framework he has built for himself, and nowhere is this more the case than in his treatment of the incarnation.

CHAPTER 5

Divine Power and the Incarnation

Several themes in Tertullian's teaching on Christ converge on the idea of divine power. Tertullian's doctrine of the incarnation keys in to his notion of divine omnipotence not only through the *creatio ex nihilo* but also through his conception of the Logos. He picks up, as already seen, the tenor of second-century theories of creation through the Word. It is now possible to show more fully how the doctrine of the incarnation develops from this seed principle. It will become clear that, for Tertullian, the divine freedom in creation establishes the suitability of the resulting cosmos to host a free and almighty act of incarnation. Tertullian finds the way open for him to associate Christ with the creator (the very one despised by Marcion) through a common divine power. Moreover, the unrivalled power of God can achieve entry into the human finite sphere despite the problems posed for the divine immutability. What is more, the ministry of Jesus discloses his great power and therefore divine identity as the *spiritus*. Finally, the famous dictum of Tertullian, 'It is certain because it is impossible' is not without relevance to the question of divine omnipotence in the incarnation.

The Logos background

Tertullian's struggle for an absolute divine freedom in creation produced a Logos concept which has often bruised his reputation, namely the notion that the divine will generated the Logos temporally for the purpose of creation. Not all the texts called to testify against him carry equally damning weight. It is purely controversial considerations for instance, which make him postulate in *Adv Hermog* 18 that there exists nothing unborn and created except God alone, and in a sense that even wisdom, *which was out of the Lord*, was not without a beginning, for it,

> was born and created (*nata et condita*) at the moment when in the mind of God it began to be actuated for the arrangement of the works of the world.

From the fact that even wisdom is in some sense 'born', Tertullian is arguing chiefly for the beginning and subjection also of matter, which includes evil: 'Evil (matter) employed by a good power (Christ) would mean a stronger power employed by a weak one, an "unborn" power by a "born" one.' A 'born' power does not employ an 'unborn' power. For Tertullian this proves not so much that the wisdom had no beginning for in a sense it did have one. His point is that matter similarly had one. Tertullian succeeds in reinforcing his doctrine of *creatio ex nihilo* but the gain is expensive, for in this quite optional postscript he has made creation essentially a free act of the Father alone in a way which would have won him the applause of the Monarchians.

Attempts have been made to rescue Tertullian from the classic subordinationist ring of apparently assigning uncreatedness to the Father alone. E. Evans in particular has sought to show that Tertullian is merely carried away by his own argument,[1] adding that *Adv Hermog* 20 later speaks not of the creation of even wisdom but of creation through wisdom.[2] This tallies with *Adv Prax* 6 where the primary generation is not of wisdom itself but of the projected world *in dei sensu*,[3] a perception of the matter shared by Wazsink.[4] The passage goes on to say,

> 'The Lord created me'... establishing and begetting, of course, in his own consciousness (*in sensu suo*).

As it happens, it does not matter a great deal to an understanding of Tertullian's Trinitarian formulation whether Evans is right on this score or not, since most commentators are agreed that Tertullian is heir to the traditional Logos conceptuality, which in his hands undergoes no radical change to exclude subordinationist overtones. As before, the Word emerges primarily as the agent of creation. Evans, in fact, finds a similar case to *Adv Hermog* 18 in *Adv Hermog* 45, where Tertullian says that first wisdom was created, 'the beginning of his ways for his works'.

Even here, however, Tertullian means that 'creation' was the beginning of wisdom's operations, of its ways (*viae*) rather than of its existence (*esse*). 'Created' (*conditam*), moreover, could just as easily be

[1] E. Evans, *Against Praxeas*, 217.
[2] Ibid.
[3] Ibid.
[4] Waszink, op. cit. 133, n. 157.

translated 'established' or 'founded'. The Logos, or wisdom, is the *agent* of creation and perhaps only in this sense had a beginning.

These points made, however, one cannot erase the affinity between Tertullian's Logos theology and that of his predecessors. Most scholars agree that Tertullian has at least read and approved Theophilus of Antioch's bold introduction of the *logos endiathetos* and *logos prophorikos* into Christian vocabulary. As R.M. Grant concludes,[5] Theophilus held that the reason of God existed undifferentiated within God. This *logos endiathetos* was, however, generated along with wisdom as *logos prophorikos* for the creation of the world. Since both *logos prophorikos* and wisdom (sometimes identified with the Spirit) are expressions of God's mind, no clear distinction between Word and wisdom is apparent except through the incarnation concept implied in Luke 1:35.[6] Grant, in fact, finds clear subordinationism in Theophilus, in which Word and wisdom are 'subordinate agents through which God acts',[7] and in which the Word could be sent anywhere because, unlike God himself, it was capable of location in time and space.[8] Nevertheless, the Word 'was God and was of God's nature (*ek theou pephykos*)'.[9]

Whilst some affinity emerges between this scheme and Tertullian's, some differences also appear. Tertullian is strongly biblical and devoted to the historic events of the Gospel. It is more to his purpose to cultivate the centrality of the Son, though he turns to the language of the Logos for help and produces the unhelpful notion that the expressing of the external Logos is identical with the generation of the *Son*. As a later chapter will discover, by means of such categories as *substantia*, *status* and *potestas*, he supplies further terminology for the equality and unity of Father, Son and Holy Spirit, and to this degree at least, moves beyond the approach of Theophilus in the direction of later Trinitarianism. And of course he exploits more fully the Sonship material in John's Gospel. Some of the earlier ideas, however, leave their mark, and they are not merely significant but crucial for understanding the direction of Tertullian's thought.

Two of these assume special importance. First, the origination of the Word in God as Thought is the basis of the Word's title to deity. Theophilus claimed that the *logos endiathetos* was originally '*ek theou pephykos*'. In the same way, Tertullian found that the Thought of God was divine by virtue of its being in God. Deity, however, was not something communicated through generation, as only later, more

---

[5]R.M. Grant, *Early Christian Doctrine of God*, 83.
[6]Ibid.
[7]Ibid. 82.
[8]Ibid. 84, on the basis of *Ad Autol* II 22.
[9]Ibid.

refined Greek formulations of eternal generation could imply. Rather, deity qualified the Word in a prior way as the appropriate subject for external expression. That is, being internal to God, the Word partook of the same substance and power as the Father.[10] Secondly, the sharply distinguished Logos stages in Theophilus conform to Tertullian's preoccupation with an 'economic' Trinity, his concern with the *dynamic*, the going forth of God. Of course, we cannot be sure, whether Tertullian actually drew his particular material from Theophilus directly or indirectly, or even only followed popular coinage adopted by Theophilus. But the way of thinking he used belonged to this setting rather than to the later more refined formulations which saw in the Trinitarian relations patrocentric communications of the divine essence. In a discussion of Tertullian's thought, therefore, 'derivation' does not denote the transmission of divine substance (and analogously of divine power), but the origination or status of the Word and Spirit *in* God.

On the other hand, Tertullian almost certainly knew of the dangers of the two-stage theory as highlighted by Irenaeus, who saw in it 'something which might lead the unwary to the false Gnostic view which assigns to the Logos a beginning of prolation'.[11] Although probably concurring with the belief of Irenaeus that the Word was always with the Father (*Adv haer* IV 20.3–4), Tertullian nevertheless also fell heir to the economic and 'temporalist' atmosphere which pervaded second century speculation on the Logos. *Adv Prax* 7, for instance, provides an example. The 'nativity of the Word' coincides with the creation fiat. Here God generates the Word for action and the Word advances to distinct subsistence.

In Tertullian and others, all this Logos talk survived alongside the more personal terminology of Sonship. Writers, both earlier this century and more recently, have detected a fair degree of tension between the two

---

[10]G.L. Bray argues, 'the verbum was latent in God's essence...'; 'The Legal Concept of Ratio in Tertullian', *Vigiliae Christianae* 31 (1977) 94–116 (pp. 113, 115). Some aspects of the article have been criticised by R. Braun in 'Chronica Tertullianea', *Revue des Études Augustiniennes* 24 (1978) 323–324. Cf. A. Heron, op. cit. 41, 48. It is difficult to see how Dörrie can maintain his claim that in Tertullian and Theophilus the going out of the Logos is related not to creation but to the word as spoken to the human creature: H. Dörrie, 'Der Johannesprolog in der frühchristlichen Apologetik', *Kerygma und Logos. Beiträge zu den geistesgeschichtlichen Beziehungen zwischen Antike und Christentum. Festschrift für C. Andresen*, Göttingen, Vandenhoeck/Ruprecht, 1979, 150.

[11]H.A. Wolfson, *The Philosophy of the Church Fathers*, Vol. 1. *Faith, Trinity, Incarnation*, Cambridge, Mass., Harvard University Press, 1964, 200–201.

models,[12] with the Son-concept slowly gaining the ascendancy over the Logos-concept.[13] Various reasons offer themselves for the strength of such a development. T.E. Pollard[14] traces the tension to that between Logos-subordinationism and the Rule of Faith. The Rule of Faith comes out on top because of Tertullian's respect for John's Gospel.[15] In Tertullian, then, the Logos model sustains a drag from the Johannine alternative of a more personal, even exalted, divine Son. However, the drag can work the other way, so that the Sonship idea modifies itself under the impact of the divine transcendence elements so typical of Logos theologies in Tertullian's time.

At this point the *potestas* looms again. In *Adv Prax* 16 Tertullian assaults the modalist view that the Father himself came down throughout redemptive history to enact his various judgements. Rather, says Tertullian, the *Son* carried out these acts of power.

To him was given by the Father

> all power (*omnis potestas*) in heaven and in earth, the Father... has delivered all judgement to the Son... they will not be all unless they have been of all time.

So it was the Son who came down in judgement upon the tower of Babel, Sodom, etc., and who was the subject of revelation and companionship.

Tertullian argues for assigning these Old Testament activities exclusively to the Son because of the metaphysical attributes of the Father, especially invisibility and omnipresence. He seems to realise that this is proving too much, calling into question the deity of the Son. He hastens uneasily to comment on the surprise of finding even the Son visible and local, and blusters on to say,

> from the beginning the whole course of the divine ordinance has come down through the Son... thus the one God, that is, the Father, has always done those things which (in fact) have been performed by (the agency of) the Son.

Although consolidated by a large number of Old Testament texts this unsatisfactory section looks suspiciously like a concession to Gnostic and similar ideas of God's remoteness. It seems to fall back upon the old

---

[12]B.B. Warfield, *Studies in Tertullian and Augustine*, London, Oxford University Press, 1930, 19; T.E. Pollard, *Johannine Christology and the Early Church*, Cambridge University Press, 1970, 62.

[13]Evans, op. cit. 36–37; T.E. Pollard, op. cit. 70.

[14]Pollard, op. cit. 63. The Rule of Faith, according to Pollard, bursts the old Logos framework. Cf. Warfield, op. cit. 86–88.

[15]Pollard, op. cit. 65.

Logos ideas, dressed up in Sonship language, in order to bridge the gulf between the one God of monotheism and the unruly and untouchable world which lies far below him. A passage in the preceding *Adv Prax* 15 strengthens this suspicion:

> It was the Son always... who wrought by the authority (*ex auctoritate*) and will (*et voluntate*) of the Father.... For the Father acts by consciousness, whereas the Son sees and accomplishes that which is in the Father's consciousness.

Tertullian is picking up an earlier tradition of finding the Son in the theophanies.[16] The influence of contemporary Platonism has been blamed for the trait in Justin[17] and Theophilus.[18] Irenaeus, on the other hand, not only sets out to destroy a Gnostic perception of God but also to beat out a mystical path to some sort of vision of the apparently invisible God.[19] Tertullian falls heir to both emphases. His passion for the transcendent majesty of God, combined with his inherited pluralist Trinitarian thought, drives him at first into the camp of Justin and Theophilus. But the perceptiveness of Irenaeus restrains him,[20] so that the theophanies eventually mark not so much an inequality of persons as a difference of persons,[21] and in any case they fall into the category of visions and dreams.[22]

In spite, then, of an influential subordinationist legacy, Tertullian often succeeds in making the cosmological background to the Son emphasise his true and full divinity rather than erode it. All the same, subordinating tendencies will yet be seen to invade the Son's relationship to divine power.

Creation, power and incarnation

Tertullian's chief Christological indebtedness to Irenaeus surfaces in the earlier writer's inclusion of Christ in the unique status attaching to creatorship. At least one scholar has noticed that in the Irenaean Rule of Faith, the first article affirming God as One and creator leads into a second designating the Son of God also as involved in creation, and

---

[16]Ibid. 270–272.
[17]P.G. Aeby, *Les Missions Divines de Saint Justin à Origène*, Paradosis 12, Fribourg University Press, 1958, 9, and on Justin's subordinationism, with emphasis, on p. 13.
[18]Ibid. 17.
[19]Ibid. 45–46.
[20]Ibid. 69.
[21]Evans, op. cit. 275.
[22]Ibid. 276.

destined to recapitulate all things in himself. Irenaeus, of course, bends this confession to his *recapitulatio* scheme of redemption in a dynamic framework.[23] By this scheme Irenaeus solved the tension facing the apologists when they had to affirm both the unity of God in the two Testaments and the newness of Christ.[24] Tertullian does not devote much time to the progressional and mystical elements so important to Irenaeus,[25] but the correlation of creator and re-creator through incarnation remains. What is more, Tertullian's stress on divine power in the incarnation follows a precedent in the work of Irenaeus. For Irenaeus the same force underlies creation and incarnation.[26] Indeed, the renewal of the creation requires the entry of the creator[27] so that the divine Word has the power of God in his humanity.[28]

For Tertullian, the relation of Christology to creation doctrine assumes yet greater importance because of his conflict with such opponents as Marcion. Associating Christ intimately with the creator-God so contemptuously dismissed by Marcion is the hallmark of Tertullian's work, a feature at its height in Book IV but present throughout. Two passages will do to highlight what I mean. In *Adv Marc* III 3 Tertullian first of all points out that Christ's miracles were predicted and guaranteed in advance by the prophets of the Old Testament creator:

> Those miracles are no sufficient reason for (your) acceptance of Christ, the more so as those miracles would have been capable of proving that Christ belongs to the creator and no other.

Again in *Adv Marc* IV 6 he says, comprehensively,

> Christ must be adjudged to be the creator's if he is found to have administered the creator's ordinances, fulfilled his prophecies, supported his laws, given actuality to his promises, revived his miracles, given new expressions to his judgements, and reproduced the features of his character and attributes.

---

[23]B. de Margerie, *La Trinité Chrétienne dans l'histoire*, Paris, Beauchesne, 1975, p. 106. Cf. G. Wingren, *Man and the Incarnation: A Study in the Biblical Theology of Irenaeus*, Edinburgh/London, Oliver & Boyd, 1959, 84–86, 103.

[24]Cited by J.E.L. Van der Geest, *Le Christ et l'Ancien Testament chez Tertullien. Recherche terminologique*, Nijmegen, Dekker, Van de Vegt, 1972, 82–83.

[25]Even here S. Otto thinks Tertullian too expounds the *recapitulatio* in a lost work: 'Der Mensch als Bild Gottes bei Tertullian', *Münchener Theologische Zeitschrift* 10 (1959) 276–282 (p. 277).

[26]G. Wingren, op. cit. 84.

[27]Ibid. 86.

[28]Ibid. 103.

Christ arrives upon the earthly scene armed with the unique power and authority of the Old Testament creator and displaying that power in impressive ways, including the miracles.

Further concrete examples of the union in cosmic power between Christ and creator frequently crop up. *Adv Marc* IV 20, for instance, introduces the connection of omnipotent creation and cosmic ownership, reviewed earlier, into the question of Christ's identity:

> Now who is this, that commands even the winds and the sea? Some new ruler perhaps, and controller of the elements which have belonged to that creator who is now subdued and dispossessed? By no means. These elements had recognised their author even as they had of old been accustomed to obey his servants.

Here Tertullian is going beyond his immediate aim of showing Jesus to be in complicity with the creator. He shows, even worse than Marcion feared, that Jesus actually *is* the creator God. Hence he emerges as *auctor* as opposed to servant. Later on in *Adv Marc* IV 29 the theme of the creator's consequent ownership as Lord (*dominus*) connects with judgement. The master in Luke 12:22–59 comes home suddenly like a thief in the night. Tertullian protests against Marcion's literal interpretation identifying the owner as a thief. The owner cannot also be literally a thief with all the traits of bad character which that involves and which Marcion holds against the creator.

And besides, Christ himself as the Son of Man comes in judgement against those who were not prepared: 'I take him to be a judge, and in the judge I lay claim to the creator.' Christ too warned of judgement and so becomes implicated in the sternness of the creator so disparaged by Marcion: 'Christ belongs to him for whom he demands obedience by reason of fear.' A compact of sternness, judgement and fear holds between the creator and the Christ so prized by Marcion. On occasion Tertullian passes beyond the notion of Christ as a mere representative of the creator in judgement to Christ as judge in his own person. So a line finally becomes visible from omnipotent creation, through consequent ownership and right of judgement to the Christ who exercises it.

Another passage, unsubtle in its sentiments, reinforces the point of *Adv Marc* IV 29 in the chapter following. Having associated Christ the sower with the creator upon whose earth he farms, Tertullian turns to the parable of the leaven. The leaven belongs to the creator too, for after it comes the oven and the furnace of hell. The judgement and the kingdom belong to Christ and so he is the creator's Christ. The judgement also implies Christ's hold on authority and order because the naming of tribes and apostles has a common significance (*Adv Marc* IV

13), for it is only by order that God proves his power.[29] The Christ shares in the power-defined prerogative of the creator. Power is the thread which binds Christ to the creator and positions him within the 'not-creation' sphere.

There was, however, a more fundamental connection between creation and incarnation. If the creation itself flowed from the hand of a benign creator and was itself good, it presented no obstacle as host to the good God himself.[30] Only if the world in fact were not good, or lay beyond redemptive action, should we have to relieve God of responsibility for its beginnings.[31] All creation belonged to him as its free originator and therefore became an appropriate medium of his deepest interaction with humanity. A creation from pre-existing material imported the threat of an essential substance which could obstruct the entrance of God the 'creator' into the world. The belief in a power over the material world prompted the declaration in *Adv Marc* V 14:

> For in this will consist the power of God in using a similar substance (the flesh) to accompany salvation.

For Tertullian the doctrine of *creatio ex nihilo* also set up a distinction between God and any other reality, so that laws governing the created things did not bind the creator. He falls back on this distinction to defend the incomprehensibility of the incarnation. He seems to assume the widely held doctrine of divine changelessness. However, although God does not by nature change, he *may* change and yet remain what he is.[32]

With regard to the incarnation, however, Tertullian highlights not just the creation in general but the human world in particular. In *Adv Marc* II 3 he wants to secure the idea of a worthy creation and so further enhance the status of humanity as the image of God within it. So he starts with the goodness, 'which created time... which established the beginning' and which existed before both. This goodness

> must be taken to be eternal, ingenerate in God, and everlasting, and on that account worthy of God.

This is the natural property of one who is called creator. Such goodness had provided an impressive place for humanity to live (*Adv Marc* II 4). This place of probation was a 'good thing' out of which the human creature could have progressed into 'God's supremely good thing'. The

---

[29]Van der Geest, op. cit. 128.

[30]E. Evans, *Tertullian's Treatise on the Incarnation, The Text Edited with an Introduction, Translation and Commentary*, London, SPCK, 1956, xviii–xxiv.

[31]Ibid. xxii–xxiii.

[32]Cf. ibid. 100.

agent of the creative act emerges as none other than the Word,[33] and the deed chiefly aimed at confirming men and women in the material creation as the image of God (*Adv Marc* II 4). *Goodness* formed the human person, breathed in soul and gave dominion to enjoy and govern.

Tertullian finds himself in possession of a twofold platform for constructing a doctrine of the incarnation. First, the calibre of the creation on the double basis of God's goodness and his capacity as 'Not-creation' to generate such a work. Secondly, the Word's involvement in the work of creation makes him just right for incarnation, since

> To this good work (God) appoints also a supremely good agent and administrator, his own Word.

The relevance to the incarnation becomes even more pointed just here. For Tertullian, what we now term 'the image of God' in the human being (*imago Dei*) owes its character not only to the Word's action in creating but also in some sense to the Word's form. The image follows the form of Christ, or the Word incarnate, as prototype:

> For whatever expression the clay took upon it, the thought was of Christ who was to become man. (*De res* 6)

It is significant that this statement appears at a crucial point in Tertullian's attempted vindication of his theological scheme as a whole, culminating in the assertion of a bodily resurrection through incarnation and redemption. This all serves to underline the impregnable position that the Word's involvement in the *creatio ex nihilo* commanded in his system. Behind the suitability of the creation as host to this Word towers the supposition ironically implied earlier, in *Adv Marc* II 2: 'But now God the almighty, the Lord and maker of all things, is made subject to criticism.'

The might of the creator alone ensures the potential of the world to accommodate the Christ's entry. Any other kind of God, such as Marcion's 'higher' god, lacks the qualifications to have a Christ. Equally, the world, the creator and the creator's Christ, in whom 'the one and only real and objective (*substantia*) divinity showed itself' (*Adv Marc* II 29), display a common share in the primordial goodness, the goodness of the mighty creator which shines through this world and becomes visible personally, in Christ.

To sum up, then, Tertullian made the omnipotence of God as creator the foundation for later statements about the credibility of the divine Word's entry into the world. But it also provided a ground for

---

[33]Meijering in *God, Cosmos, History*, 256, comments that Irenaeus seeks to show that creation and redemption in Christ do not conflict, ending up with a theology of creation as much as one of redemption.

unequivocal statements of the full integrity of Christ's humanity. The consigning by Marcion of the material universe to the realm of an inferior creator god in conflict with a higher 'good' god, led to the disparaging of human existence and gave rise to a docetic Christology. Tertullian, therefore, comes back to the question of Christ's true humanity again and again,[34] with firm denunciations of docetic views.[35] The Christ was inseparable from the clay (*De carne* 8, *De res* 6).[36] God even assumed the human condition through the normal means appointed by himself, namely birth (*Adv Marc* III 11, *De carne* 1, 18), something logically entailed in authentic fleshly existence.[37]

Tertullian saw the roots of a docetic view of Christ ultimately in an underlying doctrine of God, in Marcion's case of one who was neither creator nor restorer of flesh. He sarcastically observes: 'in this (he is) too supremely good' (*Adv Marc* III 8). For Tertullian, only the powerful origination by God of his earth rendered the incarnation credible.

Even the famous statement in Romans 8:3 that the Son was sent in the 'likeness' of sinful flesh affirms, rather than undermines, the tangible, earthly character of Christ's humanity. It means truly flesh but without the sin of flesh (*De carne* 16, *Adv Marc* V 14).[38] The same understanding

---

[34]See further E. Osborn, *The Beginning of Christian Philosophy*, Cambridge University Press, 1981. Some texts which especially emphasise the fleshliness of Christ are *Adv Marc* III 8, IV 10, IV 14 and *De carne Christi, passim*, but especially chapters 1 and 18.

[35]Hence Marcion is 'the archetype of all heresies which deny the real flesh of Christ' (R.D. Sider, *Ancient Rhetoric and the Art of Tertullian*, 56).

[36]Cf. E. Evans, *Tertullian's Treatise on the Resurrection*, 212–213; T.P. O'Malley, 'The Opposition *caelestia-terrena* in Tertullian', F.L. Cross, ed., *Studia Patristica*, Vol. X, Berlin, Akademie-Verlag, 1970, 190–194 (p. 193); J.E.L. Van der Geest, *Le Christ et l'Ancien Testament chez Tertullien*, 213.

[37]J.P. Mahé comments on the correlation established by Tertullian between the death of Christ and the genuine birth: 'Éléments de doctrine hérétiques dans le *De carne Christi* de Tertullien', E.A. Livingstone, ed., *Studia Patristica*, Vol. XIV, Berlin, Akademie-Verlag, 1976, 48–61 (p. 52).

[38]Tertullian makes a famous observation in *Adv Prax* 27 on the distinctness of the divine and human substances, although he does not, according to Grillmeier, disclose the exact manner of their conjunction, being interested mainly in distinguishing Christ the person from the Father as a person: A. Grillmeier, *Christ in the Christian Tradition*, Vol. 1 *From the Apostolic Age to Chalcedon (451)*, London, Mowbrays, 1975, 129. Grillmeier has obviously felt the weight of R. Cantalamessa's arguments in 'Tertullien et la formule christologique de Chalcédoine', F.L. Cross, ed., *Studia Patristica*, Vol. IX, Berlin, Akademie-Verlag, 1966, 139–150.

Support for Cantalamessa appears in M. Colish, *The Stoic Tradition*, Vol. II, 22. The suggestion by Cantalamessa of Tertullian's indebtedness to the Christology of Melito is another matter and is questioned by S.G. Hall: 'The

applied to the statement in 1 Corinthians 15:50 that flesh and blood cannot inherit the kingdom of God. This spoke 'not of the substance but of the conduct', for the substance came into being at the hands of the creator.

The career of Christ assumes importance here too. Tertullian can argue from divine power in the bodily resurrection of Christ to the bodily hope of the believer. He then moves directly to the full bodily humanity of Christ. From the words of Romans 8:11 ('He that raised up Christ from the dead shall also give life to your mortal bodies') he concludes the general resurrection of the flesh itself and from that the truly bodily nature of Christ himself. But at the same time the weakness of the bodily existence of Christ formed not just a medium for the divine power and a witness to it. It was also a cushioning of the might of God. As *Adv Marc* II 27 has it,

> God would not have been able to enter into converse with men except by taking to himself those human thoughts and feelings by which he might reduce the force of his majesty, which human mediocrity was utterly unable to bear, by virtue of a humility, unworthy indeed of himself but necessary for man, and consequently worthy even of God, since nothing is so worthy of God as the salvation of man.[39]

This is especially true of the lowest point of the divine abasement, namely the cross. According to *De carne* 5 the indignity of the cross proves the fact of Christ's normality as a human being through natural birth. But it also becomes the focus of his divine power as a selection of quotations illustrates:

> By this virtue of the cross... he is even now winnowing all the nations through faith... as he will afterwards winnow them by judgement. (*Adv Marc* III 18)

> Why should not Christ be said to have reigned from the tree, ever since by dying on the tree of the cross, he drove out the kingdom of death? (*Adv Marc* III 19)

Christology of Melito, A Misrepresentation Exposed', E.A. Livingstone, ed., *Studia Patristica*, Vol. XIII, Berlin, Akademie-Verlag, 1975, 154–168 (p. 159).

[39]Cf. Van der Geest, *Le Christ et l'Ancien Testament*, 219–220. He convincingly shows how *maiestas* translates the Old Testament idea of divine glory and for Tertullian highlights a contrast between the majesty of the Son of God and the *humilitas* or abasement of the humanity: *Le Christ et l'Ancien Testament*, 219–220. *Adv Marc* II 27, according to J.-P. Mahé, crystallises Tertullian's argument against Marcion: the abasement of God is for the salvation of people (*Tertullien: la chair du Christ, Introduction, texte critique, traduction et commentaire*, Paris, Source Chrétiennes, 1975, 122).

All peoples have been receiving the call into his kingdom ever since God has reigned from the tree. (*Adv Marc* III 21)

Adv Marc V 5 repeats the claim of Paul that the cross is the power of God at work in grace. Such grace can come only from the creator, whom all agree to be the one offended by the human race. This points to power at work in a Christ belonging to the creator. The argument is effective, but Luther for one would not have wholly approved of the scheme. Tertullian's 'theology of the cross' still sometimes looks too much like a 'theology of glory'. The power of the cross sometimes looks like that of an omnipotent creator looking for a new world to conquer, rather than of the slain servant. A true theology of the cross would not have needed to 'reduce the force of his majesty' for it would have been expressed in terms of a might renounced in servanthood. Tertullian misses the New Testament messianic tones of the Son of Man in loss and humiliation. This is a muted note in Tertullian and profoundly affects the balance of his work.

Power, incarnation and salvation

The power springing from the creator's potency finds expression, finally, in the activity of his Christ. *Adv Marc* IV 8[40] celebrates the power and authority which in Christ releases the demoniacs and, to Marcion's distaste, commands the fear of the demons. When, however, Tertullian in this passage speaks of Christ's driving 'the demons out not by any power of his own (*non propria potestate*) but by the creator's authority', he is not contradicting himself and denying possession of a creator's kind of power to Christ. He is only rejecting the Marcionite antithesis between the power of the 'good' God and that of the creator-god. The power Christ exercised belonged to just that creator-god. In fact, the whole sentence carries an ironic strain, beginning, 'Christ fell also under another bad mark'. In his usual biting way, Tertullian points out that the fear and hostility of the demons would mean, on the Marcionites' own assumptions, that Jesus as the Son of the 'good' God acted inappropriately in harnessing fear. For Tertullian, of course, the explanation is less problematical. Jesus acted with the same power and effect as the creator because he embodied the creator's qualities of both severity as judge and goodness as saviour.

The miraculous ministry of Jesus followed from his power as creator, held in common with his Father.[41] By his deeds he advertised his title to

---

[40]See also *Adv Marc* IV 9, 24.

[41]J. Moingt, *Théologie Trinitaire de Tertullien*, 4; *Répertoire Lexicographique et Tables*, Paris, Aubier, 1969, 156.

the creating and ruling *potestas* of the very creator-god derided by Marcion. Tertullian leaves the precise nature of Christ's power-status at this undeveloped stage because he wishes here not so much to speak up for the Son but for the creator whose words the Son speaks. The speaking is important as part of *Adv Marc* IV 9 indicates:

> Even in this (Christ's healing by touch of a leper), Marcion sees an 'opposition', that whereas Elisha needed a material help and made use of water... Christ by the act of his word... immediately put the healing into effect... as though I could not claim the word he used as part of the creator's property... that power did with a word produce at an instant this great fabric of the universe. How better may one discern the Christ of the creator than by the power of his word?

Tertullian debunks Marcion's dualism not only by reminding him that words themselves belong to the world of the creator but also by fixing on the fact that the 'word' first of all activated an immense and unrivalled power that called everything into being. Speaking a mighty word bound the Christ to the creation from the beginning. More striking still, the word of the creator and the word of the creator's Christ were one.

That unity extended for Tertullian to all the works of Christ in his saving career. The case of the ten healed lepers contradicted Marcion's law–grace dualism, because although Jesus upheld the law of priestly examination he also 'cleansed them as they went... by silent power and unaided will (*tacita potestate et sola voluntate*)' (*Adv Marc* IV 35). Conformity to law and free exercise of goodness and power therefore actually meet here. But a momentous conclusion follows:

> the Lord does his works in one way by himself, or by his Son, in another way by the prophets... especially those works which are evidences of his might (*virtus*) and power (*potestas*)... being his own works are more excellent in glory and power... different from those done by agents.

The works done by Christ broke the dualisms of law and grace, of creator and good God, because they come as the works of God himself (*qua propria*), being

> free and sovereign therefore, but without setting aside the law of the Old Testament creator. The miraculous power here stems from the creator, the *dominus* himself. The Son proves to be in turn authoritative and lawful dispenser of the divine prerogative of power. *Adv Marc* I 20 lends some weight to the approach: 'So also he was found to be God through his might (*virtus*).'

Granted, the precise occasion of power (Evans translates 'act of power'), drawn from the discussion of Philippians 2:1–7, remains unclear. It may indicate the incarnation, the resurrection or even the endurance of the cross, if indeed we are right to assume he has in mind a particular act of power. What does emerge is the meeting in Christ of divinity and power. *Power* establishes Christ's equal status with the Father. Justin Martyr has been understood to identify the Son this way as subsisting power.[42] In Tertullian's *De carne* 14 two passages stress this power of Jesus in his career as Saviour. The first asks, 'Then was not the Son of God competent by himself to deliver man?' and concludes that denial here produces two saviours one of whom, Jesus, proves not up to the task. The second passage answers the question posed by the first one:

> For as the Spirit of God and the power (*virtus*) of the Most High he cannot be held to be lower than the angels, seeing he is God, and the Son of God.

For the *kenosis* passage to register a genuine lowering of the Son, it must not imply that Christ was possessed by an angel. He was, according to Tertullian, the divine Son whose deity finds best expression in the titles *spiritus* and *virtus*. It was the climax of a great work of salvation-renewal. Tertullian fails to accomplish as much as Irenaeus had achieved with this idea. In *Adv Marc* IV 1 he settles for showing that 'renewal' does not mean 'antithesis' as Marcionite theology claimed. The one who ordained the change involved in saving renewal also foretold it. A difference of facts does not mean an opposition of powers (*distantiam potestatum*).[43] Jesus Christ as the vital element of change and renewal in the world shares in the power of the one God of creation and renewal, and restores the honour of that God.[44] Christ does not merely become the occasion for the creator's refashioning and renewing but himself actively carries out the work and emerges as 'the one and only real and objective divinity... both kind and stern' (*Adv Marc* II 29; cf. IV 11).

Against Marcion all this does not lack some impact. But the stress on divine power shrouds the warmth, humanity and humility of the New Testament portrayal of Jesus. The problem here lies with what is not said, what, in Tertullian's eyes, cannot to Marcion be said. The more Christ emerges in sympathetic unity with people, the easier it seems to be for Marcion to detach him first from the creator God as severe, and then from God as powerful. Tertullian will not at this point take the risk, though in his treatise on the *Flesh of Christ* full humanity surges to the foreground as the apologist becomes locked even deeper in battle

---

[42]C. Oeyen, 'Die Lehre der göttlichen Kräfte bei Justin', F.L. Cross, ed., *Studia Patristica*, Vol. XI, Berlin, Akademie-Verlag, 1972, 215–221 (p. 221).

[43]Evans actually translates 'difference of authorities'. This no doubt valid rendering does not seem quite strong enough for Tertullian's argument.

[44]Van der Geest, op. cit. 80.

with docetic views. Tertullian's reaction here did not secure his end without some cost to the balance in his view of Christ.

Power, incarnation and immutability

As early as the second century the coherence of the incarnation idea had come under scrutiny, especially as sketched by Tertullian. Can the one standing on the creator side of the almighty *creatio ex nihilo* appear also on the other side, as created as well as creator? The very concept of power so close to Tertullian's heart surely presented the chief philosophical obstacle to the central Christian teaching. Tertullian answered with customary unexpectedness and appropriated the seemingly menacing evidence in his own favour. The omnipotence of the creator did not stand in the way of incarnation but supplied the only real guarantee of its possibility. In *De carne* 3 even a full human nativity of the Son did not bring the structure tumbling down:

> Your idea was that to God nativity is either impossible or unseemly. I answer, that to God nothing is impossible except what is against his will.

It is in his power to change into a man without ceasing to be God.[45] Tertullian's admission of divine immutability could have indicated acquiescence in the uncompromising form of that principle found quite early in Christian thought, or it may have been an *ad hominem* device.[46] At any rate a perennial obstacle to conceptualising the incarnation in ancient thought becomes of no account on the grounds of God's omnipotence. Later theology would try to match immutability with incarnation. Tertullian simply says God can change if he wishes to:[47]

> Will you deny this to the more mighty God, as though his Christ had not the power (*non valuerit*), when truly clothed with manhood, of continuing to be God?... But nothing is on equal terms with God (*sed nihil deo par est*): his nature is far removed from the circumstances of all things whatsoever.

---

[45]Evans, *Treatise on the Incarnation*, 96.

[46]Cf. Evans, op. cit. 99. He thinks it may have been Marcion who said *conversum* and Tertullian for the sake of simplicity and the argument argues from it for the moment. Both Evans and Mahé (*La chair du Christ*, 124) are clear that immutability is not the real nub of the discussion.

[47]J.L. Gonzalez, 'Athens and Jerusalem Revisited: Reason and Authority in Tertullian', *Church History* 43 (1974) 17–25 (p. 20). Evans, op. cit. 100, reminds us that at *Adv Marc* I 4 a similar argument rules out any parity of earthly kings with God's power and rank.

The justification of the incarnation stems from God's unlimited power, though it is worth noting that a rationalisation has already crept in which Greek Christian theology later refined. Tertullian's imagery of the divine nature 'clothing' itself with the human nature implied to later minds a model of unity requiring no modification in the divine qualities anyway.[48] Tertullian does not exploit this possibility. The divine power is sufficient rationale in itself. The distinction of rank between creator and creature reflected the omnipotent work of creation ('nothing is on equal terms with God'), so guaranteeing that God can cross the gulf without diminishing in the process. Cantalamessa finds a Stoic principle here[49] but does not completely convince Braun,[50] whilst Mahé opts for a different source altogether.[51]

A passage in *De carne* 16 seems to follow the same type of reasoning as the earlier chapter, only with a special stress upon that aspect of creation power which produced the human world:

> As earth was changed into this flesh without a man's seed, so also the Word of God was able, without coagulation, to pass into the material of that same flesh.

The statement does not come in an indefinite form, 'it was possible for', but a positive one, 'the Word of God was able' (*dei verbum potuit*). It lay within the divine omnicompetence of the Word, through whom the human world came into being, to enter that same world of existence. Tertullian will not entertain any compromise over this divine ability. For example, in *De carne* 11 he tackles the view that takes Christ's flesh to be invisible soul which has tangibility in Christ by receiving an *apparently* fleshly form. He resents the implied suggestion that it would lie beyond God's power, even on that strange hypothesis, to make soul visible without giving it a false (viz. 'fleshly') identity. It would evidence serious impotence, not to mention falsehood, if God did not enjoy enough power to display the soul as it really was. Even though Tertullian does not share his opponents' ground, he hypothetically accepts it in order to press home the more fundamental assertion, that of the divine power and integrity. He would not accept any theory of the incarnation which was deficient on these two scores. *Adv Marc* V 14 encapsulates it perfectly:

---

[48]J. Daniélou vindicates Tertullian's thought by saying that he does not envisage a change of substance, but the assumption of a strange substance, *Origins of Latin Christianity*, 220.

[49]R. Cantalamessa, 'Incarnazione e immutabilità di Dio. Una soluzione moderna nella patristica?', *Rivista di filosofia neo-scolastica* 67 (1975) 631–647.

[50]*Revue des Études Augustiniennes* 22 (1976) 310.

[51]Mahé, op. cit. 330, where Theophilus and Athenagoras are particularly mentioned, though one must recognise Stoic traces in these authors also.

'In this will consist the power of God, in using a similar substance (a fleshly substance) to accomplish salvation.'

Power, incarnation and divine identity

To Tertullian's mind, the unique identity and status of Christ himself is a question of power.

> The majesty of God (*sublimitas dei*)... the temple... above the top of the mountains (*super summos montes*) meaning Christ, the catholic temple of God, in whom God is worshipped, established above all the heights of strengths and powers (*constitutum super omnes eminentias convirtutum et potestatum*). (*Adv Marc* III 21)

The final phrase 'established above' refers to Christ since he is the 'catholic temple'. The accumulation of *sublimitas*, *virtus* and *potestas* supplies a powerful tribute to Christ's divine status in Tertullian's eyes. Something similar happens in *De carne* 16 where Christ's flesh 'sits on high in heaven at the right hand of the Father' and will again come in the 'eminence' of the Father's glory. Nor does Tertullian restrict this status to the ascended or glorified body. As so often in the second-century apologists, Christ's earthly deeds of power signal deity,[52] so that 'Christ is found to be God through his might (or possibly 'act of power': *per virtutem*) as he is found to be a human by reason of his flesh' (*Adv Marc* V 20). The same distinction between divine might and real humanity crops up again in *De carne* 9:

> it was only for his words and might, solely for his doctrine and power (*doctrina et virtute*), that they were astonished at Christ as man.

And all this, he argues, in contrast to the otherwise ordinariness of his humanity. Similarly *Adv Marc* IV 7 observes that the strength (*vis*) and power (*potestas*) of his speech were a matter of wonder. But *Apol* 21 provides the strongest example of all. Tertullian quite happily admits that the lowly position of Jesus made people think him a mere man, perhaps a magician. But with a word he exorcised, healed and raised dead people as well as commanding the natural forces. It all showed that he was the divine Word, 'attended by power and reason... the same being who by his word still made as he had made all things.' Tertullian

---

[52]According to J.W. Jacobs, with particular reference to *Adv Prax* 24, both Tertullian here and Hilary in *De Trin* VII 37 believe that the Father becomes visible in the Son not corporally but when the Son manifests his miracles and signs in the Father's power: 'The Western Roots of the Christology of St Hilary of Poitiers: A Heritage of Textual Interpretation', E.A. Livingstone, ed., *Studia Patristica*, Vol. XIII, Berlin, Akademie-Verlag, 1975, 198–203 (p. 200).

had already in the same chapter mentioned that this Christ is God from God and that his second coming will be in majesty of deity displayed. The works and power, not being traceable to the humanity, stem from that fact.

The ultimate power attributed to Christ by Tertullian, tailored into an argument against Marcion, aims to secure the same point. Christ had 'obtained power to judge, and by it of course the power to forgive sins[53] (for he who judges also acquits)' (*Adv Marc* IV 10). He first shows that the creator's power to judge implies also the power to forgive, a prerogative attributed by Marcion only to the supreme higher God. The title Son of Man proves 'that he who was forgiving sins was both God and man.' Elsewhere he attacks the notion of an 'angelic' flesh of Christ, not just for the standard anti-docetic reasons of the time but also because the Christ who was God and possessed divine power needed no such improper aid to complete his saving work (*De carne* 14). As observed earlier, Tertullian rejected the idea of 'two shapers of salvation (*duo salutis artifices*), the one quite powerless without the other.' *Artifex* underlines once again the tie-up between mighty creation and mighty renovation. The identity of the Christ emerges through his possession of the divine power to save.[54] These unmistakable Christological statements disclose a theological habit of sometimes approaching the question of Christ's status through the ever-recurring theme of divine omnipotence.

Tertullian's use of the term *spiritus* to denote the divine substance sometimes has the effect of underlining the deity as power. In *De carne* 19 he describes the announced conception to Mary through the Spirit as the 'power of the Most High' (Luke 1:25), and equates it with the incarnating Word of God (John 1:14), an act of creation more than generation:[55]

> The Word is God's, and with the Word is God's Spirit, and in the Spirit is God's power, and God's everything that Christ is.

Here the question looms of the relation of *spiritus* to the Word, dealt with at some length later. On the one hand *spiritus* denotes the 'third in the sequence of divine majesty'; on the other hand it picks out the nature

---

[53]Aeby rightly takes the apparent *delegation* of power from the Father to be the consequence only of humiliation in the incarnation (P.G. Aeby, *Les missions divines. Saint Justine à Origéne*, 72).

[54]Cf. H.R. Niebuhr: 'Tertullian is a Trinitarian who understands that the God Who reveals himself in Jesus Christ is the creator and the Spirit also; but within that context he maintains the absolute authority of Jesus Christ....' (*Christ and Culture*, New York, Harper & Row, 1956, 51).

[55]E. Evans, *Treatise on the Incarnation*, 167.

of divinity itself. In the second sense, it often lies in close association
with the notion of the divine power. Take *Adv Prax* 27 for instance:

> Jesus is composed of flesh as man and of spirit as God: and on that
> occasion the angel, in respect of that part in which he was spirit
> pronounced him the Son of God... the apostle (confirms the fact that
> he is) of both substances.

Spiritus does duty to define the deity of Christ. Here Tertullian,
following common second-century precedent, risks the dangers of
obscuring any distinction between 'spirit' as a description of God's
substance and 'spirit' as the third person (a use which actually crops up
later in the chapter). He goes on to attach 'spirit' to the theme of power:

> And to such a degree did there remain the proper being of each
> substance, that in him the spirit carried out its own acts, that is
> powers and works and signs.

We may conceivably have here a reference only to the Holy Spirit at
work in the ministry of Jesus, but the mention of 'substance' rules this
out in favour of a pointer to the divine identity of Christ.[56] *De carne* 5
emphasises even further the association of the Spirit-substance with
power:

> The powers of the spirit of God proved him God, the sufferings
> proved there was the flesh of men. If the powers postulate the spirit,
> no less do the sufferings postulate the flesh.

Hence, Tertullian grounds Christ's divine origins in the *spiritus* quality
of his works. The method especially suits him on the matter of the virgin
birth, to which he appeals for settling the heavenly, divine spirit-origin
of Christ in *De carne* 19 and *Adv Marc* V 8, V 9, V 17.

We find ourselves here in the field of standard contemporary
reasoning, but in Tertullian's case a new element arises in the more
prominent role of power, particularly with regard to his teaching on
redemption and the Trinity. In two important places this role comes to
the surface: *De praes* 13 and *De carne* 14. The latter reads,

> For as the spirit of God, and the power of the Most High, he cannot
> be held to be lower than the angels, seeing he is God.

Tertullian harbours such an entrenched habit of speaking in power
language that even the incarnation, a doctrine terminating upon the
servanthood of God in the flesh, comes to expression in the unlikely
terms of divine power. Rank and power surface everywhere, and

---

[56]Cf. A. Grillmeier, op. cit. 121: 'The *Logos*, or as Tertullian says, the "*Sermo*"
or even the "*spiritus*", the spirit in Christ, is the only subject of the incarnation.'

although intended to uphold a Christology very close to that which came to definition in the fifth century, they modified the tone of New Testament incarnation teaching. Forced by Marcion to accept a contest between power and grace, he became unduly defensive towards power and fell into the trap of crowding out the divine grace and love as keynotes of the incarnation.

Power, incarnation and impossibility

Study of Tertullian's Christology has led us deep into the Christological question and has raised to view his commitment to the duality of Christ's person. The passage just discussed comes on the heels of a quite mature Christological statement:

> That these two sets of attributes, the divine and the human, are each kept distinct from the other, is of course accounted for by the equal verity of each nature, both flesh and spirit being in full degree what they claim to be.

Tertullian is making an argued case for the duality of the natures and their full, unimpaired integrity. To deny these facts, he argues, in fact contradicts Jesus himself and questions his integrity. A rational case indeed. But a now infamous passage occurs precisely at this point and bears the stigma of alleged irrationality. This, one of his most celebrated epigrams, reads,

> The Son of God died: it is utterly credible – because it is out of place (*et mortuus est dei filius: prorsus*[57] *credibile est, quia ineptum est*). And he is raised from the dead. It is certain – because it is impossible (*certum est, quia impossibile*).

It is now well publicised that Tertullian did not say, '*credo quia absurdum est*'.[58] Interest lies for us in the authentic text and in particular in the word *impossibile*, which seems to revel in the omnipotence of God and the words of Jesus, 'what is impossible with men is possible with God.'

Three main approaches to the justly famous passage have attracted support. The first insists that whatever Tertullian said, what he actually meant, and seriously, was: 'I believe because it is unreasonable (*credo*

---

[57] *Prorsus* is accepted by Evans though absent from some other texts. It does not affect our analysis.

[58] R.H. Ayers dispatches the widely used text in his article, 'Tertullian's "Paradox" and "Contempt For Reason" Reconsidered', *Expository Times* 87 (1976) 308–311.

quia absurdum est).' Weighty advocates support this view.[59] If correct it confirms suspicions of irrationalism. It is true that occasionally Tertullian attacked the schools but invariably he had in mind philosophical mutants such as Gnosticism and Marcionitism, which, being close to Christian thought, offered a more menacing challenge to the absolute majesty and power of God. Moreover, the chapter *De carne* 5 itself dwells upon the irrationality of Tertullian's opponents, accusing them of holding Christ's character and self-testimony in mutual contradiction. Further, if we find irrationality extolled here, such an alleged flight to paradox on Tertullian's part ought to appear more pervasively in his works, or at least more frequently, as is usually the case in such theologies. A call to irrationalism seems both out of place and out of character.

On every hand we find Tertullian plundering the apparatus of the philosophers, though admittedly never becoming a true philosopher in the process. A great burden of proof lies upon those who wish to say that here in *De carne* 5, Tertullian abandons and abuses the apparatus together with all the rational equipment of his deeply engrained rhetorical training. Almost any alternative explanation therefore warrants an airing.

A second view, then, is the suggestion of V. Decarie[60] that Tertullian simply echoes the defiant decision of the apostle Paul in favour of the cross in the teeth of Jewish and gentile antipathy. God has chosen the weakness and folly of the cross, rather than the glory of his consuming power, to accomplish salvation. Although contrary to the world's values and way of thought, Tertullian is not ashamed of it. On this view Tertullian accents in his famous dictum the *indignity* of the incarnation, or more precisely, *the cross*. The approach has its merits. Tertullian has after all, in *De carne* 4, defended the appropriateness of the incarnation, and everywhere shows himself to be a friend of paradox and irony. *De carne* 5, however, concentrates attention not so much upon the *appropriateness* as upon the *truth* or *actuality* of the incarnation. Tertullian goes to great pains to show that the powerful deeds and veracity of Christ point to that central mystery. We perhaps should not convert 'impossible' to 'unthinkable'. Bare possibility is the matter under dispute and the *impossibile* should not find itself swallowed up in the *ineptum*. Moreover, in the chapter, and even the book as a whole, Tertullian primarily concerns himself with the incarnation itself rather

---

[59]Cf. H.A. Wolfson, 'Philosophy of the Church Fathers', 102–106, and E. Gilson, *History of Christian Philosophy in the Middle Ages*, New York, Random House, 1955, 45.

[60]V. Decarie, 'Le paradoxe de Tertullien', *Vigiliae Christianae* 15 (1961) 23–31.

than with the cross, important though that is. These difficulties do not so much eliminate Decarie's approach as justify looking at a third possibility, not so far removed from his.

R.H. Ayers has suggested a solution along the lines of examples in the Aristotelian 'topica'.[61] The argument of Tertullian follows the dictum that a thing is to be believed if it is too improbable to be invented. We have here a contemporary, rational philosophical argument, though, Ayers admits, not a very strong one. On this view the death of the Son of God is 'impossible' in terms of the things which people imagine as possible. This attractive view, if it could prevail to a stage of consensus, would be particularly valuable to us. It would provide yet another example of Tertullian's perception of the incarnation as a supreme and overwhelming example of the power of God, overcoming all obstacles against the general human assessment of what *is* possible. The saying would form not a statement of irrationality but would cite a supreme instance of the divine omnipotence.

---

[61]See R.H. Ayers, 'Tertullian's Paradox', and his book, *Language, Logic and Reason in the Church Fathers. A Study of Tertullian, Augustine and Aquinas*, New York, Lubrecht & Cramer, 1979.

CHAPTER 6

Power and the New Creation: Divine Omnipotence and the Church

R.F. Evans says of Tertullian's work that he never devoted himself to such a sustained study of the Church as could have given rise to a treatise entitled 'On the Church', yet in his writings the problem of the Church is nearly pervasive.[1] This especially applies in relation to the identity, unity and holiness of the Church, together with its relations to society at large.[2] But Evans sees the most compelling interest of Tertullian's ecclesiology in the question of the Church as a historical community, indwelt by the Spirit and awaiting the end of all things, so that the 'themes of the Spirit and eschatology are themes of the most crucial urgency for Tertullian'.[3] The dependence upon previous writers, typical of Tertullian's handling of cosmology, incarnation and Trinity, therefore appears much fainter in his treatment of the Church. He is writing to the changing situation, especially in relation to persecution. The needs of the hour required fresh statements. All the same a debt to Irenaeus will become obvious.

We cannot of course dismiss the divine omnipotence from the field of vision here, taking in the wider question of individual Christian experience. The doctrine of God's power not only lies behind Tertullian's preoccupation with divine authority (*auctoritas*), but also impinges directly upon the apologist's doctrine of the Church, however

---

[1] R.F. Evans, *One and Holy*, 4.
[2] Ibid.
[3] Ibid.

sporadically, sometimes with far-reaching consequences. Moreover, creation, incarnation and eschatology all touch upon ecclesiology and trade with it. Our study will confine itself, however, to the more direct interaction of Tertullian's themes of power and ecclesiology.

Creation, ownership and grace

Earlier consideration of Tertullian's doctrine of creation uncovered a deep-seated belief in the *creatio ex nihilo* as the root of God's ownership of everything and especially of the conditions controlling his own relationship to the human world. So, judgement and grace, with command and forgiveness, rested upon the divine ownership. The ownership which commanded obedience also promoted grace, particularly in the area of divine lordship towards a believer. *Adv Marc* V 6 provides a useful example of how Tertullian saw this point as needing emphasis against Marcion's dualism. If the human being exists as divine 'property' in God's image, the product of divine 'breathing', if

> man is both the property and the work and the image and the likeness of the creator... then Marcion's (good) god is dwelling entirely on someone else's property, if it is not the creator whose temple we are.

Tertullian continues with the claim that only the creator who made the humanity, now built into a renewed temple, can lay claim to it. Any attempt to meddle by some other god, especially the one invented by Marcion, comes down to trespass on forbidden property. Creation and mercy belong to the same God, that one whose creative power tags him as the re-creator through Christ. Tertullian carries that power into the sphere of judgement. God the creator, no other, comes forth as the avenger against those who destroy the new temple. Tertullian can cite Marcion's own favoured apostle Paul: 'if anyone destroys the temple of God he shall be destroyed'... by the despised creator of course.

Creation, ownership and grace meet again in a passage from *Adv Marc* V 11, already cited, and which again looks to Paul. The treasure of the Spirit held in the clay vessel of the body belongs once more to the powerful creator, 'the glory is the creator's, and it is his vessels that savour of the excellency of the power of God'. More of Paul surfaces in *Adv Marc* V 7. Tertullian focuses upon the words of 1 Corinthians 8:4–6 in which Paul discredits any rival god to the biblical one. The God of Jesus Christ originated all things and stands as the one 'for whom we exist'. The correlation of creation, ownership and redemption through Christ finds its way to completion here. The creator comes out on top as God of all, for 'from him are the world and life and death, and these cannot belong to that other god'. If, as seems likely, 'from him' carries a retributive sense, then again creation additionally unfolds into judgement.

Adv Marc IV 38 supplies a final example of the way creation-ownership connects with grace. Here Tertullian handles the question of Caesar's penny put to Jesus, and the answer of Jesus rests on the principle that human beings should be returned to the maker who stamped his image upon them. Omnipotent creatorship invites full allegiance. But what then of Marcion's allegedly 'good' god? Tertullian dispatches him with an air of finality:

> Let Marcion's god go and fetch coinage for himself... except that one has to do this who has not a penny of his own.

The argument bars a god from operations of grace and kindliness in a territory which he has not established as his own *absolutely* through the *creatio ex nihilo*. Especially does it bar the way to human religious allegiance to such a god. Marcion's dualism of creation and grace remains impossible.

In more specific features of divine grace, particularly forgiveness, we find that the connection of power and grace still holds. In *De pudic* 21 for instance, the power of forgiveness is nothing other than the *potestas* which comes from God. The same majesty of divine power (*maiestas divinae potestatis* of our earlier discussion) can re-focus from subjection to forgiveness. Here the God over the temple, the *dominus*, the source of human life and health, the God with powers of judgement, also meets the creature. The same omnipotence which invites obedience also mends fracture. Between these two lies the full scheme of grace in the incarnation, the cross and the resurrection. The power which both commands and restores contains the whole story of God's dignity and power.

Creation and re-creation

Adv Marc II 29, examined earlier, sounded some echoes in Tertullian of the Irenaean theme of re-creation through the Christ of the creation.

Other texts repeat the idea. Hence *Adv Marc* IV 37 claims that the Son of Man saves what was lost, both body and soul and 'in full accord with the creator he promised salvation of the whole man.' Again in *Adv Marc* V 17 Tertullian discusses the assurance of Ephesians 2:10 that Christians are God's workmanship in Christ. In respect of our substance he made us, 'but in respect of grace he has created us'. It is not surprising that in *De carne* 17 Tertullian picks up the view of Irenaeus, though without mentioning him, that regeneration life begins with the virgin birth: 'into a virgin no less needed to be introduced the Word of God, constructive of life'.

Three principles emerge from the various texts. First, the incarnation aims at a new creation. Secondly, this achievement ranks in power with the original *creatio ex nihilo*. Thirdly, the Word of God assumes in this renovating operation his unique position and role in the original creation. One mighty work, redemption, replicates another, creation. *Adv Marc* IV 7 underlines the balance. Tertullian justifies Christ's severe rebuke to the demons who impertinently gave the impression that Christ had come for destruction (of them) rather than recovery (of the human). He did indeed come to destroy them but supremely came for a creation rather than a destruction. The famous paradox passage of *De carne* 5, discussed earlier, stresses that the incarnation presents 'the one and only hope of the whole world' and although strictly beneath God's dignity it is 'for our advantage'. The extraordinary power which makes incarnation (the impossible) possible bends itself to the renewal and salvation of the world. The incarnation takes for its single goal, redemption after the pattern of the *creatio ex nihilo*. *De carne* 6 says just that:

> Christ… being sent to die, had of necessity also to be born, so that he might die… the project of dying is the reason for being born.

A similar tribute in *Adv Marc* V 14 puts the connection between the creator's power and redemption in a crystalline way: 'For in this will consist the power of God, in using a similar substance to accomplish salvation.' The constitution of Christ's person forms the context. Tertullian takes his stand upon the full bodily humanity of Christ, a full incarnating for a full renewal of the race. The essence of God's power consists in the Spirit of God's healing of the flesh of sin. God accomplishes this by means of an *authentic* incarnation, the very zenith of his saving power. Without such power no salvation, renewal or new creation could be hoped for. Naturally, we are speaking of a real incarnation of flesh, certainly not the clothing of the Son with an angel (*De carne* 14), a docetic-inspired idea which questioned the Son's power or competence to deliver humanity from within its own skin without unwarranted outside aid:

> To what purpose then was she also clothed with an angel, except perhaps as an attendant to help him in the accomplishment of man's salvation? Then was not the Son of God competent by himself to deliver man whom the serpent by himself and unattended had overthrown?

For Tertullian, one may not compromise the absolute power with which Christ inaugurated the new creation or else the true and authentic vulnerable humanity would perish also.

Power, Spirit and the Church

The debate over an alleged progression from a binitarian to a Trinitarian structure in Tertullian's thought stands in the way, at this point, of any instant discussion of his teaching on the Holy Spirit and power. The main critical and historical issue revolves around the place of Montanism and its allegedly decisive bearing on the direction of Tertullian's thought, particularly in *Adversus Praxean* (though with Braun I leave aside here the ingenious suggestion that 'Praxeas' was in fact none other than Irenaeus).[4] Some scholars have detected a fundamental difference between Tertullian's Trinitarian doctrine in *Adversus Praxean* and those writings generally agreed to have preceded it. The most important names attached to this discussion include Loofs,[5] Kretschmar[6] and Stegman[7]. Facing the opposite way we find Moreschini,[8] Bender,[9] Fortman[10] and Braun. Braun argues that since up to *Adversus Praxean* Tertullian's doctrinal concerns have been *christological* and *soteriological*, it is difficult to assert that his Trinitarianism comes to us as totally new. In his work against Praxeas these elements emerge because modalism and Montanism have drawn them out.[11] If the progression theory is correct it seems strange that so much of *Adversus Praxean* limits itself to the discussion of the Father and the Son.

[4]See R. Braun, 'Chronica Tertullianea', *Revue des Études Augustiniennes* 23 (1977) 339–340, reviewing this idea by S.G. Hall.

[5]F. Loofs, *Theophilus von Antioch Adversus Marcionem, und die anderen theologischen Quellen bei Irenaeus*, Leipzig, 1930, cited by G. Kretschmar, *Studien zur frühchristlichen Trinitätstheologie. Beiträge zur Historischen Theologie*, Tübingen, Paul Siebeck, 1956, 23.

[6]Kretschmar, op. cit. 23–27.

[7]See R. Braun, review of C.A.B. Stegman, 'The Development of Tertullian's Doctrine of *Spiritus Sanctus*' (Dissertation: Southern Methodist University, 1979), 'Chronica Tertullianea', *Revue des Études Augustiniennes* 27 (1981) 328–329.

[8]R. Braun in a review of C. Moreschini's 'Tradizione e innovazione nella pneumatologie di Tertulliano', in 'Chronica Tertullianea', *Revue des Études Augustiniennes* 27 (1981) 329.

[9]W. Bender, *Die Lehre über den Heiligen Geist bei Tertullian*, München, Max Heuber, 1961, 148–149.

[10]Fortman, *The Triune God*, 112. He reminds us that in Tertullian's tracts on Modesty, Baptism and Repentance the same co-ordination appears of the Holy Spirit with the Father and Son even though the latter two probably come in the 'pre-Montanist' phase.

[11]Op. cit. 329.

In fact, Kretschmar himself holds back from maintaining the *decisive* influence of Montanist prophecy upon Tertullian's work, noting the caution of even Loofs[12] himself.

There is no need to conclude a discontinuity between the theology of *Adversus Praxean* and the apologist's earlier work (assuming indeed that everyone is working with a sound chronology). Changes of concern will naturally produce changes in content. A full Trinitarian doctrine in an earlier work would have sometimes proven highly inconvenient for his rhetoric, and it may even have suffered relegation to the background just for that reason (cf. *Adv Marc* I 5 and I 15). This makes all the more remarkable the consistency with which one theme persists: the divine omnipotence. So right into *Adversus Praxean* Tertullian claims to be doing what he has always done, namely defending the *monarchia*, the unique rank of the one God.

All in all, it should cause little surprise to find the Holy Spirit included in the rank of one mighty creator God as early as the *Apologeticum*. In fairness, however, the full conception of the Holy Spirit as power reaches its highest definition in the 'Montanist' phase. The Spirit is the 'third in the sequence of majesty' (*Adv Prax* 3) and '"vicarious" Lord' (*De virg vel* 1).[13] The absence in the earlier works of such specific descriptions of the Spirit as a subject of power surely stems from the nature of the earlier apologetic. However, the association of *spiritus* and power proved inevitable.[14] Turning from *spiritus* as *substantia* to *spiritus* as *persona*, as Tertullian does in *Adversus Praxean*, would have proved impossible without a parallel movement from 'power' to '*a* power', a *species* of power.

Langstadt argues that for Tertullian the power belongs to the one deity and therefore is the one power in Father, Son and Spirit, 'the

---

[12]Kretschmar, op. cit. 23, n. 4 where he recognises that the ideas of *Adv Prax* 8 have appeared earlier in *Apol* 21. Braun for his part quite readily recognises a greater elucidation of Tertullian's Trinitarian thought in later work (his review of Stegman, op. cit. 328–9). P. Gerlitz supports a development theory, but his authority turns out to be the familiar Kretschmar: *Ausserchristliche Einflüsse auf die Entwicklung des Christlichen Trinitätsdogmas, Zugleich ein Religions– und Dogmengeschichtlicher Versuch zur Erklärung der Herkunft der Homousie*, Leiden, E.J. Brill, 1963, 18.

[13]Gerlitz thinks that in this chapter the Spirit is both a *Wesenbestimmung* of God and a *vis*, or *dynamis* (ibid. p. 17).

[14]According to H. Karpp, during the Montanist period the idea grows that the Holy Spirit comes in power to take hold of the prophet and the human must make space for the Spirit (*Schrift und Geist bei Tertullian*, Gütersloh, C. Bertelsmann Verlag, 1955, 49).

power that is the Spirit that is God'.[15] The Spirit, however, is *given*, which Langstadt sees happening in two ways in Tertullian's thought, first by participation by all members of the Church and secondly in a full way to the prophets, apostles, confessors and martyrs:

> The full gift of the Spirit is the gift of Spirit in the fullness of his deity and therefore also in the fullness of his power: the power of prophecy, the power of miracles, the power of absolution from unforgivable sins.[16]

By identifying 'the Spirit' with merely 'Spirit' (the fullness of deity and power) Langstadt at least illustrates just how much in Tertullian the *spiritus* of the Trinity points to powerful deity.[17] Hence in *De pudicitia* the apologist writes, 'What is power? The Spirit, and the Spirit is God.'[18] Tertullian's strong soteriological interest, typical of the early writers, yields a fresh interest in the Spirit as sanctifier of his people, the 'vicarious power' of the Logos for applying his redemptive work.[19]

The Spirit and the Church

Tertullian does not only deploy the Spirit's individual status within the divine *potestas* for his doctrine of redemption. With the Spirit, as with the Son, a crucial relation to creation comes to light. According to *Adv Prax* 12 the sanctifying work of the Holy Spirit springs from his involvement in the powerful work of creation. The Father creates together with both Son and Holy Spirit so that both Son and Spirit act as powerful subjects.[20] Equally the Spirit's work in the sacrament of baptism stems from his powerful operation as a third person in the rational ordering of the watery earth[21] (*De bapt* 3). *De bapt* 4 goes on to argue that just as the Spirit in all the immense power of creation hovered over the primal waters, so he similarly did over the water of baptism, ready at the invocation to extend the same power in sanctifying efficacy. Tertullian still takes this line in *Adv Prax* 31, which specifically counts

[15]E. Langstadt, 'Tertullian's Doctrine of Sin and the Power of Absolution in *"de pudicitia"'*, K. Aland & F.L. Cross, eds, *Studia Patristica*, Vol. II, Berlin, Akademie-Verlag, 1957, 251–257 (p. 255).

[16]Ibid. 255–256.

[17]Cf. Gerlitz, op. cit. 17.

[18]E.J. Fortman, *The Triune God*, 111.

[19]Warfield, op. cit. 87.

[20]Cf. Bender, op. cit. 95. He rejects the view of K. Adam that Tertullian resembles Hermas in assigning so much power to the Son that nothing remains for the Spirit, basing his comments upon the presence, for Tertullian, of the Holy Spirit at creation.

[21]Ibid. 96–97, citing *De bapt* 8.

the Spirit in with the Father and the Son. A trenchant Montanist claim, that the emergence of the Spirit in the New Prophecy indicates attainment of creation's goal, possibly lurks in the text.[22] In this case we cannot rule out an implied correlation of the Spirit with the *creatio ex nihilo*.

For Tertullian, then, the sacrament of baptism demonstrates the omnipotence of God and takes its empowerment from the Holy Spirit himself. The power operates in a way similar to the miracle at Bethsaida, restoring the candidate to divine likeness and surpassing John's baptism by bringing true forgiveness.[23] The Spirit derives his mighty renewing power from his participation in the primal creation. Tertullian remains consistent in the face of Marcion's dualism. Holding to a 'sacramental' sphere of the re-creating Spirit's power,[24] he again champions the goodness of the material creation as even surpassing natural goodness. Just as the apologist quite happily implicates Christ in the mighty production and sphere of creation, so he associates the Spirit of renewing grace with the sphere of nature. Grace means power. Power means creating. He cannot separate the potency involved in the original creation from that involved in the whole scheme of grace. In Theophilus[25] and Irenaeus[26] we already have antecedents for Tertullian's standpoint. The attention to power running through Tertullian's theology leads in the direction of a Trinitarian theory involving the Spirit as a 'Third' in the power of divine creatorship. Certain specific soteriological roles, however, fall to the Spirit. It seems likely that Irenaeus, rather than Montanism, should take the credit for these. It was Irenaeus who first highlighted the connection between the Spirit as creator and the Spirit as re-creator. In his *Adv haer* III 17.2 the Holy Spirit, as the Breath of God in Genesis 2:7, mediates the emergence of the human creature. The Spirit's sanctifying presence stems from that powerful creating act. This holds whether we are talking about actually

---

[22]P. Langlois, 'La théologie de Tertullien', in *Bibliothèque de l'École des Chartes*, 125 (1967) 438–444 (p. 441).

[23]Cf. B. Leeming, *Principles of Sacramental Theology*, London, Longmans, 1963, 45.

[24]Ibid. 43.

[25]Grant draws attention to the citation of Ps. 32:6 in *Ad Autol* I 7, and argues that wisdom for Theophilus must be identical with the *pneuma* or power by which the heavens were made. R.M. Grant, 'Theophilus of Antioch to Autolycus', *Harvard Theological Review* 40 (1947) 227–256 (p. 253).

[26]Aeby points out that in Irenaeus the activity of the Spirit in creation is similar to that of the Word and that mention of both belongs to the Rule of Faith. Conversely, God does not need angels to create but creates solely through word and wisdom (*Les missions divines*, 65). He cites particularly *Adv haer* I 22.1; IV 20.1.

effecting union between a person and God (*Adv haer* V 1.2), making the person fit for immortality and God's indwelling (*Adv haer* V 8.1) or cleansing in preparation for the life of God (*Adv haer* V 9.1).[27] The Spirit becomes the chief agent in the ascent to God.[28] The same Spirit descends upon the disciples at Pentecost bringing several languages for the simple reason that he possesses power over all the nations.[29] The approach augments the Irenaean stress on the Spirit as life-giving Spirit for the Church.[30] The descriptions mainly spotlight the prerogative of the Spirit as stemming from his involvement in the primal creation, and his *potestas* enjoys a divine rank pointing in the direction of the divine goal in creation. For Irenaeus the argument buttresses his theology of the *recapitulatio* of human destiny.

Irenaeus, then, provides a very clear precedent for the notion found in Tertullian that the special powers and operations of the Spirit in the renewal of the race do not differ from those of the primal act of creation. But Tertullian returns to the *potestas* of creation for a concept which will establish the unity and equality of the Spirit with the Father and the Son, in order to advance the Paraclete's prominence in the post-apostolic Church. The idea, already present in earlier tradition, receives, of course, a special accent in the 'Montanist' period.

The authority and power of the Spirit emerging from this construction meet us in *Adv Prax* 13: 'we... being disciples not of men but of the Paraclete'. *Ad mart* 3 encourages the martyrs to engage in the spiritual struggle in which God stands as their president, the Holy Spirit the trainer, and Christ the master. In *De bapt* 15, where baptism relates to the one body, Tertullian's gloss, 'one Church in the heavens', points to the kingdom soon to fall with power upon the nations.[31] Baptism forms the oath of allegiance and entry to that kingdom.[32] The military-sounding oaths of Mithraism, reflecting loyal promises to general and emperor, became mirrored in Christian baptism with its promise of obedience to God.[33] They belonged to a 'shadow empire', in which, in the Spirit, Christians became part of a new kingdom of power. Here Christians gave themselves over to the one God and the one Spirit of power and renewal. To this source we can trace Tertullian's vision of the

[27]Fortman lists these features, op. cit. 105.

[28]Aeby op. cit. 63. He cites *Adv haer* III 24.1 in support.

[29]*Adv haer* III 17.2, cited by Aeby, op. cit. 61.

[30]T. Marsh, 'The Holy Spirit in Early Christian Teaching', *Irish Theological Quarterly* 45 (1978) 101–116 (p. 113).

[31]R.F. Evans, op. cit. 9.

[32]Ibid.

[33]H. Demougeot, 'Paganus, Mithra et Tertullien', F.L. Cross, ed., *Studia Patristica*, Vol. III, Berlin, Akademie-Verlag, 1961, 354–365 (pp. 361–362).

Christian life. The political and hierarchical ethos of western Christianity stems in some measure from this imperial-sounding tone of Tertullian's rhetoric. Loyalty to the universal emperor transposed very neatly into loyalty to his representatives upon earth, especially if held in place by Tertullian's doctrine of the monarchy of God, in which the one divine rule may descend by degrees to others than the Father (although Tertullian has in mind only the Son and the Spirit). Congar has rightly spotted how easily an empire-driven model can go further and issue in the ultimate fusion of power: political monotheism.[34]

But the Paraclete with his power showed loyalty too, and gave assistance to the persecuted Christians.[35] For that matter, all Christians enjoyed such assisting power through the Spirit. *De idol* 24 pictures the Spirit as the power of the wind which drives the ship of faith between the perils which threaten it. As the energising force of Christian experience,[36] the Holy Spirit with his sanctifying power is sufficiently important to appear in the Rule of Faith.[37] Tertullian roots the effectiveness of the Christian's prayers in the *potestas* of the Spirit (*De orat* 1).[38] This internal work of the Spirit will reach its peak in the resurrection (*De res* 40), where the Spirit's *strength* or *reality*, rather than his personality, dominates the landscape. An indwelling sanctification by the Spirit forms a down-payment of coming resurrection (*De res* 51) and the Spirit will be the animating power (*De res* 46).

The climax of Tertullian's thought, however, comes in his later work where the divine power of the Spirit arms a polemic. First, he claims the Spirit's power exclusively for the fresh life coming through the New Prophecy. The powerful operation of the Spirit upon the prophet focuses that power, an irresistible power.[39] Secondly, the Spirit's power settles Tertullian's dispute with the establishment on the special prerogative of absolution.

In the vast subject of divine–human relations two threads control the discussion, and both relate to power. The first concerns accountability and the second concerns forgiveness. For the first we turn to *De paen* 4, which speaks of the requirement of human obedience, in which 'the majesty of divine power (*maiestas divinae potestatis*) has the prior right'. Divine dignity and majesty consist of power, a power which lies behind all God's dealings with the human world. But the same power brings

[34]Y. Congar, 'Classical Political Monotheism and the Trinity', *Concilium* 143, *God as Father. Religion in the Eighties*, Edinburgh, T. & T. Clark, 1981, 31–36.
[35]Karpp, op. cit. 47. He is thinking of Tertullian's sentiments in *De fuga*.
[36]Bender, op. cit. 142.
[37]Ibid.
[38]Ibid. 142–143.
[39]Cf. Karpp, op. cit. 49.

forgiveness through the Spirit and the same divine exclusiveness jealously guards it.[40] In *De pudic* 21 too, the *potestas* which underlies creatorship and control over creation also extends forgiveness of sins. *Potestas*, as opposed to *disciplina*, denotes the power by which God can forgive sin.[41] Significantly, he then introduces the Holy Spirit: 'It goes with the Spirit of God.' The power remains uniquely God's and, by inference, the operation remains God's, though it takes place through the Spirit at work in the messengers. However, Tertullian exploits a difference between the apostles' *doctrine* and their *power*. The bishops may succeed to one but not to the other. That other, in fact, comes from God[42] in the gift of the Holy Spirit, which does not attach to the episcopal office as such.[43] The power of absolution comes in God the Holy Spirit through a spiritual man (*homo spiritalis*), 'one who like a prophet or apostle has the Spirit',[44] and it 'belongs by definition to the Church.' *De pudic* 21 in Langstadt's paraphrase runs,

> *Potestas* (the) power of absolution from sin which otherwise is unforgivable, is one and the same with the power which manifests itself in the working of miracles. It is the personal charisma of prophets and apostles: and it belongs by definition to the church if the church *proprie et principaliter* is the Spirit. The church therefore can forgive any sin through a *homo spiritalis*, one who like a prophet or apostle has the Spirit. But *potestas* is not a power which can be claimed by the bishop by virtue of his office.[45]

A diagnosis emerges of the relation between the ecclesiastical power given in the Church and the power of the Spirit.[46] The real power present in the Church, more strictly, is the *Spiritus* ('*Spiritus autem deus*'). This same power surged into view in the miracles and belonged

---

[40]See F.E. Vokes, 'Penitential Discipline in Montanism', E.A. Livingstone, ed., *Studia Patristica*, Vol. XIV, Berlin, Akademie-Verlag, 1976, 62–76 (p. 66).

[41]E. Langstadt, op. cit. 255.

[42]Ibid. 252. See also W.P. Le Saint, '*Traditio* and *Exomologesis* in Tertullian', F.L. Cross, ed., *Studia Patristica*, Vol. VIII, Berlin, Akademie-Verlag, 1966, 414–419. Both De Labriolle and Von Campenhausen note that Tertullian jealously guards the power of forgiveness exclusively for God: P. de Labriolle, *La crise Montaniste*, Paris, Leroux, 1913, 441, 447–448; H. Von Campenhausen, *Ecclesiastical Authority and Spiritual Power in the Church of the First Three Centuries*, London, A. & C. Black, 1969, chapter 9. Compare also W. Telfer, *The Office of A Bishop*, London, Darton Longman & Todd, 1962, 124.

[43]Cf. W.P. Le Saint, *Tertullian: Treatises on Penance. On Penitence and On Purity. Translated and Annotated*, London, Longmans Green & Co., 1959, 280.

[44]J. Daniélou, op. cit. 440–441.

[45]E. Langstadt, op. cit. 252.

[46]De Labriolle, op. cit. 447.

therefore to the charismatic Church rather than to the institutional Church.

These sentiments, of course, aimed at a particular purpose in a particular situation, but the conviction that the powerful Spirit creates the Church belongs to a fundamental theological structure in Tertullian. This is because 'the Church is really the Spirit in whom is the Trinity of the one divinity' – a statement that probably any 'catholic' under other circumstances would have happily confirmed.[47] Commonly, Christians thought of the Church as a body of people renewed and revivified in the Spirit. The Holy Spirit, then, occupied for Tertullian a prime position in the life of the Church, arising from his involvement in the divine power of creation, rule, re-creation and resurrection. Ample precedents appear in the earlier apologists, particularly in Irenaeus, a fact which alone removes Tertullian's general pneumatology from the category of being purely and simply Montanist. We cannot say without qualification that Tertullian and Irenaeus had not 'found a necessary and satisfactory place and function for the Spirit in their thought'.[48] The precise relationship of the Spirit to Father and Son in an essential Trinity remained undefined, as it was to for a long time, but the place and function of the Spirit had begun to take shape. A model based on the concept of power had underlined the status of the Holy Spirit in Tertullian's exposition of the Church as a sphere of the kingdom and power of God.

[47]J.N.B. van den Brink: 'Reconciliation in the Early Fathers', E.A. Livingstone, ed., Studia Patristica, Vol. XIII, Berlin, Akademie-Verlag, 1975, 90–106 (p. 97).

[48]R.P.C. Hanson, The Attractiveness of God. The Doctrine of God in the Early Church, London, 1973, 123. He later recognises, however, that Tertullian, like Irenaeus, gave a fuller and more perceptive place to the Holy Spirit in the Trinity. D.L. Holland finds the references to the Holy Spirit in the Hippolytan creed to be adrift theologically and present only because of baptismal and confessional practice: 'The Third Article of the Creed', E.A. Livingstone, ed., Studia Patristica, Vol. XIII, Berlin, Akademie-Verlag, 1975, 189–197 (p. 197). He also, however, thinks the creed does not adequately reflect the pneumatology that was beginning to emerge (p. 193).

CHAPTER 7

Power and Consummation

The setting of Tertullian's eschatology

The question of corporeal existence illustrates how easy it was for Christian eschatology to conflict with received wisdom in much of the Hellenistic world. For many Greek writers no lasting value attached to the physical material frame. It served at best only as a stepping stone to incorporeal existence and at worst, in a well-worn phrase, as a prison-house for the soul. Such schools did not welcome a doctrine of bodily resurrection.[1] Greek preference more often looked to a disembodied immortality,[2] if indeed it entertained any hope of survival at all. So powerful was this tendency that even Jewish writers sometimes stumbled at the idea of corporeal renewal,[3] Philo especially betraying hesitation on this score.[4] Possible support for a bodily resurrection in the Aristotelian unity of body and soul[5] mostly produced a naturalism where neither body nor soul survived death.

---

[1] So G. Florovsky, 'Eschatology in the Patristic Age: An Introduction', K. Aland & F.L. Cross, eds, *Studia Patristica*, Vol. II, Berlin, Akademie-Verlag, 1957, 235–250 (p. 245). Resurrection meant for many Greek writers permanent imprisonment in the flesh, and according to Celsus, fitting only for an earthworm.

[2] A.J. Visser, 'A Bird's Eye View of Ancient Christian Eschatology', *Numen, International Review For the History of Religions*, 14 (1967) 4–22 (p. 5).

[3] Ibid.

[4] Ibid.

[5] Florovsky, op. cit. 246–247.

The context for Tertullian's controversial writings belongs to eclectic movements more open than he to contemporary influences but also Christian in flavour. The more famous Gnostic[6] and Marcionite[7] systems feature strongly. Tertullian writes major works against both, but he especially confronts Marcion's dualism at every turn, since it challenged his key themes of creation, incarnation and resurrection. Irenaeus and the *regula fidei* had already interacted strongly with Gnostic thought – a stubborn fact unaffected by modern speculation on the alleged respectability of Gnostic systems within ancient Christianity.[8] Tertullian, however, wrote when the main Gnostic crisis had passed.[9]

We are concerned here with specific targets of Tertullian's fire and certainly not the vast polychrome field of 'Greek philosophy in general', though Hermogenes, Marcion, the Gnostics, and even the Monarchians, showed a great receptivity to some commonplace philosophical currents. All the same, I do not think we can afford to ignore the observation of Florovsky that a predisposition to ideas of permanence and recurrence was common,[10] that the notion of novelty became obscured where a belief in the completeness and perfectness of the cosmos prevailed,[11] and that the notion of eschatology itself diminished or disappeared altogether in such schemes.[12] As it happens, Tertullian's stress upon kingdom, history and eschatology obviously did not spring from desire for philosophical engagement with the Greek schools. He worked mainly with biblical categories within a Latin frame.

[6]According to G.W.H. Lampe the theme of the soul's ascent to heaven replaces the parousia in the various Gnostic systems, 'Early Patristic Eschatology', in 'Eschatology. Four Papers to be read to the Society for the Study of Theology', Scottish *Journal of Theology, Occasional Papers*, No. 2, London, Oliver & Boyd, 1957, 1–35 (p. 18).

[7]Lampe, ibid., notes that according to Marcion as well as Basilides, the soul imprisoned in the body is alone saved.

[8]According to D.L. Holland, the *regula fidei* of Tertullian and Irenaeus faithfully reproduced a mainstream tradition ('Some Issues in Orthodox-Gnostic Christian Polemic', E.A. Livingstone, ed., *Studia Patristica*, Vol. XVII/I, Oxford, Pergamon Press, 1982, 214–222). H.J. Carpenter (cited by Holland) also recognises the consensus lying behind the statement of the Rule of Faith on creation, 'Popular Christianity and the Theologians in the Early Centuries', *Journal of Theological Studies*, NS 14 (1963) 297.

[9]Holland, op. cit. 216.

[10]Florovsky, op. cit. 240. For the Stoic doctrine of conflagration and renewal see the perceptive treatment of J. Mansfeld, *Providence and the Destruction of the Universe*, 129–188, and M.L. Colish, *The Stoic Tradition*, Vol. I, 24–25, 29–31, 182–183, 255–256, 314–317.

[11]Ibid.

[12]Florovsky, op. cit. 241.

Among the known cosmological options the idea of a 'cyclic' universe found much favour in Roman Stoic thought. The theme of periodical successions of identical worlds eventually found new detailed expression in the Stoic doctrine of *palingenesia* (rebirth) and *apokatastasis ton panton* (restoration of everything).[13] In *this* matter, Stoicism only minimally acted upon Tertullian.[14] It became very easy for some systems to elevate the status of the cosmos itself and endow it with qualities traditionally divine, as Hermogenes did – and attracted the venom of Tertullian. To have a meaningful eschatology, let alone a belief in corporeal resurrection, Christian writers needed to underpin their work with a coherent doctrine of creation.[15] Tertullian could not, even if he wanted to, turn around all the schools committed to the eternity of matter or to the cyclic view of the universe. Rather, he consolidated earlier Christian writing by placing the *creatio ex nihilo* right at the base of the Christian theological scheme, including eschatology. His was an apologetic theology containing a latent challenge to some contemporary currents by asserting a fully omnipotent creator wholly committed to the directing of his universe.

The influence of Christian writers

Tertullian picked up the legacy of earlier Christian writers in many themes. One of the more important was the conviction that in some sense the last times had already begun. The Church anticipated the consummation by its participation in the Holy Spirit and so stood in a territory of both fulfilment and expectation of final consummation.[16] Tertullian lived with these two concerns, namely the Spirit of power whose operations were the very *dynamis* of God upon earth, and the subjection of the cosmos to the divine rank or power. It may be that already a mysticism or pneumatology was beginning to nudge aside the second-century eschatology,[17] but on the whole Tertullian still reflected it. The second century stressed 'two advents, the first in humility and the

---

[13]Ibid.

[14]H.B. Timothy professes to find the Stoic view in *De res* 12, though it is likely that rhetoric and an argument *ad hominem* come into play here. For Timothy's account of Tertullian's indebtedness to Stoicism see *The Early Christian Apologists*, 47–48.

[15]Florovsky, op. cit. 243.

[16]Lampe, op. cit. 19. Cf. Florovsky, op. cit. 236: 'The story of salvation was still in progress.... The kingdom of the Spirit had been already inaugurated.'

[17]Lampe, op. cit. 19.

second in royal power'.[18] The stronger 'apocalyptic' futurism flowed mainly from the less theologically-bound quarters of early Church life,[19] but nevertheless the theologians, too, talked of an ultimate and final consummation.[20] The theory that eschatology survived because of the Church's sacramentalism rooting the faith in history[21] must be balanced by the recognition of the place that historical and eschatological themes enjoyed as of the structure of the faith.[22]

Justin Martyr led the way in elaborating the implications of the eschatological hope. Resurrection belief especially, he argued, remained an indispensable condition for Christian faith[23] and explained why Christians were persecuted.[24] Justin left the resurrection belief in no obscurity.[25] It belonged to the Church's confession[26] and its celebration lay behind the Christian worship on the first day (or 'eighth' day) of the week instead of the last day.[27] The risen body connected with the very body that died.[28] He rejected one of the Greek options of natural immortality and saw in everlasting life a wonder and miracle of the divine power.[29] The mighty power of Christ's kingdom will come to an earthly millennial expression centred upon Jerusalem before the final consummation,[30] though the millennial aspect, with its possible political connotations, he shrewdly avoided in the apologetic works.[31] All the same, it betrays a preoccupation with the divine omnipotence and the impact of that power upon God's own creation. It is possible that

---

[18]E. Ferguson, 'Canon Muratori, Date and Provenance', E.A. Livingstone, ed., *Studia Patristica*, Vol. XVII/II, Oxford, Pergamon Press, 1982, 677–683 (p. 681).

[19]Lampe, op. cit. 24.

[20]According to Florovsky, the goal 'beyond history' regulated history, op. cit. 238. W.H.C. Frend maintains that dread of the end was such that tolerance towards the Roman empire was the lesser evil, 'Church and State, Perspective and Problems in the Patristic Era', E.A. Livingstone, ed., *Studia Patristica*, Vol. XVII/II, Oxford, Pergamon Press, 1982, 38–54 (p. 45).

[21]Op. cit. 22–23.

[22]See Florovsky, op. cit. 238–239.

[23]Visser, op. cit. 8.

[24]*Dialog* 17; 118.

[25]*Dialog* 32; 36; 53; 82; 100.

[26]*Dialog* 85.

[27]*Dialog* 41.

[28]*Dialog* 80.

[29]*Apol* 10.

[30]Justin believes in this final destruction of all things by fire, but unlike the Stoics excludes God the creator from it (Grant, 'Theophilus of Antioch', p. 253).

[31]Visser, op. cit. 9.

Tatian, Athenagoras and Theophilus held to a similar millenarianism, muted for the same reasons.[32] Theophilus, influenced by the Apocalypse,[33] probably expected the divine power to display itself upon the earth. He also held to a general bodily resurrection (*Ad Autol* I 13, II 38),[34] although notions of divinisation or attained immortality also crept in.[35] Like Justin he espoused the ideas of *ekpurosis* (conflagration) and *apokatastasis* (restoration) but rejected cyclic views.[36] The divine power which accomplishes this upheaval will also execute judgement (*Ad Autol* I 14). Certain key themes significantly developed in Irenaeus and Tertullian crop up in Theophilus but lack a doctrinal programme or scheme into which the ideas of eschatology may be fitted. For this we need Irenaeus.

Tertullian and Irenaeus

The eschatology of Irenaeus takes a vivid shape through the expectation of an Antichrist which parallels, according to Lampe, the 'recapitulation' achieved by Christ.[37] The kingdom does not simply evolve but needs a powerful divine intervention to cut short the ascendancy of the Antichrist.[38] That intervention presented the ultimate hope, but in the giving of the Holy Spirit the 'last times' already loomed.[39] The divine power, poised to destroy finally all opposition, operated already through the Spirit of power.[40] So the permanently present power of God in his Spirit resolved the tension between future and present. As for the general scheme which enfolds this eschatology, Irenaeus begins with the doctrine of the *creatio ex nihilo*. D.S. Kim[41] has uncovered the centrality of creation to Irenaeus' scheme. It means that nothing is impossible with

[32]Ibid.

[33]W. Bauer, *Orthodoxy and Heresy in Earliest Christianity*, Philadelphia, Fortress Press, 1964, 78.

[34]Cited by Grant, op. cit.

[35]Grant, ibid. 253–255. Cf. especially *Ad Autol* II 27.

[36]Grant, ibid. 253–254. Cf. *Ad Autol* II 37,38.

[37]G.W.H. Lampe, op. cit. 29.

[38]Ibid.

[39]*Adv haer* III 11.9. For Patristic approaches to the idea of the 'the last times', and the view of Irenaeus in particular, see W.C. Van Unnik, 'Der Ausdruck, "In den Letzten Zeiten" bei Irenaeus', *Neo-Testamentica et Patristica (Festschrift to O. Cullmann)*, Leiden, E.J. Brill, 1962, 292–304 (especially pp. 302–304).

[40]Van Unnik suggests that this theme eases the problem of the delay in the parousia, op. cit. 303–304.

[41]D.S. Kim, 'Irenaeus of Lyons and Teilhard de Chardin: A Comparative Study of "Recapitulation" and "Omega"', *Journal of Ecumenical Studies* 13 (1976) 69–94.

God, as faith rather than philosophy reveals; that creation is both subject to God and subject to change; and that the knowledge of God arises from his self-revelation and providence.[42] Humanity's destiny lay in growth through the Holy Spirit to a perfection originally designed by God.[43] The redemptive recapitulation of this journey by Christ the second Adam *therefore embraces all the dispensations of time.*[44] It aspires not simply to the restoration of some pristine order but to the perfection of creation.[45] The vision of final Christian redemption thus also enfolds within itself the concept of 'deification', or more correctly 'participation in God'. Consummation includes a new unity with God as authentic human fulfilment which in turn supplies a focus for God's own glory, 'mediated in God's love and omnipotence'.[46] The divine omnipotence, then, terminates upon the everlasting goodness of the creation.

Between that consummation and the present process associated with the immanent Spirit lies, for Irenaeus, the millennium in which the earthly kingdom arrives in fullness of power, perhaps even continuous somehow with the present process.[47] *Adv haer* V 32.1 sees in this reign the time when those who are worthy shall become 'accustomed gradually to partake of the divine nature',[48] and the climax in which the omnipotence of the lord of history finds fulfilment.[49] The recapitulation of Christ reaches to all things and demonstrates God's deserved primacy, 'drawing all things to himself at the proper time' (*Adv haer* III 16.6).[50] Believers, who have suffered so much, come to participate in the reign and power of God (*Adv haer* V 32.1), rounding off a process of human

---

[42]Kim, op. cit. 73.

[43]Ibid. 73–74.

[44]Ibid. 76.

[45]Ibid. 83, 86.

[46]Ibid. 87.

[47]See P. Bissels, 'Die frühchristliche Lehre vom Gottesreich auf Erden', *Trierer Theologische Zeitschrift* 84 (1975) 44–47 (p. 45). A.P. O'Hagan is satisfied at least that true cosmic renewal is involved in the millennial concept, thus altering the natural order and introducing a new one: *Material Re-Creation in the Apostolic Fathers*, Berlin, Akademie-Verlag, 1968, 37.

[48]O'Rourke Boyle sees this stage as the final preparation in knowledge for the heavenly kingdom: 'Irenaeus' Millennial Hope: A Polemical Weapon', *Recherches de Théologie Ancienne et Médiévale* 36 (1969) 5–16 (pp. 15–16). Cf. Kim, op. cit. 87; Lampe, op. cit. 25; E. Ferguson, 'The Terminology of Kingdom in the Second Century', E.A. Livingstone, ed., *Studia Patristica*, Vol. XVII/II, Oxford, Pergamon Press, 1982, 669–676 (p. 670).

[49]Daniélou sees Irenaeus expressing here the sacredness of the world and of history; J. Daniélou, 'La typologie millenariste de la Semaine dans le Christianisme primitif', *Vigiliae Christianae* 2 (1948) 1–16 (p. 9).

[50]O'Rourke Boyle, op. cit. 14.

ascent supported wholly by the power of God.[51] The millennialism of Irenaeus does not just spring from a blitz on Gnosticism but also from a conviction that God is competent to achieve the original aim of his creation. Other things may distinguish his task from that of Tertullian's,[52] but this particular motive supplies the key to the continuity of their thought. Both based their certainty upon the power of God expressed in creation, incarnation, resurrection and cosmic redemption. Of this mutual belief the millennial reign served as a shared banner. In fact, of course, millenarian teaching did bar the way to both Gnosticism and Marcionitism by confirming the integrity and worth of matter.[53] In one text of *Adv haer* V 28.3, the millennium (probably the end of the millennium signalled by the general resurrection as in *Adv haer* V 35.2[54]) also introduces the judgement.[55]

Anticipating, and perhaps influencing, Tertullian, Irenaeus suffers no embarrassment at having a good God who also puts humanity to judgement. A real God is not just good but also tests those upon whom he shall send his goodness (*Adv haer* III 25.2–5). Goodness and wisdom go together in the judicial power, 'because he is Lord and judge, the Just and Ruler over all' (*Adv haer* III 25.3). The *power* of God by which he rules upholds the effectiveness of his moral supremacy. Finally, Irenaeus makes an appeal to Plato,[56] who held that God was both good and just 'having power over all things… as the beginning and the cause of the creation of the world'. Whatever Plato intended by his words, for Irenaeus they prove the proposition that divine power, denoted by the standing that goes with creatorhood, fixes a twofold function in the one God: both judgement and goodness. And with judgement goes resurrection. Tertullian will come to make more of this, but already in Irenaeus we meet a double resurrection with an eye to judgement (*Adv*

---

[51]Cf. Bissels, op. cit. 47.

[52]H. Finé identifies the difference between Tertullian and Irenaeus on the millennial reign as a difference of stages, Tertullian's being the more final (H. Finé, *Die Terminologie der Jenseitsvorstellungen bei Tertullian. Ein semasiologischer Beitrag zur Dogmengeschichte des Zwischenzustandes*, Bonn, Hanstein, 1958, 43).

[53]O'Rourke Boyle, op. cit. 7–9, 12; S. Wood, 'The Eschatology of Irenaeus', *Evangelical Quarterly* 41 (1969) 30–41 (p. 38).

[54]Wood, op. cit. contests J. Lawson's claim (*Theology of Irenaeus*, 282) that in Irenaeus the judgement takes place *before* the millennium. Problems in locating the judgement haunt millennial systems.

[55]J. Daniélou notes that the material is missing from the Latin text and offers a rendering of the Greek which places judgement in the seventh day and execution in the eighth (eternal) day, op. cit. 10.

[56]W.C. Van Unnik believes Irenaeus is drawing attention to Plato's having some knowledge of the God who judges, 'Two Notes on Irenaeus', *Vigiliae Christianae* 30 (1976) 201–213 (p. 207).

haer II 23.5). The power of God bestows the double edged gift of immortality.[57] The same power, wisdom and goodness which created from God's own free will also endow with 'everlasting permanence' received from 'the power of the Unoriginate' (*Adv haer* IV 28.3). Ultimately, Irenaeus can take a stand on the very space that Tertullian will later occupy:

> For if he does not vivify what is mortal, and does not bring back the corruptible to incorruption, he is not a God of power... that flesh shall also be found fit for and capable of receiving the power of God, which at the beginning received the skilful touches of God.[58] (*Adv haer* V 3.2)

Resurrection depends entirely upon God's reputation as a God of power, and that in turn finds authentication in the original power of creation and more especially the remarkable production of the human creature,[59] enhanced by the special place Christ enjoys as the source and goal of human likeness to God.[60] For Irenaeus, as later for Tertullian, the pronouncements of the Rule of Faith, culminating in resurrection, coalesce around the unifying notion of the creator's *potestas*.[61]

Creation, power and consummation

The dominance of the *creatio ex nihilo*, seen at every point so far, touches Tertullian's eschatology also. *Adv Hermog* 34 provides just one striking example:

> The fact that everything sprang from nothing will ultimately be made plausible by the dispensation of God which is to return all things to nothing.

A large number of biblical references follow (mainly from the Old Testament and in poetic contexts), but they do not dispel the worry that the preoccupation here with annihilation conflicts with the more New

---

[57]Wood, op. cit. 32–33.

[58]The translation is Wood's, op. cit. 33–34. Cf. Florovsky, 'Eschatology in the Patristic Age', 239.

[59]G. Pelland, 'Dans l'attente de la résurrection: Un thème central de l'évangelisation dans l'Église ancienne', *Science et Esprit* 28 (1976) 125–146 (pp. 129–30).

[60]Pelland, op. cit. 135.

[61]A. Hamman stresses the centrality of Christ's resurrection victory to the Irenaean Rule of Faith: 'Resurrection du Christ dans l'antiquité chrétienne (II)', *Revue des Sciences Religieuses* 50 (1976) 1–24 (p. 5).

Testament theme of *consummation*.[62] Tertullian, however, means it, for he continues, 'all things produced from nothing will in the end come to nothing'.

This seems a dangerously bold card to play for the modest gains that accrue to his hand, and we may wonder why he did not flinch from it. Chapter 11 may have already given the semblance of an explanation: 'whatever things are ascribed to evil, are (also) to be attributed (to matter), in accordance with the fact that its condition is evil'.

For Tertullian only the most drastic purification will remove evil, the very dissolution of the material itself, not because material is evil but because this is the only way to destroy the evil which has contaminated it.[63] He believes of course in the immediate reconstitution of all things thereafter. Whilst for him the 'conflagration' takes its origin from the New Testament, as it did for Theophilus, yet it seems as if the thoroughness of the Stoic *ekpurosis* has influenced Tertullian's picture, one fostered by the drive to stress divine might. Plainly such a doctrine requires the *creatio ex nihilo* for its support, but, as Irenaeus (and the New Testament itself) had shown, the *creatio ex nihilo* need not lead to such an overkill. Both *consummation* and *renewal* supply categories in which the creator's free omnipotence over his material can find eschatological expression.

However, both the New Testament and Irenaeus do share with Tertullian a hold on the idea of judgement as a legitimate manifestation of the divine power. Tertullian expressed it in his own way of course:

> I have long ago established my contention that the creator's power is twofold, that he is both judge and kind. (*Adv Marc* V 11)

Earlier we saw these words as counting Christ in with the creator's power, as in *Adv Marc* IV 39, where the second coming of Christ, all admit, brings severity with the kindness. It forces Marcion to concede that either there are two Christs, each appropriating one or the other activity, or that Christ's God is none other than the judge. *Adv Marc* I

---

[62]One may contrast with this Meijering's estimation: Irenaeus is ambiguous on the fate of the universe but at root believes with Plato that the world does not deserve destruction. Rather it deserves consummation (*God, Cosmos, History*, op. cit. 248–262). Irenaeus, against Gnosticism, stresses the durability of the world, and Tertullian, against Hermogenes, stresses the contingency of all things. But for Irenaeus durability is assured precisely from the world's contingency, its dependence upon *God* (*Adv haer* V 36.1). The chronology and function of the millennium can be very unclear in Tertullian (see *Apol* 48, *De res* 11).

[63]Grant considers that Theophilus derived his doctrine of the cosmic burning from 2 Peter 3:10, expressed in Stoic terms (*ekpurosis, apokatastasis*) but, like Justin and Christians generally, rejecting the notion of a recurrent destruction in *Ad Autol* II 17, 37, 38 especially (Grant, op. cit. 253–254).

27 has already exploited Marcion's unthinking acceptance of the 'good' God as 'Lord':

> Fool: you call him lord (*dominum*), yet deny he is to be feared, though this is a term suggesting power (*potestas*) and with it fear.

The 'good' God, that deplored creator, took with the Christ himself the title 'Lord' and inspired a fear that appropriately went with it. On this basis why should the God of Jesus Christ not also be our judge, argues Tertullian in *De res* 14: 'Judge because Lord (*dominus*)... Lord because Maker (*auctor*)... Maker because God'?

Bodily resurrection, however, supplies the clearest link in Tertullian between creation and eschatology. The stigma of 'innovation' does not attach itself to this move since it comes down from the earlier writers.[64] The resurrection, like the creation, would reveal God acting in power for those who worshipped him and suffered for him.[65] Tertullian thought the doctrine of the resurrection of decisive importance and put the revival of interest in it down to the credit of the new prophecy in *De res* 63.[66] Perhaps, but he himself introduced the subject much earlier. In *Apol* 48 he wrote:

> why could you not again come out of nothing into being, by the will of the very same Author whose will brought you into being out of nothing?... Your doubts, I suppose, will be about the reality of God, who set together the mighty frame of this universe out of what was not.

The language reverberates with the *creatio ex nihilo*. A slightly fuller quotation would have yielded the word *nihil* five times. Tertullian, like Irenaeus and probably following him, correlates primal creation and the act of resurrection, and in an early and seminal work at that. Some have detected in this balance a bulwark against dualism, since a Christ related only to non-physical existence would have led straight towards dualistic thinking.[67] That unity came to be anchored in the creed by the words,

---

[64] Tertullian is anxious to make this very point when paying tribute to what he calls the apostolic Church in *De praes* 36. In his account of the catholic faith, 'even in Africa', he follows a line from confession of the creator to resurrection of the flesh, even though the crucifixion is not mentioned. Cf. *De praes* 13, already discussed.

[65] R.M. Grant, *Augustus to Constantine*, 141.

[66] He actually says, 'But yet God almighty (*Deus omnipotens*), while in these last days... he pours out his Spirit upon all flesh... has also put life into the struggling faith of the resurrection of the flesh....'

[67] E.C. Blackman, *Marcion and his Influence*, 96.

one God as creator, raiser of the dead and judge.[68] In *Adv Marc* V 10 Tertullian refers the reader to what generally is taken to be his *De resurrectione carnis* (since he honours Marcion with a brief mention at the opening of it) for a fuller handling of the resurrection. A much fuller treatment of the themes of *Apol* 48 occurs there. *De res* 11 asks,

> must we not reckon up the might (*potentia*), the power (*potestas*), the freedom of action (*licentia*) of God himself, asking whether he is not great enough to be able to rebuild and restore... if out of nothing (*ex nihilo*) God has built up all things, he will be able also out of nothing (*de nihilo*) to produce the flesh reduced to nothing (*in nihilum*)... the restitution of the flesh is easier than its institution.

Both the vocabulary and the symmetry of the argument call up the *creatio ex nihilo*. The use of power-vocabulary, wedded to the *creatio ex nihilo*, underscores the divine power as the guarantee of final bodily restoration. True, Tertullian wisely admits in the same chapter that in fact the power merely to create from pre-existing material would not call into question the power to restore, especially as both bare pre-existing material and death itself form a kind of non-existence. But this concession forms an argument *ad hominem* once again, rather than labouring to establish grounds already argued out in the work against Hermogenes. Tertullian sees the bodily resurrection as just a part of the total cosmic restoration, a task formidable to all except the one who calls the very universal matter into being. Tertullian's argument from chapter 5 to chapter 17 makes the *creatio ex nihilo* the centrepiece of his case,[69] and begins with the familiar claim that the whole universe of things exist as God's servants because called into being solely by his voice.

However, the human species enjoys a special status in the creation because constructed by the breath of God's mouth and because 'things' serve them. The world lying around humanity, then, exists under greater contingency than the human race itself, a fact which discloses not just the *power* of God to restore but the *worth* of the humanity that he restores. A two-fold root for the general resurrection emerges from Tertullian's treatment.[70] First, the power which could generate from nothing all things, including the human world, will certainly prove adequate for the task of resurrection (though taken in isolation, the power to shape from pre-exisiting material might, hypothetically, come up to the challenge). Secondly, the things so wonderfully and powerfully called into existence bear witness to the special worth of humanity and

[68]Ibid. 96–97.
[69]R.D. Sider, 'On Symmetrical Composition in Tertullian', *Journal of Theological Studies*, NS 24 (1973) 405–423 (p. 420).
[70]Cf. *De res* 14.

the coherence of the resurrection doctrine. Such is the sentiment expressed in the rhetoric of *De res* 9: 'God forbid that (he) should abandon the receptacle of his own breath, queen of his own creation.'

In Tertullian's hands, then, the apologists' traditional doctrine of bodily resurrection remains intact. From the common store of *testimonia*[71] he used the appeal to resurrection in nature's own life, which displayed clear instances of the divine power (*potestas*) and parables of the resurrection (*De res* 13). As with Irenaeus, the doctrine of judgement fastens the idea of resurrection to creation because the general resurrection makes possible the kind of judgement most appropriate to a God who is both Lord and Maker (*De res* 14). The final bodily resurrection assumes a central position. In *De res* 2 bodily resurrection is lined up last of all in the links fastening the doctrine as of creation to that of Christ, but it really forms the main battleground with heretics. They dismiss bodily resurrection because they wish to dismiss Christ from the sphere of the flesh and of the creator. In their view God did not create, Christ did not partake of the creation and the created flesh cannot hope for salvation. The serious intention of this view lay in the hope of a theodicy which, under dualistic tendencies, sacrificed the *power* of God to secure God's goodness. But, for Tertullian, loss of power endangered also the worth of the creation, the possibility of incarnation and the reality of the Christian hope. To his mind, a system extending from the uncompromised *creatio ex nihilo* through incarnation to resurrection offered the clearest test of whether a view took as its starting point the biblical account of redemption or a current, however serious, philosophical question. Here Tertullian provides a contrast with Origen.[72]

Inconsistencies haunt his approach, however. For the elegance and rigor of a second *creatio ex nihilo*, Tertullian actually sacrificed the one thing he needed to defend his case against Marcion: the worth of the present creation. The world was so bad that it called for a total conflagration and re-creation. It is likely that a hankering for the Stoic conflagration and re-constitution (*apokatastasis*) fed into Tertullian's thinking here. But it also betrays a millenarian, triumphalist and defeated posture in the apologist's struggle with the problem of evil. More mellow answers were to hand in Irenaeus and, for that matter, in the New Testament itself.

---

[71]*De res* 12. E. Evans finds the same argument, whatever its limits today, in several of the early Christian writers (*Tertullian's Treatise on the Resurrection*, 226).

[72]Steinmann, *Tertullien*, 211.

Consummation, power and history

The influence of Stoicism has been correctly detected in Tertullian,[73] touching on his eschatology in the areas of sin, conflagration, fatalism and anthropology. Other salient features of his end-times scheme seem relatively unscathed from a philosophical shaping. As we noticed earlier, Tertullian broke with Stoicism's fatalism and tendency to limit the divine power. His *creatio ex nihilo* also challenged neo-dualism arising in some Roman Stoicism. A radical beginning implies a radical climax. In Tertullian the circle of fatalism fell foul of a personally directed divine providence with its impending free act of dissolution.[74] Tertullian really straightened out the Stoic circle into a linear concept of history and reality.[75] An omnipotent God who initiates, rules and terminates, contained no comfort for those who had grown accustomed to simple faith in the self-contained perpetuity of its universe.

To the linear history Tertullian added the enhancing conviction that the end was already pressing in upon the Church.[76]

> Fix your eyes on the courses of the world, the gliding seasons, reckon up the periods of time, long for the goal of the final consummation, defend the societies of the churches, be startled at God's signal, be roused up at the angel's trumpet, glory in the palms of martyrdom. (*De spect* 29)

But chapter 30 goes on to celebrate this spectacle's fast approach, a sentiment embraced by Tertullian through a range of his works not just during his 'Montanist' period (*De monog* 7, 11, 14; 16; *De paen* 1; *Ad ux* 15;[77] *De exhort* 9). His understanding of the Lord's Prayer betrays this

---

[73]H.B. Timothy, *The Early Christian Apologists*, 47–50. Some of his examples in Tertullian could, however be put down to rhetoric and especially Tertullian's habit of arguing *ad hominem*.

[74]The apparent devotion to cyclic themes in *De res* 12 should not be pressed. Tertullian closes his inventory of nature resurrections by stressing that they form only illustrations of the fact that *God* is a 'a restorer of all things'.

[75]According to J. Pelikan, only Tertullian's philosophy of history made it possible for him to give voice to an eschatological hope, 'The Eschatology of Tertullian', *Church History* 21 (1952) 108–122 (p. 109).

[76]Tertullian was committed to the proximity of the return of Christ well before his defection to the Montanists, W.P. Le Saint, *Tertullian: Treatises on Marriage and Remarriage: To His Wife; an Exhortation to Chastity; Monogamy*, London, Longmans, Green & Co., 1951, 115, n. 13.

[77]In this text he cautions even against having children since they will go to God before their parents.

expectancy.[78] The strength of his prayer for the coming of the kingdom uncovers his passionate interest in the vindication of God's own historical involvement in the world.[79] Certainly, the kingdom's coming, although it involved a millennial interlude, primarily promised the judgement of God that would put right a world off-course (*Adv Marc* IV 24), but more than that it would bring sternness, tears, and the oven of *final* conflagration (*Adv Marc* IV 30). Tertullian has in mind the consummation of history which lies beyond the millennium. This proves of much greater significance to him than the millennium itself. This is why the *regula fidei* refers to both the resurrection and the judgement but not to the millennium, even though both Tertullian and Irenaeus were Chiliasts. It is likely that *Apol* 48 describes the millennium when it speaks of the 'border-line that gapes between[80]... hung like a curtain before that eternal dispensation'. It shall, however, pass away, making way for the judgement and for eternity. Whatever this phase is, Tertullian perceives it as an interim period, whilst the real business of God's history and powerful summation lie either side of it. *Apol* 21 calls the culmination a display of the 'majesty of deity'.

Tertullian and Irenaeus share a common belief in a literal millennium involving a bodily resurrection and followed by a judgement and an open eternity (*Adv Marc* III 24), but Tertullian's interest differs in not extending to the lavish glory of a renovated earth. He focuses upon the glory and power of *God* who ends the world's course, judges its deeds and dissolves it in favour of another order. In this order only the bodies of human beings survive the purifying fire (*De res* 5). Tertullian also makes a major shift of attention to a *heavenly* kingdom with a Jerusalem, lowered, quite literally, from above (*Adv Marc* III 24). In *Adv Marc* III 24, he does refer to a work of his, now lost, which allegorises and so universalises the kingdom promises to the nation of Israel that it is assumed to betray the influence of Irenaeus' *Adv haer* V 31–36.[81] But he does not even muster this material against Marcion, so underlining his lack of interest in the present earth's potentialities. He looks more intensely for the vindication of God's rule and power over history through the creator's dissolution of it. He can allegorise the holy land in

---

[78]Lampe notes, op. cit. 27, that the Latin of *De orat* 29 is '*tubam angeli expectemus orantes*'. Cf. the universal tone of Tertullian's handling of 'Your kingdom come' in *De orat* 5.

[79]R.F. Evans, *One and Holy*, 5.

[80]The text may or may not carry an allusion to the millennium (T.R. Glover, *Apologeticus*, 216, note b).

[81]So Evans suggests in his text of Tertullian's *Adversus Marcionem*, part 1, 247, note 1. See, however, *De res* 26, shortly referred to.

De res 26 so that it becomes purely spiritual.[82] A pessimism about the historical process in itself brought confidence to rest on the *parousia* alone.[83] In contrast to Irenaeus, Tertullian highlighted with greater passion and elaboration the aspects of divine power which stressed God's freedom and transcendence over the creation, culminating in a reign of the saints to offset the sufferings of the martyrs (*De spect* 30, *Adv Marc* III 24).[84] He exploited the division which he saw between the visible, secular power, which preyed upon the martyrs, and the sceptre which directed even the ordering of the times. His writing work started with a defence of persecuted Christians but found final confidence in a very imminent transformation of human flesh, a feature of Montanism,[85] in a radically different future.

For Tertullian, judgement, resurrection and dissolution naturally rest upon the divine power. The miracle of the leprous hand attributed to Moses offers a set of three signs, 'the triple power of God (*trina virtus dei*)' which will subdue the devil, raise the flesh and then 'prosecute all blood with judgement' (*De res* 28). The first promise especially implies the entire obedience of history, including its darker aspects, to the omnipotent will of God.[86] All that opposes God and persecutes his people will have to bow before that power that raises and judges. This is the territory of the almighty creator:

> to whom can (Paul's) teaching rightly belong... but to him to whom all things... belong since the beginning, and from whom also are the times, and that dispensation of the fulfilling of the times? What has Marcion's God ever done?... That mighty power... in raising him up

[82]Lampe, op. cit. 25–26. And according to *De res* 26, the oil is divine unction, the water is the Spirit, the wine is that of the soul (whereas Irenaeus insists on its materiality), whilst the holy land itself is nothing other than Christ's own flesh.

[83]J. Pelikan, op. cit. 111–112.

[84]Lampe, op. cit. 25. Cf. C. Cooper who notes that Chiliasts emphasised, 'that the millennium here on earth was compensation for all the troubles of the preceding millennia': 'Chiliasm and the Chiliasts', *Reformed Theological Review*, (1970) 11–21 (p. 19).

[85]J.G. Davies has noted the apologetic agenda shared by Tertullian and Montanism, in 'Tertullian, *De resurrectione Carnis* 63: A note on the Origins of Montanism', *Journal of Theological Studies*, NS 6 (1955) 90–94 (pp. 91–92). D. Powell holds that only the imminentism of the New Prophecy distinguished it doctrinally from the Church in general, 'Tertullianists and Cataphrygians'. See the review by R. Braun in 'Chronica Tertullianea', 1975, *Revue des Études Augustiniennes* 22 (1976) 312–313 (p. 312).

[86]*De fuga* 1 sheds light on *De res* 28, by attributing persecution to the devil only by the permission of the omnipotent divine will and relative to the ultimate eschatological moment of settling up.

from the dead and setting him at his own right hand, and subjecting all things to him, was wrought by (the creator God). (*Adv Marc* V 17)

Tertullian reserves ultimate consummation to one who can claim to be almighty creator.

Consummation, power and judgement

The suggestion seems correct that Tertullian conditions his broader attitude to eschatology from his already settled conviction about impending judgement upon an evil world.[87] However, he swings between claims of a universal belief in judgement (*Apol* 48, *Ad nat* I 19) and a lament about universal apathy towards that belief (*De spect* 30). The latter probably more accurately reflects the true state of things, except for superstitious fear of the caprice of the gods. Philosophy particularly showed little interest in a divine originating omnipotence which also finally wraps up the human age according to his fixed moral standards. This is what Tertullian really meant by judgement (*De spect* 20, 22).[88] Marcion's distaste of a God of judgement all but provided the rationale of his system. Tertullian, on the other hand, asserts the centrality of judgement as a divine-like activity, 'the substance of the apostle's preaching' (*Adv Marc* V 13). Marcion was a devotee of Paul, but Tertullian finds in Paul's teaching a God who originates creation, law and Gospel and who visits judgement upon the creation he produced.

Marcion, however, was grappling with the problem of evil, as we noticed earlier. Tertullian did not altogether ignore this issue. He resorted occasionally to a freewill theodicy, but more often he made the divine omnipotence turn defence witness. In *Adv Marc* II 13 he argued that the much praised quality of goodness in God was really quite useless and academic unless it rested on the almightiness that went with the power of judgement. This led to the conclusion that,

in effect is he almighty (*omnipotens*), in that he is mighty (*potens*) both to help and to hurt. It is a lesser thing to show nothing but favour because of inability to show anything but favour (*quia non aliud quid possit quam prodesse*).

[87] J. Pelikan, op. cit. 110. Tertullian, according to Pelikan, was convinced that the moral and religious conditions of degeneracy fulifilled biblical predictions for the end time (*De praes* 1; *De pudic* 1; *De bapt* 8; *De monog* 16).

[88] P.G. Van der Nat provides the setting for this description: 'Tertullianea', *Vigiliae Christianae* 18 (1964) 14–31, 129–143 (pp. 142–143). He rightly detects that for Tertullian divine wrath hits the shows because they are idolatrous. Cf. *De idol* 1 in which Tertullian finds all sin to be a form of idolatry.

Here the dangerous tendency to base goodness upon power, rears it head once again. All the same, the certainty of judgement, according to Tertullian, restrained Christians from taking vengeance, precisely because the Lord was 'just in estimating... potent in executing' (*De pat* 10).

Mainly, however, divine judgement draws attention simply to divine power. This insight, argues Tertullian, commands recognition in every human soul (*De test* 2). Even the habit of uttering curses admits 'that his power over us is absolute and entire.' These unconscious concessions concede that God is both the kind of God to judge and powerful enough to get it right. So whence 'is judgement but from power? To whom does supreme authority and power belong, but to God alone?' By making its unwitting confession, the soul concedes that omnipotence belongs intrinsically to the definition of God.

Once again the doctrine of creation enters the picture. In *De testimonio animae* Tertullian includes in the soul's perception a creator who judges. At his lightning and thunders people tremble whilst receiving blessings in his creation (*Ad Scap* 2). These present portents of the divine wrath point to a God who controls and intervenes in nature and history.[89] The creator and Lord of nature, the ultimate judge, will not accept sacrifices because everything is his already. The connection between creating and judging appeared in Tertullian as early as *Apol* 17. God enters as 'the fashioner of the whole fabric of the universe'. But God disclosed himself in works which not only delight us but also excite fear. Even the human soul by its various appeals to God as bringer of recompense acknowledges this very God as Judge. The line runs clearly in the chapter from God as Creator, displayed in works of power, to God as ultimate Judge.

The logic of this summary appears more elaborately in the work against Marcion. Marcion uses a curiously modern argument that a good God cannot be also a judge, although he recognises the god of the Old Testament as 'Judge and Lord, the creator of man' (*Adv Marc* I 25). On this account, however, the Old Testament God cannot be the God of Christ. Tertullian is able to associate Christ with the work of judgement[90] and then to underline his assertion that such powers can spring only from the creator God. So the 'garden' of Christ's kingdom in the mustard seed parable belongs to the Creator (*Adv Marc* IV 30). But

[89]Tertullian sometimes traces the judgement of God in history and nature: *Adv Marc* II 2, II 11; *Apol* 18, 40; *Ad Scap* 1; *De pat* 2, 5.

[90]For texts in Tertullian referring to judgement by God or by Christ, see, V.C. De Clercq, 'The Expectation of the Second Coming of Christ in Tertullian', F.L. Cross, ed., *Studia Patristica*, Vol. XI, Berlin, Akademie-Verlag, 1972, 146–151 (p. 150).

'the fire of judgement with its sternness and tears' follows. The parable of the leaven sends the same message. The leaven in Christ's kingdom goes to the furnace (of hell) showing the God of Jesus, even Jesus himself, to be a judge. In the same way, *Adv Marc* V 16 argues from Marcion's revered Paul in 2 Thessalonians 2, where Christ's second coming brings with it the very trappings of judgement that Marcion has stripped away from Christ and his 'good' God. Judgement falls because people do not know the God who judges. Which God could this be, asks Tertullian, except a God known through the natural world which belongs to him and which his power generated. *Adv Marc* IV 39 dwells on the distress that judgement brings to the nations. But Marcion cannot detach this distress and severity from the blessings, the goodness, that also accompanies it. The good God of Jesus Christ turns out to be the 'severe' creator also. Omnipotence alone joins what Marcion can only sever: goodness and judgement. Even Jesus himself returns from the dead through the promise by that 'mighty power of (the creator's) in Christ' (*Adv Marc* V 17).

Goaded by Marcion, Tertullian attempts the ambitious reconciliation of justice and goodness by appeal to the divine omnipotence.[91] His attempts warrant a closer scrutiny. Earlier we met the words of *Adv Marc* II 13, in which Tertullian claimed that God is almighty (*omnipotens*) in that he is mighty (*potens*) both to help and hurt. A feeble God can *only* show mercy. Omnipotence, on the other hand, will guarantee both mercy and judgement. The justice of God reveals God 'in his perfection both as Father and as Lord... as Father in kindly power' (*patrem potestate blanda*). So although in places justice arises from sin and the need for restraint (cf. *Adv Marc* II 11), in significant passages it displays the brooding power necessary to give validity to the divine goodness:

> goodness and justice are in such close association and agreement that the separation of one from the other is inconceivable... his goodness constructed the world, his justice regulated it.... By an act of justice this whole world was established and set in order... (justice) came into existence simultaneously with that goodness which is in the origin of everything. (*Adv Marc* II 12)

The same power which undergirds God's kindly dealings with humanity also flows out in judgement. The *Apologeticum* had already argued,

---

[91]See the comments of P. Stockmeier on Tertullian's discussion of suffering and persecution. Tertullian's explanation over against the dualistic answer of Marcion lies of course in the oneness of God and more particularly in God's authority and strength: 'Gottesverständnis und Saturnkult bei Tertullian', E.A. Livingstone, ed., *Studia Patristica*, Vol. XVII/I, Oxford, Pergamon Press, 1982, 829–835 (p. 833).

especially in its opening appeal, for a contrast between evil that springs from unsound judges and the health that flows from the competence and soundness of divine judgement, so that real justice and truth actually underwrite goodness and mercy.[92] Such power coincides for Tertullian with that which drew all things into existence from nothing. Tertullian has of course achieved his goal by simply setting the problem one stage back. Marcion's complaint is not just that judgement and goodness cannot cohabit in the same creator's world. Rather it focuses on what kind of creator it is who makes a world which comes to judgement. Later Latin thought learnt that power alone cannot lend sufficient support to goodness. Divine wisdom, however inscrutable, must also enter the equation. The main value of Tertullian's argument here, therefore, is negative: you cannot have guaranteed goodness without power as guarantor. No more than that is before us, and its negative quality leaves a vacuum which should be occupied by a fuller account of how this guarantor has fully displayed divine love and infinite grace. This inadequacy, we have seen, left a mark upon Tertullian's view of the Christian life.

Consummation, power and resurrection

Tertullian infers the power of final judgement directly from God's role as creator, as well as from the human creation's accountability and the omens of judgement in nature. Similarly, bodily resurrection springs from the supreme power to call all things from nothing. The proximity of these themes to each other in Tertullian occasions no surprise.[93] His preoccupation with fixing on the one authentic divinity becomes acute in the discussion of resurrection and judgement.[94] There certainly is a resurrection to judgement (De res 50). Indeed De res 56 grounds the resurrection in the necessity for justice to be done in respect of reward and retribution. The soul alone cannot inherit God's recompense, for it would be unjust for the body to do the work and the soul to make off with the wages! But fair play is not the whole story; God's own demand and requirement touch upon the question of resurrection. It requires a person to come to judgement 'in full being', justifying God's 'craftsmanship (dei artificio)', 'authority (arbitrio)' and 'rights (iure)' (De res 60). Artificio recalls the cognate term denoting God's title as creator

[92] De paen 2 describes justice as precious in God's sight and De res 14 insists that both help and punishment display righteousness.

[93] J Steinmann has commented also on the necessity, in Tertullian, of resurrection for judgement: Tertullien, 207.

[94] F.J. Cardman, Tertullian on the Resurrection, Dissertation, Yale University, New Haven, Conn., 1974 (microfilm) 161.

(cf. *artifex* in *De res* 5), whilst *arbitrio* carries the ring of absolute freedom with the creation. Resurrection, then, serves to provide for a 'Maker' the most appropriate form of judgement (*De res* 14). Power over creation fixes the nature of the judgement and guarantees the absolute power to bring it about. Belief in a coming resurrection looks to many supporting evidences:

> the dignities of the substance (the body) itself, the power of God (*vires dei*), instances of that power (*exempla earum*), the reasons for judgement, and its implications. (*De res* 18)

One can hear the complaint mounting here that Tertullian opts for this scheme only in order to rub out Marcion. It is the theology of infighting rather than of the essence of the faith. Such it might be if it did not occur in the more standard description of the Christian faith in the early *Apol* 18. Having identified the Christian God as the one who made the universe and especially fashioned the human being, it goes on to describe the judgement in these terms:

> the dead... shall be raised, refashioned and reviewed, that their deserts of either kind, good or evil, may be adjudged.

The link between bodily resurrection of the body and creation-power crops up again in later chapters (23 and 48) and in *Ad nat* I 19. The pattern, then, does not originate narrowly in some polemical motive. From the beginning his theological vision of the consummation lived from a seminal notion of divine omnipotence.

Consummation, power and the Rule of Faith

Tertullian shared with his opponents the conviction that theological debate ultimately concerned the question of salvation. Resurrection, therefore, did not just function as a condition of reward and punishment. In fact, this was not even his leading thought. One conviction animated his enquiry, namely that God was mighty to save and the crowning feature of this salvation was restoration in corporeal form. Earlier in this study it emerged that an omnipotent God of creation lies at the base of this hope. In *De res* 2 Tertullian argues that the real purpose of the heretics is to introduce another kind of god altogether. However, they rightly sense that this will not be done easily, so they play upon the doubts felt by some concerning the resurrection. Then in a crucial thrust, he diagnoses the process of defection from belief in a resurrection to defection from belief in a god offering any kind of hope:

they are first caused to crash in respect of the resurrection of the flesh, and afterwards crash in respect of the unity of the deity.

Tertullian resents Marcion's attack on the resurrection of the flesh, effective only because of that hope's vulnerability when taken in isolation. This attack clouds Marcion's real purpose. That purpose aims to remove the uniqueness of God, a tenet of Christian near-unanimity. Tertullian claims the correctness of his own, alternative, method, namely moving from the unity of God the Creator to the resurrection of the flesh.[95] The claim amounts to a twofold statement. First, the divine omnipotence of the Creator underlies all teaching on incarnation and eschatology. Secondly, his system does not strictly pass straight from the idea of God as creator to that of God as raiser of the dead. True, sometimes Tertullian guillotines the argument this way, leaning on both the freedom of the divine power (*De res* 6) and the appropriateness of resurrection through divine power (*De res* 42, 57). The heretics reject the resurrection plainly and simply because of disbelief in the power of God (*De res* 36), but God is capable of using the allegedly distasteful operation of resurrection (*De res* 6), to which 'the whole revolving scheme of things' (*De res* 12) already bears witness, to effect the changes he wants (*De res* 7). All the same, the line from creator to restorer runs *through incarnation*.[96] To Tertullian's mind, creation and re-creation do not constitute an all-sufficient system. A *Christian* system proceeds through the Christ who became human, the Word and original archetype of human existence in the creation (*De res* 6). Most importantly of all, there is no novelty here. He speaks of nothing other than the Rule of Faith itself, which under his care remains unbowed in the face of blatant attempted innovation. The divine monarchy promises an 'incorruptibility' to be put on with a view to a new order (*De cult fem* II 6). What is the resurrection, then, but the ultimate and lasting display of the divine and gracious power of the mighty creator and his Christ lying at the heart of Tertullian's message. It is the Rule of Faith itself.

---

[95]Cardman seems correct in maintaining, against Mahé, that Tertullian speaks here not just of a logical order but of the programme he himself adopted. So *Adversus Marcionem* precedes *De Carne Christi*: ibid. 231.

[96]See Cardman, ibid. 13, 28.

CHAPTER 8

Divine Power and the Trinity

Divine power and monotheism

So far, the evidence has pointed to a foundational and strategically cohesive significance for the doctrine of divine omnipotence in Tertullian's Rule of Faith. But when Tertullian defended and explained the Rule of Faith he frequently found himself also defending Trinitarian foundations. In fact, he took up the question of the 'plurality and ordinance of the Trinity' in order to show that it not only squared with the Rule of Faith but indispensably helped to maintain it (*Adv Prax* 3). His mind ventured here beyond questions of the Logos alone to the Trinitarian 'economy'.

Exploration of Tertullian's scheme immediately runs up against the varied evaluations of it in modern scholarship. However, most commentators agree that some kind of tension lies open to view. Bernard Lonergan homes in on the apparent contradiction between counting the Son in with the Father as God and saddling the Son with temporal descriptions as a derived portion of the divine substance under the command of the Father.[1] Lonergan salvages from all this the virtue of its being a necessary positive step in the process of dialectical development in dogma. M.F. Wiles, on the other hand, thinks Tertullian, like so many second and third century writers, simply and unhelpfully fell into the trap of subordinationism in his obsessive struggle against

---

[1] B. Lonergan, *The Way to Nicea: the Dialectical Development of Trinitarian Theology*, London, Darton Longmans & Todd, 1976, 49.

Monarchianism.[2] G.L. Bray, however, takes a radically different line, arguing that, like most of the early writers, Tertullian strove most of the time to defend a monotheism[3] of creator and Father of the universe.[4] Certainly, an all-pervading conviction of unique divine power points in this direction, especially in the *Apology* and the works against Marcion and Hermogenes. G.C. Stead also detects a fundamental standard monotheism, indebted to the likes of Irenaeus, but coming into tension with the pluralism inherited, and exploited, from other earlier apologists.[5] Monarchianism, however, carried the traditional stand on God's uniqueness into pure undifferentiated monotheism, and Tertullian's concern with this sprang as much from his doctrine of the incarnation as from any other source. He knew well enough that Adoptionism and Monarchian pronouncements converge.

What is clear in his development of Trinitarian thought is that Tertullian employed the power-theme to strengthen his concept of the divine unity. Although a Stoic doctrine of divine omnipotence has been found at the root of baptismal efficacy in *De baptismo* 1–2,[6] a specifically Christian power-model arose. Irenaeus immediately springs to mind. In his vindication of an unimpeded divine creator over against Gnosticism he certainly influenced Tertullian, as earlier discussion indicated. The 'two hands' of God, the Son and the Spirit, do not meet us as subordinate intermediaries but as God's *own* activity.[7] Frequently the divine equality of the Son and the Spirit stemmed from this place in the creation.[8] Theophilus of Antioch also associated the divine power with the Logos and described God's nature in terms of power, even heaping up words from the vocabulary of power (*ischus, kratos, dynamis, energeia*) in *Ad Autolycum* I 3 and II 15. Although sounding a little Stoic, all he wrote assumed an underlying biblical creator described at the beginning of the treatise (*Ad Autol* I 4) as Almighty (*Pantokrator*) adding a number of texts following from the Psalms).[9] And through the Word came the

[2]M.F. Wiles, *The Making of Christian Doctrine. A Study in the Principles of Early Doctrinal Development*, Cambridge, University Press, 1967, 124.

[3]G.L. Bray, 'The Patristic Dogma', P. Toon and D. Spiceland, eds, *One God in Trinity*, London, Marshall Morgan & Scott, 50. Equally suspect seems the theory of W.R. Schoedel that early Trinitarian thought took its lead from the speculations of polytheism, 'A Neglected Motive for Second Century Trinitarianism', *Journal of Theological Studies*, NS 31 (1980) 356–367.

[4]E. Evans, *Against Praxeas*, 247.

[5]G.C. Stead, 'Divine Substance in Tertullian', *Journal of Theological Studies*, NS 14 (1963) 46–63 (p. 65).

[6]J.-C. Fredouille, op. cit. 329.

[7]J. Lawson, op. cit. 132.

[8]Ibid. 125.

[9]*Ad Autol* I 4.

making of all things, since he is power (*dynamis*) and wisdom (*Ad Autol* II 22). An accompanying quotation from John 1:1–3 locates the Word in the realm of creatorship. It is likely that even Marcellus of Ancyra took up the power-language of Theopilus,[10] preferring to present the Logos as *dynamis* and *energeia*[11] though the Greek use of these words was much more subtle than the Latin use of *potestas*. All the same a Roman parallel lies to hand in Hippolytus who speaks of 'two persons and one power' and draws the oneness of God from the oneness of the divine potency (*Contra haer* 8). Hippolytus, however, seems to fall short of the developed Trinitarian structure of Tertullian and lacks the use of *substantia* to give tightness to the divine unity.[12] One thing is clear: Tertullian has neither plucked the notion of unifying power from the air, nor adopted a model likely to be suspect amongst his contemporaries. Tertullian could claim to be using a widely current basis for his approach to unity.

It springs, especially in Tertullian's thought, from God's status as creator. God is the 'one-only-God' because nothing existed alongside him (*Adv Hermog* 17). The *creatio ex nihilo*, in other words, explains why only one God is there. A number of texts put the name Father to this status of creatorship,[13] a well deployed weapon in the face of Marcion's dualism (e.g. *Adv Marc* V 5). Indeed, in the wider tradition of the early Church, the title 'Father' enjoyed prominence more as a name of the creator than a name in the Trinity.[14] The difference between these two uses became obscured wherever the Logos 'expressed' (*prophorikos*) seemed to be merely one of the first stages in the creator-Father's creating activity. Although this helped Tertullian to put the Word, or Son, on the divine side of the creator–creation duality, the traditional subordinationist legacy of the earlier apologists still survived with vigour.[15]

Tertullian harnesses the Logos speculation to fill out his case for a *creatio ex nihilo*. Paradoxically, he thus underscores the uniqueness of God rather than the pluralism of that tradition. The process comes to

[10]E. Pollard, op. cit. 248–249.

[11]Ibid. 254–255.

[12]B.B. Warfield, *Studies in Tertullian and Augustine*, 90–91.

[13]J. Moingt, *Théologie Trinitaire de Tertullien*, 4: *Répertoire Lexicographique et Tables*, 140.

[14]J.N.D. Kelly, op. cit. 83; G.L. Bray, 'The Patristic Dogma', 50; J. Pelikan, *The Christian Tradition, A History of the Development of Doctrine*, Vol. 1. *The Emergence of the Catholic Tradition (100–600)*, Chicago, University Press, 1971, 103.

[15]G.L. Bray, 'The Filioque Clause in History and Theology', *Tyndale Bulletin* 34 (1983) 91–114 (pp. 112–113).

view against Hermogenes especially. He had postulated the eternity of matter and advanced the idea that it furnished the material for the primal creation. In *Adv Hermog* 17 Tertullian rejects this view as subverting not only God's uniqueness but also his power, because his creating work now received its rationale and shape from the determining qualities of the material and not from his own will (*Adv Hermog* 17). Such a suggestion was contrary to God's sovereignty expressed by Paul in Romans 11:34. In his own wilfully controversial way, Tertullian replicates the language of Hermogenes and comments that God had a far more suitable material for the creation of the world than matter, namely his wisdom (or spirit). A shocking materialism seems to loom, strengthened by Tertullian's view elsewhere of the soul as material. However, the full sentence runs, 'It is out of this that he created, creating *by means of* it and *with* it' (emphasis mine). The comment turns out to be a piece of rhetoric basing the creation on the *agency* of wisdom as opposed to the arbitrary external pressure of co-existent matter, the ruling notion in Hermogenes. Tertullian could not hazard the creation upon something non-rational.

It is easy to see from Tertullian's handling of the matter why he valued Seneca. Seneca too, in *Ep* 65, criticised the notion that the material contributed anything to creation when challenging the claim of Aristotle to find multiple causes for the creation (more precisely, the material, the maker and the design). Seneca argued for a single, first and general cause: creative wisdom, the deity. Tertullian brings this motif of *creative wisdom* and rational agency powerfully to the front in the earlier *Adv Hermog* 14:

> it is in his wisdom that he made all things first, since, by inventing and arranging them, he had already made them in it (*in qua cogitando et disponendo iam fecerat*).

Although following up with the unnecessary hypothetical concession that God *could*, though did not, use both matter and wisdom[16] he certainly wishes to say that only wisdom could really provide the necessary *initium* for the creation. The principle which could not be surrendered was simply this: 'it was more appropriate to him to make them of his own will than of necessity'. The Word-wisdom tradition, albeit a risky model, served to shield the axiom that God produced all

---

[16]Perhaps it was a desire to retrieve Tertullian from this fate which led Holmes to translate the earlier phrase (*in qua cogitando et disponendo iam fecerat*) with, 'because by mediating and arranging his plans therein, he had already done (the work of creation)' (noted by Waszink, *Treatise Against Hermogenes*, 136. He goes on to reject the translation).

things *freely* and *rationally* in his almightiness, and that means *ex nihilo*.[17] And there is more. In chapter 19 Tertullian takes the '*in principio*' to mean 'in power'. Immediately in the next chapter he asks us to acknowledge 'that power' in the wisdom in which all things were created.[18] The couching of divine unity in terms of power germinates here and was to come to full flower in *Adversus Praxean*.

Again, it is necessary to say in passing that Tertullian's move does not altogether constitute an innovation. For one thing the general link of Logos-wisdom with creation enjoyed a distinguished pedigree.[19] Justin and Tatian especially used the power model this way. Justin calls the Logos 'the first power after the Father' (*Apol* 32 10), being begotten as a rational power from him (*Dial* 61, 105). Tatian, in *Ad Graecos* 5, speaks of the 'beginning' as 'the power of the Logos (*logou dynamis*)', so that 'he himself was all power (*dynamis*)'. However, the same subordinationist tendency of Justin persisted in Tatian with the Logos 'coming forth from the power (*dynamis*) of the Father'. Whereas even Origen spoke of origin and source in terms of eternal generation, Tatian placed it in the area of power and will, threatening a thoroughgoing subordinationism, whatever safeguards he intended. All the same, views which see Tatian as the end of the road for the Logos model seem substantially correct. The problems had become too great for it to express the relationship both of the Son to the Father and of the Son to created things owing their existence to the Son.[20]

In Tertullian a new sense of the almightiness of God and of his rational free[21] creation comes to the surface. The biblical categories of both Sonship and almightiness now assume a new importance. In *Adv*

---

[17]Tertullian never defends a *sheer* force or *dynamis*, but only one informed by both reason and goodness. Cf. *Adv Marc* II 29: 'the goodness and the judgement, combine to produce a complete and worthy conception of a divinity to which nothing is impossible (*divinitatis efficiunt omnia potentis*)'.

[18]G. Armstrong spots a connection in *Adv Hermog* 18 between creation through Wisdom and creating without any material, *Genesis in der Alten Kirche*, 103.

[19]For parallels in Justin, Athenagoras, Tatian and Theophilus, see A. Heron, 'Logos, Image, Son', 48–58.

[20]Ibid. 58.

[21]*De paen* 1 provides one of the clearest expressions as rendered and discussed by W.P. Le Saint: 'Reason (*ratio*)... a property of God's, since there is nothing which God, the creator of all things, has not foreseen (*providit*), arranged (*disponit*), and determined (*ordinavit*) by reason....' Le Saint sees an intended sequence of planning, ordering and executing creation (*Tertullian: Treatises on Penance. On Penance and On Purity. Translated and Annotated*, London, Longmans Green & Co., 1959, 137). 'Foreseen', though lexically sound, seems a little weak for *providit*. Le Saint certainly intends more than mere prescience.

Prax 17 the term 'almighty' belongs to the Son just as much as to the Father. In the next chapter the Son may enjoy worship, and in the following chapter the Son equally lays claim to the creation *ex nihilo*. God alone spreads out the heavens and calls them into being with his voice, but it is the Son who makes such claims, 'because he alone served the Father's operation'. Tertullian appeals to biblical texts, though ones more suitable to the Spirit (Ps. 33:6; Isa. 44:24).[22] Psalm 33:6 in the Logos tradition had discerned a subordinated Son coming out for creation only at the will of the Father. Now the text serves to locate the Son in the not-creation distinct from the creation, the not-God.

For all its usefulness, however, the *creatio ex nihilo* does not at once meet all Tertullian's needs. It proves insufficient for even an 'economic' model of the Trinity, because there is an undisguised space where the Holy Spirit ought to be found. The writing against Praxeas carries the power-theme further in the direction of other supporting notions little exploited before his work.[23]

Monarchia

Behind much of Tertullian's thinking on power as something wielded in the world lies the notion of the *monarchia* (single rule), which regularly expressed the Church's monotheism in robust active terms. The idea, as well as the word, had however a wider currency. Yves Congar has reminded us that Aristotle, and later Apuleius, classed the ideal of one ruler amongst their first principles of philosophy and that this insistence underpinned the political absolutism of both Alexander and Caesar. So, although passing through the filter of Philo and such Christian pioneers as Justin and Theophilus, the now respectable 'Christian' *monarchia* tradition still owed some debt to non-Christian roots.[24] *Adversus Praxean* especially puts us on the track of Tertullian's thinking on the subject. A famous passage introduces the subject very early:

[22] It is striking how little place, even in *Adversus Praxean*, Tertullian finds for the Holy Spirit as third Person. In *Adv Hermog* 31; 32 the Spirit seems a component of creation itself.

[23] Irenaeus, led to face the 'supra-creation' question in *Adv haer* II 28.3, evaded it as not revealed in Scripture and sent a clear signal to Gnostics whose scheme depended upon divine emanations before creation. All the same, in *Adv haer* IV 14.1 Irenaeus argues that before creation the Word glorified the Father, 'remaining in him; and was himself glorified by the Father'. B. de Margerie (whose footnote wrongly read IV 4.1 in the 1975 edition) reminds us that this also strikes at Gnostic thought (op. cit. 110).

[24] Y. Congar, 'Classical Political Monotheism and the Trinity', *Concilium* 143 (1981) 31–36 (pp. 31–32).

I say that no kingdom (*dominatio*) is in such a sense one man's own...
single... a monarchy (*monarchia*), as not to be administered[25] also
through those other closely related persons whom it has provided for
itself as officers. (*Adv Prax* 3)

Tertullian appeals here to the economy (*oikonomia, dispensatio*[26]) or
'administration' to stave off the charge of 'overturning' the long-
cherished teaching of 'the one-only monarchy' supporting everything.
His defence hangs on the administration of the imperial monarch's rule
through the *dispensatio* of appointed officers. This is not a yet more
chronic slide into a subordinationism which disperses the rule to
numerous powers. He is simply saying that monarchy suffers subversion
only by the intrusion of an *alien* and *independent* authority,[27] as he
explains later: 'Overthrow of monarchy (takes place) when another
kingship (*alia dominatio*) is imposed, with its own character and quality.'
And Tertullian can think of an example: Marcion, of course. Now he is
ready to turn the tables on his opponents and accuses the 'Monarchians'
themselves of undermining the *monarchia*, because they reject the
administration by which it operates (*Adv Prax* 4). He falls back on 1
Corinthians 15:24–28 where the kingdom transfers from Son to Father,
so disclosing a *monarchia* capable of multiple authority. The text could
of course also support the idea of a 'successive' exercise of power which
favours the Monarchian case.[28] But Tertullian has more to say. He sees
the Trinity proceeding by degrees (*Adv Prax* 13) and not undermining
the monarchy, whilst the Holy Spirit is the 'preacher of one monarchy'
(*Adv Prax* 30).

But does *monarchia* in Tertullian point primarily to the idea of *order*
or to *power*, even domination? J. Daniélou favours the Stoic influence
and therefore the notion of order, controversially maintaining the
priority of the *Octavius* of Minucius Felix[29] over Tertullian's *Apology*.

---

[25]Evans, *Against Praxeas*, 197, says that *administretur* should be taken to mean
oikonomeitai. After some textual emendations he summarises Tertullian as saying
that Latin Christians had allowed their understanding of *monarchia* in the
political sense of the throne of Caesar, to govern their notion of the divine unity,
and have taken *monarchia* to mean single ruler, occupier of the throne, whereas
the real sense of *monarchia* in Christian language is not one ruler, but the empire
itself.

[26]B. Botte, 'Oikonomia: Quelques emplois spécifiquement chrétiens', *Corona
Gratiarum. Miscellenea Patristica, Historica, et Liturgica* (for E. Dekkers), Bruges,
M. Nijhoff, 1975 (p. 9). Cf. E. Evans, op. cit. 192.

[27]Evans, op. cit. 146.

[28]Ibid. 202, 205.

[29]J. Daniélou, *Origins of Latin Christianity*, 189.

He enjoys support from Van der Geest.[30] However the majority of authorities that I can find stress the sense of the *potestas* in the *monarchia* idea. The text of Tertullian points in that direction: according to H.A. Wolfson, in *Adv Prax* 3

> whatever power the Son possesses, and… the Holy Spirit possesses, comes from the Father. By this unity of power he means what we have described as unity of rule.[31]

So the Son and the Holy Spirit share in the supremacy of the Father.[32] Tertullian does not wish, then, to depart from the established conviction of the single and sovereign rule of the one almighty God over against the many gods of polytheism,[33] and he is confident that the 'economy' does not destroy this concern.[34] *Monarchia* and *potestas* are synonyms,[35] though not perfectly so, for the *monarchia* focuses only upon the *exercise* of power. Undoubtedly, the imperial model hovers close to Tertullian's thinking, possibly with the idea of a co-regent in the background of the *oikonomia* idea.[36] The absoluteness of some imperial rulers may even have provided an illustration, within limits, of the divine rule.[37]

The disagreement about whether order or power dominates Tertullian's choice of the monarchy model really points to varying opinions on the relative importance of Greek and Latin influences upon him. The Greek influence on Christianity drove towards a sense of harmony in the universe and of an order where culture and experience could find fulfilment, whereas the Latin writers thought more practically and politically, bringing all life under regulation.[38] Hence Origen represents the triumph of the Greek ethos, but Tertullian, with his vision

---

[30]J.E.L. Van der Geest, op. cit. 128.

[31]H.A. Wolfson, *The Philosophy of the Church Fathers*, Vol. 1: *Faith, Trinity, Incarnation*, 328–329.

[32]R.H. Ayers, op. cit. 55.

[33]J. Moingt, *Théologie Trinitaire de Tertullien 3: Problématiques de l'unité et des processions*, Paris, Aubier, 1966, 835.

[34]Ibid. 837.

[35]Ibid. 838.

[36]Warfield, op. cit. 78. Evans also speculates that Tertullian may have in mind Severus and his colleagues who all held the empire without any partition, *Adv Prax*, 56, a possibility strengthened by reference to that fact in *De pall* 2 and by a similar kind of use in *Suppl* 18 by Athenagoras.

[37]G.L. Prestige, *God in Patristic Thought*, London, SPCK, 1975, 94–95; R Klein, *Tertullian und das römische Reich*, Heidelberg, Carl Winter, 1968, 75.

[38]G.L. Bray, *Holiness and the Will of God*, 96, stated even more forcibly by P. Stockmeier, 'Zum Verhältnis von Glaube und Religion bei Tertullian', F.L. Cross, ed., *Studia Patristica*, Vol. XI, Berlin, Akademie-Verlag, 1972, 242–246 (p. 246).

of the divine authority (*auctoritas*), stands clearly in the Latin tradition. Both emphases found favour in early Christian thought because each spoke for monotheism and excluded a multiplicity of gods (cf. Theophilus in *Ad Autol* II 8).[39]

The case for Greek origins has enjoyed reinforcement in the theory that the whole *monarchia* idea stems from the order brought to Alexandria by Greek rule. The contrast between this and earlier polyarchy inspired Hellenistic Judaism to trace a similar contrast between the cosmic order found with Jahweh and the raging disorder of the world conceived by polytheism.[40] However, for all the attractions of this view, other considerations also claim our attention. In the first place, with regard to Tertullian's time, it seems unlikely that the nuances of the word *monarchia* underwent no change (even in Alexandria) with the coming of later Roman rule. The nature of imperial rule, the presence of Roman armies and the application of rigorous Roman regulations would surely bring the power of the personal imperial cult to the foreground and add at least this perception to that of order. Secondly, the Christian kerygma announced a new kingdom in the person of Jesus, rising in might even above Roman rule. The sounding of this keynote had reached a crescendo in the writings of Tertullian. Then again, as observed earlier, even scholars with a special interest in the Stoic influence upon Tertullian have hesitated to name it as the seminal centre of his Trinitarian thought. Lastly, a mere look at the text of Tertullian betrays a Trinitarian scheme stressing unity of power, status and majesty in the image of the Roman emperor's power. This discussion of the question of *monarchia* does not lead into arid wastes. It spotlights a concept that, for different reasons, unites Greek and Roman worlds in Christian thought around a common fervent interest, namely the preserving of monotheism.[41] That concept combined, according to J. Moingt, ideas of Greek philosophy, Alexandrian Jewish biblical theology, and reflection on the political organisation of the empire.[42] The

---

[39]From R.M. Grant, *Theophilus of Antioch. Ad Autolycum, Text and Translation*, Oxford, Clarendon Press, 1970, 37.

[40]T. Verhoeven, '*Monarchia* dans Tertullien, *Adversus Praxean*', *Vigiliae Christianae* 5 (1951) 43–48.

[41]D.L. Holland insists that early apologetic commonly focused upon monotheism against polytheism, in the case of Theophilus to the point of never speaking of the incarnation of the Logos in Christ, 'The Third Article of the Creed', 192. Cf. Congar, op. cit. 32, for the dependence of Theophilus also upon the *monarchia* in Philo. See also J. Moingt, 'Le problème du Dieu unique chez Tertullien', *Revue des Sciences Religieuses* (1970) 337–362 (p. 341).

[42]Ibid.

monotheism supported here enjoyed ascendancy over the pagan system because of the order attaching to such a powerful and absolute rule.[43]

The monarchy offered only one Lord,[44] thus prompting the question of how Christ might also merge with that lordship. Justin resorted to the traditional Logos model. The Son, generated by the will of the Father, worked by the power of lordship under his Father's authority. Irenaeus, anticipating and influencing Tertullian (cf. *Apol* 17; *De test* 5,6; *Adv Marc* I 10),[45] looked to the duality of creator and creation, as seen earlier (cf. *Adv haer* III 16.1; III 8.3; III 9.1).[46] Christ's position sprang from his role on the creator side of that duality. The same approach served Tertullian well against Marcion and Hermogenes but required a more sophisticated statement when squaring up to the Trinitarian issue.

According to Moingt, his answer lay in a theory of the communication or delegation of power from the Father as proper possessor,[47] to the Son and Holy Spirit, by analogy with a communication of divine substance. The notion presented in this way a re-statement of the unity in generic, rather than numerical, terms.[48] This highly competent account by Moingt shrewdly focuses upon all those salient issues. His attention falls upon the centrality of a vocabulary of power, the crucial nature of *monarchia* and the link between substance and power in the Trinitarian formulations.[49] But the *communication* of power does not assume quite the central and definitive importance required by his theory. Tertullian chiefly met the challenge facing him by changing the emphasis of the *monarchia* from one *ruler* to one *rule*. More important still, he finds a basis for the unity of that rule in a deeper underlying unity of rank, dignity and potency. B.B. Warfield has traced Tertullian's co-regency illustration into the very being of God himself,[50] a view of Tertullian which would probably commend itself only to a few. Yet the almightiness involved in the *creatio ex nihilo* discloses not just an activity but a status and a potentiality. Tertullian chooses to count both Son and Holy Spirit in with this sheer unlimited potency. It is a condition of their existence, read off from the inclusion of each in the work of creation. On this basis, the uniting power is an

---

[43]Ibid. 342.

[44]Ibid.

[45]Ibid. 345.

[46]Ibid. 343–344.

[47]Ibid. 355.

[48]Ibid. 360–361.

[49]W. Bender also finds a relation between the *monarchia* and the issue of *substantia*, *Die Lehre über den Heiligen Geist bei Tertullian*, München, M. Heuber, 1961, 31.

[50]Warfield op. cit. 78.

idea detachable from the *monarchia* imperial model. It is not just the *monarchia* where the Father's prerogatives are delegated by his leave, but a full unity of equality. In this equality, the one status of power associated with creatorship, and supporting the actual concrete exercise of power, belongs to all three: Father, Son and Holy Spirit.

But the tension in Tertullian's writing between these two aspects of divine power, potentiality and operation, raises an omen of succeeding tensions in Christian thought between a real Trinity and a 'political monotheism'. Both Yves Congar and Jürgen Moltmann[51] have observed these tensions, and Moltmann, especially, finds it difficult to live with the doctrine of creation in Tertullian and the Fathers. For him, the stress on the creator feeds the pattern of a patriarchal lord and a monotheism on imperial lines. It is true that, even in his working out of God's power as creator, Tertullian speaks of a divine ownership, and of an obedience which follows. But it is difficult to know how else Tertullian might have substantiated his rejection of the emperor as God, and of dualism in all its forms. Moreover, Tertullian was only invoking a biblical theme here. It is as clear in the New Testament as in the Old and is reflected pervasively in the early Christian writers. The one thing undisputed by Jewish and Christian traditions was God's transcendence over, and control of, nature. It is true that some today find the roots of oppression, especially of male dominance, in the doctrine of creation itself, but a measure of over-sophistication and speculation can sometimes weaken the case made.[52] However, we can probably trace the more overbearing traits of the power-concept mainly to the *monarchia* inherited in the early tradition, and to the ill-fated adoption of the imperial model. We have seen that the *monarchia* owes its origins to an Aristotelian political axiom and that the coming of Roman rule strengthened, and even further politicised, the Greek idea already focusing on order. Similar traits in Tertullian's thought on divine omnipotence in creation have already been exposed. The analogy of empire offers the best clue to the roots of western political theology, both ecclesiastical and civil.

---

[51]Both essays appear in the important *Concilium* 143 (1981): Y. Congar, op. cit. 33–34; J. Moltmann, 'The Motherly Father. Is Trinitarian Patripassianism Replacing Theological Patriarchalism?', 51–56.

[52]G. Jantzen, 'Who Needs Feminism', *Theology* 93 (1990) 339–343, propounds a well-known elegant theory which holds together a series of dualisms (mind–nature, soul–body, male–female) which explain the oppression of females and comes back to the *creatio ex nihilo*. It seems strange to blame the *creatio ex nihilo* for a dualism which it was designed to combat in the defence of the incarnation. See my comments in chapter 9.

Substantia

Already in Stoic thought the *substantia* ('substance') of the *Logos* stood for a kind of unity with a multiplicity of functions, but in Tertullian that *Logos* was personal.[53] It is not uncommon to spot a monism in the traditional Stoic use of *substantia*,[54] so different from Tertullian's employment of the word that Spanneut finds in Tertullian a use which does not rise much above rhetoric.[55] The most definitive work on the prevailing uses of *substantia*, that of G.C. Stead, traces a wide divergence in usage of *substantia* in contemporary literature,[56] ranging from particular or collective 'stuff' to existence itself. Applied to God the word yields a number of senses: a periphrasis for himself, a mode of existence, divine rank or unique divine 'stuff'.[57] It also links strongly in *Adversus Praxean* with *spiritus*.[58] In that writing, according to Stead, the sense prevails of divine 'stuff' or divine substratum composed of 'spirit', Tertullian's version of the divine 'corpus'.[59] This view carries great weight amongst commentators,[60] though occasionally we again hear echoes of Stead's own caution that with *substantia* we are dealing with a very fluid and imprecise word.[61] It has been taken also, therefore, to denote a distinctively Latin way of stressing the concrete reality as opposed to the mere idea.[62] Whatever may be the case, the divine substance in Tertullian serves at least to signal the divine unity. It is one and contrasts with all that is creation or 'Not-God', a fundamental use of the word determined in conflict with Marcion and Hermogenes (see especially *Adv Marc* I 7; I 14; IV 9; IV 20).

Does Tertullian's use of *substantia* extend to such a full-blown Stoic idea of divine 'stuff' that the Father actually *communicates* that 'stuff' to the Son and the Holy Spirit?[63] More strictly, Tertullian veers to a *prolation* or extension of *substantia* out of the substance of the one

---

[53]Spanneut, op. cit. 307.

[54]Daniélou, op. cit. 346.

[55]Spanneut, op. cit. 309. He makes appeal to the important work of S. Schlossmann, 'Tertullian im Lichte der Jurisprudenz', *Zeitschrift für Kirchengeschichte* 27 (1906) 413–416.

[56]G.C. Stead, 'Divine Substance In Tertullian', 58–62.

[57]Ibid. 62.

[58]Ibid. 63–64.

[59]Stead, op. cit. 62. Also his *Divine Substance*, Oxford, Clarendon Press, 1977, 161, 202–203. See also Braun, op. cit. 182, 194.

[60]J. Fortman, *The Triune God*, 114.

[61]J. Moingt, *Théologie Trinitaire de Tertullien*, 2: *Substantialité et individualité, étude du vocabulaire philosophique*, Paris, Aubier, 1966, 303.

[62]Daniélou, op. cit. 345–348.

[63]G.C. Stead, *Divine Substance*, 161 and his, 'The Concept of Divine Substance', *Vigiliae Christianae* 29 (1975) 1–14 (p. 14).

creator-Father. The main purpose of the discussion here is not to settle a highly technical and complex discussion but to locate whatever bearing *substantia* might have upon *potestas*. Some critics have in fact defended Tertullian from an alleged crude materialism in his use of *substantia*. Tertullian may simply be speaking of objective or definite reality[64] as opposed to pure abstraction,[65] in a kind of 'striking realism'.[66] Perhaps the word stretches to describing real, even permanent, being.[67]

As a background to the kind of use Tertullian makes of *substantia* certain passages assume particular importance because they may contain the notion of a substance *transmitted* from Father to Son. Attention centres on three chapters in *Adversus Praxean*, namely 9, 14 and 26. In all of them *substantia* has the appearance of a substratum, or reality common to each person of the Trinity, though the Father in particular seems equivalent to the whole substance. Take *Adv Prax* 9 for instance:

> For the Father is the whole substance, while the Son is an outflow and assignment of the whole (*pater enim tota substantia est, filius vero derivatio totius et portio*), as he himself professes, 'Because my Father is greater than I.'

Evans concludes that a certain lessening of the Son in his divine being occurs here.[68] However, our earlier caution against too crude a materialism warns against a lessening in which the Son becomes a minor portion cut off from the larger and superior mass of 'stuff' called the Father.[69] The stress falls upon *derivatio* rather than upon *portio* (although *portio*[70] does not in any case, in Tertullian, simply denote 'portion'). Tertullian speaks of a relationship of Son to Father like that of *prolatio* to its source.[71] A Stoic tradition undoubtedly lurks in the background,[72] and

---

[64]Daniélou, op. cit. 363. He acknowledges his debt to Moingt.

[65]Ibid. 217: 'name of body has to be given to what is real'.

[66]Ibid.

[67]Stead, 'Divine Substance in Tertullian', 47. Cf. p. 48 where he considers that in *Adv Prax* 26, *substantia* stands in contrast with *operatio* and *accidentia*, which suggests an equivalence with *ousia*.

[68]Ibid.

[69]Thus E. Evans, commenting on *De anima* 37: 'as substance they are incapable of increase or decrease; since Father and Son are one substance there can be no difference of magnitude between them…'.

[70]Ibid. 246: 'There is a derivation of the whole substance of the Deity into the Son.'

[71]Ibid. Cf. the approval which P. Langlois gives to Moingt's judgement that *tota substantia-portio totius* does not indicate a part of a mass but the relation of the contained with container, 'La Théologie de Tertullien', *Bibliothèque de l'École des Chartes* 125 (1967) 438–444 (p. 441).

[72]Spanneut, op. cit. 309.

this same theme of a substance flowing from its source creeps in at chapter 14 also:

> (we) must acknowledge the Son as visible because of the manner of his derivation just as we may not look upon the sun in respect of the total of its substance (*substantia*) which is in the sky, though we can with our eyes bear its beam because of the manner of the assignment (*portio*) which from there reaches out to the earth.

Adv Prax 26, also, describes the *spiritus* who is the *substantia* underlying the Word as 'a certain possession/assignment of the whole (*ut portio aliqua totius*)'. Evans' translation of *Adv Prax* 9, 'the Son is the outflow and assignment of the whole', finds backing in what follows the phrase, namely a quotation of John 14:28. It speaks of the subjection of the Son to the Father *in the work of redemption*. Significantly, the comparable quotation from Psalm 8:6, connecting with the humiliation passage of Hebrews 2:5ff., strengthens the case. These biblical passages have nothing to do with the generation of the Son . Tertullian is simply saying that in the Father we have the whole rank and quality of *substantia*, but in the Son this fullness of the whole deity flows out in assignment or expression in the divine mission of redemption. *Portio* carries the sense of extension or external expression in *De res* 16, where the body will be held in judgement because it is the 'portion (*portio*) of that which thinks, not its chattel.' The Son, on this reading, emerges as an outflow and expression of the whole deity in his redemptive servant-mission, manifesting the full majesty and love of the divine *substantia* (and not to be confused with the generation of the Son which Tertullian, as we have seen, associates with the external expressing of the Logos).

This way of understanding Tertullian fits well with his 'economic' emphasis and with the other passage quoted above, *Adv Prax* 14. Ensnared in a distancing of the wholly invisible God from creation, he defends the Son's visibility in the Old Testament theophanies and the incarnation. Just as the light and glory of the sun in the sky comes to us through the moderated expression of its beam upon earth, so the totality of God's majesty and *substantia* comes to us in the Son. The whole substance goes out in assignment and expression in the Son who makes its majesty visible without danger to the one seeing. For Tertullian, the function of the Son challenges the Monarchianist assumption of undifferentiated unity because of shared invisibility. In *Adv Prax* 26, too, the chapter opens with a reference to the remark of Philip in John 14:8, 9 where he asks, 'Lord, show us the Father and we shall be satisfied', along with the reply, 'He who has seen me has seen the Father.' Chapter 24 has explained the interchange as showing that the Son was the Father's deputy, by means of whom the Father 'was both seen in acts and heard in words and known in the Son ministering the Father's acts and words'. So perhaps *Adv Prax* 26 also focuses upon the Son in his incarnation as the *portio*, assignment or expression, of the whole, the full manifestation of the whole divine *maiestas* and *substantia*.

Of course this is not the whole of Tertullian's account of the Trinity as a single substance. He does not fall into the Sabellian trap of calling the Son divine substance only in the redemptive mission. But nevertheless as an 'assignment' of the one substance the Son does indeed reveal the Father and become visible, which the Father is not. All this does not settle, or even help to settle, the question of what the *substantia* or the *spiritus* really is. I am glad to be relieved of offering a challenge to the magisterial study of G.C. Stead in which he makes plain his view that 'in Tertullian's Trinity the *una substantia* represents the stuff or reality, called *spiritus*'.[73] Under any consideration, the Son is, for Tertullian, substance on account of his having proceeded from that which is substance. Tertullian senses the threat of finding himself in the camp of the Gnostics with their prolations which separate out aeons from their source. He turns for help to the illustrations of spring and river, sun and beam, root and shoot. These show only that the Son retains his character as divine substance and does not undergo separation away from the Father. All the same, he remains remarkably undisturbed at the prospect of conveying, even indirectly, subordinationist impressions. For him, as curiously later to Arius, Monarchianist and Modalistic trends posed the most sinister threat to the 'apostolic' faith.

Tertullian's use of substance makes weightier the power-orientated thrust of his doctrine of the Trinity. God does not just call up power as an accidental and relational act of deity. With Evans,[74] we may perhaps say that in Tertullian power is a necessary characteristic of the divine substance, though Stead is cautious.[75] When Tertullian talks about the monarchy, the one rule of power, he can find the spring of it in a substantial Trinity. The Son and Holy Spirit (*Adv Prax* 3) enjoy the status of equal possessors (*consortes*) in the substance of the Father (*substantiae patris*) and not mere sharers (*participes*). By contrast he pegs the angels as alien to the Father's substance (*alienorum a substantia patris*). Son and Spirit possess parity in divine power because they come forth from the divine substance. Even Irenaeus had said that God and his Word are 'one according to the essence of his being and power' (*Dem* 47).

---

[73]G.C. Stead, *Divine Substance*, 203.

[74]E. Evans, *Adversus Praxean*, 56.

[75]Stead criticises Evans' understanding of *substantia* in an attributive sense: *Divine Substance*, 51–53.

The power, then, can belong to the substance and not just the actions of substance (*contra* Evans).[76] When Tertullian writes in *Adv Hermog* 3 that 'Lord is the name, not of a substance (*substantia*), but of a power (*potestas*)', he is simply tying *the title 'Lord'* to God's works *ad extra* rather than to the divine essence. He discusses at this point only the divine power in the economy. Of course, *substantia* and *potestas* are not synonyms. Rather, the inner limitless potency of God belongs to the substance and being of God, the reality that is not-creation. The claim that Tertullian locates the divine unity not in something that God *has* (*potestas*) but in what he *is* (*substantia*)[77] overlooks Tertullian's deployment of *potestas* as a key focus for the divine unity. *Substantia* presents itself as the primary category, invariably mentioned first and often alone. However, *potestas* lurks implicitly in the *substantia* as an intrinsic quality of it, a potency, fortified by the supporting categories of rank (*gradus*) and quality (*status*).

Tertullian, like traditional Stoicism, tied substance closely to 'spirit'. Here a Patristic quirk can fascinate modern criticism, namely the practice of using *spiritus* to denote not only the Third in the Trinity, but also the substance of deity itself. Tertullian follows the practice with abandon. For the present it commands our attention because in Tertullian the *spiritus* belongs to each of the Trinity, and *substantia*,[78] as seen already in Stead, actually consists of Spirit.[79] The Word (*sermo*), according to one text of *Adv Prax* 7,[80] is a substance (*substantia*) consisting of spirit (*spiritus*), wisdom (*sophia*) and reason (*ratio*). True, *spiritus* has to share the honours with two other characteristics, but it does enjoy first mention.

However, a less emended, more traditional, reading of this text yields '*spiritu et sophiae traditione constructa.*' Now the substance of the Word consists of *spiritus* (its nature) by virtue of its being from *sophia* (its origin). Tertullian then means that the Word is *aliqua substantia*, 'a Person, which is a particular kind of substance', and that this substance is none other than (the divine) *spiritus*, because it is the very wisdom of God put into speech. This alternative traditional reading would sit comfortably with Tertullian's later plea that God's being *spiritus* does not rule out his being also corporeal or concrete. Any textual and grammatical grounds for the newer reading would therefore have to be

---

[76]E. Evans, op. cit. 57.

[77]Pollard, op. cit. 58.

[78]Stead, op. cit. 203.

[79]Identification of divine substance with Spirit is confirmed in the standard writings, e.g., Daniélou, op. cit. 347, Evans, op. cit. 43.

[80]E. Evans, ibid. 231.

very strong to overturn the older, more coherent, version which sits so well with the larger evidence.

The close association of *spiritus* with *substantia* and its divine rank, when added to the similar alliance of 'spirit' and 'power' in Tertullian's incarnation scheme, brings *substantia* into the centre of Tertullian's power-rooted thinking, precisely the point made by *Apol* 21, examined earlier. Some of the text bears repeating:

> we... to that word, reason and power (by which we said God devised all things) would ascribe spirit as its proper substance (*substantia*), and in spirit, giving utterance we should find word; with spirit, ordering and disposing all things, reason; and over spirit, achieving all things, power.

Tertullian does not mean that there is another, superior, quality called power overseeing the function of spirit, but that power characterises spirit.[81] *Adv Prax* 26 helps us out here by speaking of the Word's part in the qualities of the divine substance: 'Power (*virtus*) is an attribute of spirit, and will not itself be spirit.' Again in *De carne* 19 the Word is God's spirit in the sense of the divine substance, 'and in the spirit is God's power (*virtus*), and God's everything that Christ is'. The quotations, incidentally, show that power occupies a major position for Tertullian when he elaborates on the special character of divine substance. C. Oeyen thinks that he can find a similar kind of relation in the work of Justin Martyr and even Clement of Alexandria, though his conclusions seem to be unnecessarily obscured by his stress on an angel-pneumatology which he thinks dominates Justin's outlook.[82] Ayers' words prove appropriate here:

> *Spiritus* also has the unique rank or status, namely supremacy. God's *substantia* is that *spiritus* of power and goodness which alone is supreme in the whole range of being and thus cannot be threatened by contingency, change and death.[83]

To a great extent, the unique potency and powerful operations of the Three provide the basis for the divine unity in Tertullian's thought, especially where substance is concerned.

---

[81]J. Pelikan's translation may seem a little free, but helpful: 'first-begotten Word, accompanied by power and reason, and based on the Spirit', *The Christian Tradition*, 158.

[82]C. Oeyen, op. cit. 220–221.

[83]Ayers, op. cit. 53.

Community of power

The doctrine of the Trinity confronts Tertullian with a new task in relation to the divine power. Now he has to make the simple and widely accepted notion of monarchy, even under the modified sense of 'one rule', speak not just of the Father,[84] or of Godhead, but more flexibly to include Son and Spirit. He has not made it any easier for himself by working with the idea of power as a divine capacity, not just a divine act. *Adv Prax* 2 introduces his thought in a celebrated passage:

> setting forth Father and Son and Spirit as three... not in condition but in sequence (*non statu sed gradu*), not in substance but in aspect (*nec substantia sed forma*), not in power but in its manifestation (*nec potestate sed specie*), yet of one substance, one condition and one power... from whom these sequences... are reckoned out in the name of the Father and the Son and the Holy Spirit.

'Co-substantiality' (since Tertullian falls short of the more developed Greek 'consubstantiality' of Nicaea) supplies the sphere of thought for community of power. A notion of divine potency fits it all very well. Even the idea of co-regency in *Adv Prax* 3 points to an underlying title to power: the persons ruling are *tam uniti*. The Spirit, as well as the Son, finds a place in the discussion, just enough evidence to assert a threefold possession of the divine almightiness.[85] But the formula found in the opening chapters appears nowhere in the work again, giving way to a linear binitarian approach dominated by the relation of the Son to the Father. This feature, incidentally, undermines the notion that Tertullian's 'mature' doctrine sprang from his Montanist convictions, since the main work of that period, against Praxeas, frequently ignores the Holy Spirit. There is no radical swing away from earlier thought already illustrated by *Apol* 21.

Given the preoccupation with the Son, *Adv Prax* 17 provides us with a further point of departure and connects well with some words in *De oratione*: 'in the Father the Son is invoked.' There is a suggestion that the name of the Father is the Son himself.[86] *Adv Prax* 17 for its part repels the Modalists by arguing that the Son acts in the Father's name, rather than the other way round. So 'these titles and the attributes they imply are his also'. Tertullian warns the Modalists of the consequences:

> beware lest by these the Son is also shown to be of his own right God as being the Word of God Almighty (*qua sermo Dei omnipotentis*) and

---

[84]J. Moingt, *Le Dieu unique*, 348–352.

[85]W. Bender, op. cit. 33.

[86]E. Evans, op. cit. 287.

as having received power over all (*quaque omnem accepit potestatem*); and the Most High.

Tertullian plainly suffers no reticence on behalf of the Son when it comes to titles of power. Earlier on he had used four titles of the Father, but three of them find their way into the Son's pedigree: God Almighty (*deus omnipotens*), Most High (*Altissimus*), Lord (*Dominus*). They suggest a part in the divine power far beyond the redemptive work. They point to a share in the names, attributes and uniqueness of the Father. Tertullian spells this out clearly enough in *Adv Prax* 17 concerning the Son's claim in Revelation, 'I am the Lord (*dominus*), the Almighty (*omnipotens*)':

> wherever else they think the designation 'God Almighty' (*dei omnipotentis*) not appropriate to the Son, as if he who is to come were not the Almighty, when the Son of the Almighty (*filius omnipotentis*) is no less almighty (*omnipotens*) than the Son of God is God.

The Monarchians, predictably, argued from these words in Revelation that the Son is identical with the Father. Tertullian draws only the conclusion of a unity of power appropriate to an identity of divine substance. Omnipotence belongs to Christ on account of his Sonship and his being the very Word of God.[87]

But what did Tertullian mean when he spoke in this same chapter of the Son *receiving* power over everything (*quaque omnem accepit potestatem*)? Does Tertullian after all treat divine power as accidental and conveyable from Father to Son, not at all intrinsic to the substance of the Son? Certainly the phrases which follow give that impression. The right hand of God exalts the Son, and the Father *subjects all things to the Son*. In fact, however, divine power belongs to the Son on account of both substance *and* economy. The chapter in its full-roundedness draws attention both to the equally power-laden status of the Son with the Father and to the distribution of power to the Son in the work of redemption. So the Monarchians, according to Tertullian, should not shrink from pinning all the titles to power on the Son even though they can only bear to honour the Father that way. But nor should they collapse into taking the Son's exercise of divine power in redemption to imply a modalism, so treating the Son as if he were the Father, when it simply points to a distribution of power.

In tune with this more searching unity of divine power comes *Adv Prax* 22 and a comment on the words of Jesus, 'I and my Father are one': 'there are two, albeit in one power (*duo tamen... in una virtute*)'. Possibly the formula here is: plurality of works (*per opera*), one

[87]Ibid. 288–289.

indivisible *exercise* of power (*una virtus*). *Adv Prax* 19 follows the Son's power back into Proverbs 8 and the wisdom/Logos scheme. At creation we find 'Christ the wisdom and the power of God (*qui est Christus sophia et virtus dei*)'. Tertullian anticipates the danger of a purely economic understanding and charges on: 'There was then one who made, God not alone, except alone with regard to other gods.' The divine power of the Son in creation implies his unity with the Father as not-creation. By the Son also as power (*virtus*) came all things, and 'he is not alone... except... in respect of the other (gods)'. Immediately Tertullian plunges into a defence of unity of substance and the deity of the Son. The power of Father and Son in community, distinguishing them from creation including the gods, goes with the divine substance or deity itself. Tertullian repeatedly takes divine power and traces it to the divine being (though sometimes starting with its expression in the economic activity or function). His Trinitarian account falls in with a description of the omnipresent power:

> no separation but a divine ordinance (*dispositio*)... God... takes up his position everywhere – though in might and power (*sed vi et potestate*)... the Son also as inseparable, is with him everywhere. (*Adv Prax* 23)

Again a formula takes shape: two subjects but one ubiquity of power. The divine *dispositio*, part of the economy (*oikonomia*), works against the context of the Son's actual unchanging omnipresent power, a virtue of the divine substance. Similarly, *Adv Prax* 21 takes the route from power in the economy to the power belonging to divinity, that is, from the delegated judgement in power (*potestas*) to the announcement that 'the Son was always in the name of God and King and Lord Almighty and Most High'.

In spite of the many references to a power delegated in the economy, therefore, we should not narrow Tertullian's unity of power to this alone. This seems to be the flaw in J. Moingt's otherwise impressive work on Tertullian.[88] Even at *Adv Prax* 4, where *potestas* unites with *substantia*, he hangs on *potestas* the sense of a concrete, personal expression of power.[89] His case, in fact, rests largely on that passage. He reminds us that the text speaks of the kingdom being restored to the Father, and argues that the Son (and the Spirit) come to receive the power from the Father and to participate in that which properly belongs

---

[88] J. Moingt, op. cit. 833–839. Moingt believes that only with later theology do we come across the equality of Father, Son and Spirit under the essential attribute of power.

[89] Ibid.

only to the Father.[90] His case also looks to the way in which, for Tertullian, Adam is the communicating source of substance to all human souls, a pointer to the communication of the Father's substance to the Son and Spirit. Moingt traces a ready parallel between the communication of substance by the Father to the Son and a similar communication to the Son of power (considered purely as God's activity towards the world).[91] But do these 'communications' correspond in such a way? On Moingt's own account, looking to the illustration from Adam, the communication of substance best takes the description *generation*, whilst the communication of power best takes the description *delegation*. One falls under being, the other under function. If 'communication' is to be our guiding light, it would be more consistent to say that the unbounded might and *potency* attaching to the divine substance belongs by nature to the Son also.

In addition Moingt appeals to *Adv Prax* 9 and *Adv Prax* 14. In fact, however, neither of these chapters speaks of the Father's superiority of power. The former speaks of the Son's possession of substance by *derivatio* (discussed earlier) and the latter deals with the Father as invisible. We are still left, then, with an argument based largely on *Adv Prax* 4. In fairness, *Adv Prax* 4 does indeed speak of the reception of power in some sense by the Son, but certain comments seem in order.

First, it is possible that *Adv Prax* 4 clashes with the two preceding chapters as Moingt himself observes when discussing *status*. In contrast to *Adv Prax* 2, the binitarian idea seems to reassert itself in *Adv Prax* 4. The Holy Spirit looks a little like a brief afterthought as discussion turns again exclusively to the Father and Son. We should therefore be wary of assuming a connected and continuous expansion of thought from chapter 2 through to chapter 4. Secondly, even in chapter 4 there emerges no clear elaboration of the communication of the Father's substance to the Son, which is surprising if Tertullian is working with a parallel between substance and power. In fact *Adv Prax* 4 need not be taken to teach the *communication* of substance. This takes in the statement, 'I... derive the Son from no other source but from the Father's substance (*qui filium non aliunde deduco, sed de substantia patris*).' It means no more than this, that the Son does not come as an intruder to the monarchy but as of the same substance of the Father. It yields no particular information on the *mode* of the Son's participation in the substance, as it must for Moingt's infrastructure to hold. Thirdly, it eventually becomes plain why Tertullian can speak of a power and a monarchy received from the Father. The setting, it transpires, is quite a narrow one, namely the redemptive mission of the Son. It is generally

[90]Ibid. 355–356.
[91]Ibid. 360.

recognised that Tertullian has in mind Jesus' own reference to his earthly mission, as well as his directing of the Church's mission and finalising of the age. Tertullian can quickly switch within the chapter from a sentence treating monarchy as authority to one treating it as the sphere ruled over.[92] If he can make an unconscious transition like this, he can just as easily make a logical one from treating power as a capacity in chapter 2 to treating it now as active and delegated under the conditions of redemption in chapter 4.

Tertullian's argument really aims at two quite distinct points to clear himself of the charge of destroying the divine *monarchia*. First, he wants to reaffirm that the Son is not alien to the *monarchia* but belongs to the same substance of the Father which commands universal subjection. In *Adv Prax* 4 itself he pleads that only the introduction of a novel god, a rival to the creator, shatters the monarchy. He clears himself of such failure on the grounds that the Son belongs to the very substance and divine power of the creator. Secondly, he does not want the bare unity of God left by default in the hands of the Monarchian party, but wishes, with the whole work against Praxeas, to underline some distinctions which go with the unity of divine power and substance. What better place to flag these than in the economy of redemption. In a phase of the Son's human subjection the power, as now concrete and effective, passes from Father to Son and finally back again.

All the same, the argument perhaps just shelves the question.[93] Whilst the divine power has proven handy for the concept of divine unity and equality, it provides a model for plurality only by switching from the intrinsic power of the divine substance to a secondary sense: the actual concrete exercise of power. The real question is how a plurality of subjects can equally possess *absolute* power. The *monarchia* concept proves too wooden to contain such a notion. This said, Tertullian understands only too well the distinction between the Son's power possessed by substance[94] and his power as received from the Father. In *Adv Prax* 17 he distinguishes between the Son being 'of his own right

[92]E. Evans, op. cit. 202.

[93]Ibid. 202.

[94]B. Piault seems to recognise such a possession. He interprets Tertullian as saying that there is only one substance, one nature, one power and one God whilst the ranks, characteristics and manifestations are attributed to all the three names of Father and of Son and of Spirit, 'Tertullien a-t-il été subordinatien?', *Revue des Sciences Philosophiques et Théologiques* 47 (1963) 181–204 (p. 190). Aeby, op. cit. 73, on the other hand, follows Moingt in saying that, for Tertullian, the power belongs only to the Father and is transmitted to the Son at creation and ever since. Aeby, however, offers only *Adv Prax* 15 as textual support, which speaks only of the Son's achieving that which is in the Father's consciousness.

God Almighty' and as having received power over all. The tension arises from a mix of influences. There is the pressure of Hermogenes and Marcion, calling forth a defence of a single divine creating power. Then there is an anxiety to remain in line with the 'orthodox' pioneers of the *monarchia* model. On the other hand the response still bears the mark of the pluralist tradition stemming not just from the various Logos schemes but also from the New Testament account (as *Adversus Praxean* illustrates).

Tertullian is slow to realise that what he wants to achieve can come only by re-appraising the central role of the *monarchia* concept. It will not furnish the distinctions he so desperately needs and he will have to abandon to the Monarchianists at least the imperial model for power, which threatened so much all that was distinctively Christian.

Status

Braun,[95] Evans[96] and D'Ales[97] have adequately reviewed the word *status*. J. Moingt shares with these writers the view that in Tertullian status first points to the condition which constitutes the divine majesty and dignity.[98] He finds it used against Marcion to mark the one almighty creator.[99] *Adv Marc* I 7 explains Tertullian's use perfectly:

> That (objective reality) alone do I find unbegotten and uncreated, alone eternal, the creator of the universe... and restrict supreme greatness not to its name but to its condition (*status*), not to its designation but to its attributes.

In purely lexical terms 'position' can translate *status*, so Moingt correctly reminds us that the word often carries a social or political ring indicating rank.[100] We cannot for a moment afford to forget Tertullian's Latin flair for giving everything, especially God and humanity, its station. *Status*, then can fix not only a condition but also a level, placing things in their proper relation.[101] The instinct serves Tertullian well in, quite literally, putting matter in its place against Hermogenes.[102] In the writings against both Hermogenes and Marcion Tertullian has successfully fought for the solitary supremacy of that divine *status*. In *Adv Prax* 2, still wearing the

[95] R. Braun, op. cit. 199–207.
[96] E. Evans, *On The Resurrection*, 50–52.
[97] A. D'Ales, *La Théologie de Tertullien*, Paris, G. Beauchesne, 1905, 81, n.3.
[98] J. Moingt, *Unité et processions*, 834.
[99] Ibid. 831–834.
[100] Ibid. 799.
[101] J. Daniélou, *Origins of Latin Christianity*, 353.
[102] Ibid. 354.

scars of his battles, Tertullian uses this very word to count the Son and Holy Spirit in with the rank and position of the one omnipotent, unrestrained creator.

Moingt, however, has something else in store for us. He sees in a little less than half of the occurrences of *status* in Tertullian indebtedness to philosophical usage.[103] This usage points to the idea of 'origin',[104] and translates the Greek '*hypostasis*'.[105] Daniélou read Moingt on this matter and vigorously took the line that Tertullian does not follow philosophical, nor even juridical, use but turns an everyday term to his own ends. In the absence of any proof for Moingt's judgement, together with the fact that his theory brings *status* into competition with *census*,[106] his suggestion should not be seized too quickly no matter how well it fits with his views on *substantia* and *potestas*. In *Adv Hermog* 18 Tertullian writes that God, in creating through his wisdom, created through that *Sophiam* which was *non statu diversam* and which was internal and proper to him. It does not seem sound, with Moingt, to translate these words as 'not from a different origin'.[107] The basic sense of *status* as the unique divine eternal condition, the main concern of the whole book, suits the sentence perfectly. It points not to the *source* of wisdom, but to the divine quality of wisdom. Moingt's inclinations here, of course, stem from *De anima* 20–21 where all souls take their origin (*status*) from the first human soul whose origin was in the breath of God.[108] Like *De fuga* 18, also cited in support,[109] these are contexts quite remote from *Adversus Praxean*. More importantly, Tertullian does not himself employ the parallel of the human soul anywhere in his work on the Trinity, even though it would prove a useful ally in establishing a distinction of persons. *Adv Prax* 5 and *Adv Prax* 7, where Moingt sees the parallel most clearly,[110] do not even use the word *status* in the crucial passages. *Status* in these chapters seems to serve the same function as *substantia*, followed by *potestas*: to place the Son and the Holy Spirit on the same unique not-creation level as the Father. Mode of coming-to-be is not in view. Divine power, considered as level, position and rank, continues to pervade Tertullian's theology of unity.

[103] J. Moingt, op. cit. 799.
[104] J. Moingt, *Le Dieu unique*, 352.
[105] J. Moingt, *Unité et processions*, 802.
[106] Ibid. 807, 816; Daniélou, op. cit. 356.
[107] See G.C. Stead, *Divine Substance*, 203. *Substantia* in this passage means nature, status or rank.
[108] J. Moingt, *Le Dieu unique*, 358.
[109] Ibid. 353.
[110] Ibid. 359–360.

Gradus, forma and species

Gradus, forma and *species* provide in Tertullian the terms for plurality and distinction in counterpoise to *status*, *substantia* and *potestas*. *Gradus* cannot exactly translate into 'rank',[111] since we have seen that its counterpart, *status*, as well as *substantia*, already does that.[112] Moingt can resolve the matter by reading from *gradus* degrees of mediation of the divine substance along the lines discussed earlier.[113] The passage in *Adv Prax* 8 from which Moingt made this point could equally describe simply *order* or *stages*.[114] 'Step' or 'stage' seems to be Tertullian's chief interest (however attractive may be Moingt's suggestion that *gradus* stresses the internal and essential relations between the three persons in the fluidity of a transmitted *substantia* between them).[115] Precisely what the stages are does not show up all that clearly in Tertullian's writing. It could be the emergence of the Word and the Spirit in the creative work of God or the successive stages of the redemptive economy in which, to a Montanist, the Holy Spirit now predominates. Either way a shortcoming in Tertullian's scheme comes to the surface. His use of *gradus* will not yield an elegant formula. The *status* describes the creator's condition as the eternal not-creation, but *gradus* supplies only a plurality *in the economy*. We are stranded a long way from fourth-century formulations, and the weakness extends to *forma* and *species* too.

Moingt finds in *forma* the individuation which follows transmission of substance, and, again, teases us with the possibility of a distinction within internal relations. Its natural and chief sense, however, stresses visibility and aspect,[116] as Moingt himself recognises.[117] Tertullian displayed an all-absorbing interest in God's relation to the world, so *forma*, with its ring of 'external aspect', provided the perfect expression of his theology. Possibly it underlines the conviction that distinction within the Godhead goes as far back as creation. In the end, he does not expound his aim enough to provide us with a precise account. *Species* is not easy to distinguish from *forma*. Perhaps *species* is the visible aspect concretely brought into view.[118]

Moingt follows through his scheme of individuation and reads *species* as a specific thing or individual. Hence in Tertullian it highlights the

---

[111]For example, R.P.C. Hanson, *The Attractiveness of God*, London, SPCK, 1973, 78.

[112]E. Evans, *Against Praxeas*, 53.

[113]Moingt, *Substantialité et individualité*, 468.

[114]Cf. Daniélou, op. cit. 359, and E. Evans, op. cit. 53.

[115]Moingt, op. cit. 466, 506; Daniélou, op. cit. 365.

[116]E. Evans, op. cit. 54.

[117]Moingt, op. cit. 481–494.

[118]E. Evans, op. cit. 57.

respective individuality of the Son and Spirit as recipients of the transmitted substance.[119] For such an internal ontological meaning, Moingt appeals to *Adversus Hermogenem*, where indeed particularity comes to the foreground. Even there, however, *species* is the specific external form that particular things take from underlying matter, so the 'external expression' still offers the most promising translation. As with *gradus* and *forma* we find *species* to be a term suited to stress the way in which the creation discloses distinctions in the Godhead. Nevertheless, yet again, the precise connotation eludes commentators.

Status, substantia and *potestas* bring out the divine status, rank and conditions of existence as creator. Each of the three is more than a divine activity but not exactly equivalent to the Deity itself. *Potestas* especially appears as *the* divine attribute which highlights the creator's objective and concrete reality, over against all that is created. With *gradus, species* and *forma* we can see an ordered unfolding which underscores the three divine names or titles to the creative rank and potency. However, much obscurity remains. The divine rank and condition, though unique, does not preclude a plurality of persons, a triple name and title to the one underlying rank and dignity. The frailty of the *monarchia* concept to accommodate both the unity and the distinctions of Trinitarian thought becomes most obvious here. Another tactic will be needed to overturn what Tertullian sees as the Monarchianist abuse of the notion of divine power.

Persona

Although *persona* forms the first part of the celebrated formula 'three persons in one substance (*tres personae in una substantia*)', it does not command the same kind of attention or enjoy the same prominence as its partner, *substantia*, in Tertullian studies. Several reasons may account for this. In the first place, *substantia* has a known philosophical and everyday usage and has proven to be a flexible tool in Tertullian's work as a whole, whereas the sources for his use of *persona* do not seem so transparent. Equally, in the Trinitarian context, *substantia* holds a dominant position in *Adversus Praxean* for expressing the divine unity, whereas *persona* does not command the divine distinctions. As J.P. Mackey observes,

> his concept of person is extremely undeveloped.... Tertullian really
> depends upon his concept of the 'economy' by which the created

---

[119]Moingt, op. cit. 446–447.

world came to be and through which the divine governance of the world is exercised.[120]

All the same, for the demolition task in *Adversus Praxean*, Tertullian extracts maximum effect from the word, and it deserves some close attention.

The evolution of *persona* in ancient Latin seems plain enough.[121] From an original sense of theatre mask, changed by the actor according to the part he played, *persona* came to stand for both the character part itself and the part or role which a person assumes in the world. From here it was a simple matter for the word to denote any human being with a significant role in society, a personage or person of certain standing and, eventually, anyone indeed with legal rights and obligations.[122] It is this latter, juridical, development which has perhaps stimulated the greatest amount of dissension concerning the sense of *persona* in Tertullian's work, ably reviewed by Moingt.[123]

It is now commonplace to repeat Harnack's view that *persona* had a purely juridical meaning in conjunction with *substantia*. In this setting the famous formula derived from the idea of a plurality of persons having title to one property. Although Harnack himself later had doubts about the notion and although he came up against brisk opposition, the juridical emphasis survived in various forms, including the reminder that in Roman law a *persona* was the subject of a court action,[124] so that D'Alès could claim that it commanded incontestable ground.[125] Along came S. Schlossman to assail the received wisdom.[126] Tertullian was not in fact a jurist but simply had the temperament of a jurist and the instinct to provide a rational basis for Trinitarian faith.[127] Schlossman

---

[120]J.P. Mackey, *The Christian Experience of God as Trinity*, London, SCM, 1983.

[121]C.T. Lewis & C. Short, *A Latin Dictionary*, Oxford, Clarendon Press, 1962.

[122]Thus, for instance, W. Pannenberg, 'Person', F.H. Kettler, ed., *Die Religion in Geschichte und Gegenwart*, Tübingen, J.C.B. Mohr (Paul Siebeck) 1962.

[123]J. Moingt, *Histoire, doctrine, methodes*, 37–43.

[124]G.L. Bray, 'The Filioque Clause', 112, n. 46.

[125]D'Alès, *Théologie de Tertullien*, 83, n. 2. Moingt, wrongly, gives 82 for this footnote.

[126]Moingt, op. cit. 38.

[127]S. Schlossmann, 'Tertullian im Lichte der Jurisprudenz', *Zeitschrift für Kirchengeschichte* 27 (1906) 251–275 (p. 270). See also a review (to which my attention was drawn by Moingt's survey) by F. Kropatscheck, of Schlossmann's '*Persona* und *prosopon* im Recht und im christlichen Dogma', *Zeitschrift für Kirchengeschichte* 27 (1906) 363–364. He maintains that neither *persona* nor *prosopon* has any certain relation to Roman or Greek law.

prefers a Stoic explanation of the formula and *persona* now becomes a particular possession concretely of a portion of the *substantia*.[128] This brings us to the more recent theories of Kretschmar and Andresen that *persona* belongs to a 'prosopographic' tradition.[129] On these accounts, the prevalent angel-Christology of the apologists' era, in which the Son and the Spirit were celestial beings before the face (*prosopon*) of God, provided Tertullian with the type of distinction for which *persona* stood.[130] Whilst rejecting the origins of such an approach in angelology, C. Andresen nevertheless finds the distinction of persons to rest upon a Greek type of exegesis which takes account of the various 'voices' in Scripture, thereby identifying the various speakers by the words which come forth *ek prosopou*.[131] Moingt dismissed both views as they stood but later recognised some importance in them for a fair estimation of *persona* in *Adversus Praxean*. Moingt himself plainly prefers the definitive work of M. Nédoncelle,[132] which recognises certain juridical senses of *persona*, including the individual vis á vis their legal role, their social role, their civil dignity and the legal 'person' as opposed to things. Nédoncelle, however, goes further. *Persona* marks out not just a role but a real concrete existing individual whilst not excluding character, individuality and rationality.

All in all, *persona* now shapes up to look useful in four main areas for shedding light upon Tertullian's Trinitarian thought: role, individuality, personality and function. Moingt can find examples of the 'dramatic' sense of 'role' in *De carne* 11, *De pudic* 8, *De spect* 23 and *De anima* 57.[133] Even in a directly Trinitarian passage it fulfils this function, though only once:

> No, but almost all the psalms which sustain the role of Christ (*Christi personam*) represent the Son as speaking to the Father. (*Adv Prax* 11)

Even here of course *persona* also implies a concrete individual. If not, Tertullian completely capitulates to the Monarchianist view that he is trying to combat. His scheme wishes to expunge the purely 'dramatic' understanding of person that menaces a right understanding of the Godhead.[134] Hence in relation to the words of Jesus to Philip, 'He who

---

[128]S. Schlossmann, 'Tertullian im Lichte der Jurisprudenz', 407–416, particularly noted by Moingt, op. cit. 38.

[129]Moingt, op. cit. 41–43, 557–565.

[130]Ibid. 557.

[131]Ibid. 357–358.

[132]M. Nedoncelle, 'Prosopon et persona dans l'antiquité classique. Essai de billan linguistique', *Revue des Sciences Religieuses* 22 (1948) 277–299.

[133]Moingt, op. cit. 618–619.

[134]Ibid. 622.

has seen me has seen the Father', Tertullian makes it plain that he intends here no mere role or appearance of the Father in the form of a Son. Other statements of Jesus provide the clue. These separate the Son from the Father and present the Son in his own person as the way to the Father. *Adv Prax* 24 recognises, of course, the Father's deeds and acts of power in the Son, and only in this sense does the *persona* of the Son represent the Father.

The juridical background of *persona* can, if sound, assume some importance in connection with its reference to a distinct concrete individual. *Persona* signifies not a role but the subject, or object, of some action. One *persona* stands set in relation to another *persona*. Many examples emerge, even outside *Adv Prax* 24, implying a real concrete individual.[135] It seems rather unlikely that such a pervasive sense of *persona* should suddenly disappear at the writing of *Adversus Praxean*, particularly in the light of that work's objective. We also have here an explanation for why, as Moingt notices,[136] in *Adv Prax* 27 Tertullian concentrates on proving that the *Sermo* is a *res solida*, using such striking terms as *corpus* and *effigies*. We do not come upon grounds here for identifying *res* with *persona*. The two words appear in juxtaposition and are not therefore synonyms:

> The Word (*Sermo*) may be seen to be an object (*res*) and person (*persona*), and so may be capable, insofar as he is another besides God, of causing there to be two, the Father and the Son, God and the Word. (*Adv Prax* 7)

They are distinguished but intimately connected, for the passage goes on to say that the *sermo* as a *res* does not take the stigma of 'an empty thing', as borne out by the claim that,

> Whatever therefore the substance of the Word was, that I call a person, and for it I claim the name of Son: and while I acknowledge him as Son I maintain he is another beside the Father.

Perhaps a commentator could derive directly from *res* the idea of individuality in Tertullian's thinking as a stepping stone to understanding his use of *persona*. Tertullian himself, however, argued first the *substantiality* of *persona*, from its participation in the divine *spiritus* or *substantia*, and then made good his claim that the *sermo* is after all a *res* by presenting it in distinction from the invisible *persona* of the Father. He set his sights on the notion of concrete individuality.

[135]Ibid. 567.
[136]Ibid. 632.

However, as a side effect *persona* comes to clearer definition and receives content and solidity.[137]

So just how much did Tertullian intend to convey by 'person' in the debate about the Trinity, and in particular how 'personal' in the modern sense was his conception? Uncompromising lines of battle have appeared over this question. C.C.J. Webb, for instance, concludes from Tertullian's treatment of the conversations in John's Gospel between Father and Son a sense of full loving personal relationships[138] between *personae*. Webb stands amongst the legendary twentieth century defenders of a social Trinity, but this should not prejudice judgement of his approach. His perception of *persona* would make it conform in Tertullian to the modern formal concept of person, explained as the 'actual unique reality of a spiritual being, an undivided whole existing independently and not interchangeable with any other... the concrete form taken by the freedom of a spiritual being'.[139]

Perhaps Tertullian did indeed hold to such a heightened sense of personality attaching to each of the divine persons in the 'conversation' passages, but it seems more likely that he merely turned the 'prosographic' idea to good use as a suitable method of distinguishing a plurality of persons or concrete individuals on the basis of a plurality of voices. According to Moingt, taking a tradition of early theologians which identified and personalised the sacred voice,[140] Tertullian concluded from the conversations of the persons a distinction between them like that of physical individuals towards each other.

Persona, in other words, merely challenged the 'one-voice-one-speaker' concept of Praxeas by the 'three-voice-three-speakers' formula of the New Testament as Tertullian understood it. Certainly, he needed no more than this in order to neutralise that role-playing Monarchianism with which Tertullian strove in combat. But given that *Christ* is a *persona*, and that the *personae* often emerge through the Father–Son relationship developed in John's Gospel, Webb does not lack some warrant for expecting much more than merely three speakers implied in Tertullian's treatment. Even he, however, would have to concede that the emphasis falls upon *function*, that is, upon 'persons' in the *economy*. It is only here, in the presence of the active power of God, that the term *persona* can be taken as touching the subject of our enquiry. In *Adv Prax*

---

[137]Ibid. 636.

[138]C.C.J. Webb, *God and Personality*, London, Allen & Unwin, 1918, 66–67.

[139]M. Muller and A. Halder, 'Person', *Sacramentum Mundi: An Encyclopedia of Theology*, London, Burns & Oates, 1969. Cf. B.B. Warfield, 'Tertullian and the Beginnings of the Doctrine of the Trinity', *Princeton Theological Review* 4 (1906) 1–36 (p. 5).

[140]Moingt, op. cit. 561.

6 it is for the creative act that wisdom takes surer, firmer shape as *persona*. Equally, in *Adv Prax* 7, discussed earlier, the *sermo* which comes to view as *res* and *persona* makes an appearance as the creative *sermo*, incapable of being void and empty, because through it come substantial things. According to Tertullian, the plurality of persons in *Adv Prax* 12 derives from the words of Genesis 1: 'Let us make man in our image.' Then again, the very term itself makes its debut in *Adv Prax* 3 to function immediately as the plural marker of the *monarchia* which expresses itself through the divine economy. So the term quite naturally falls into association, in *Adv Prax* 14, with 'acts of power', the only sense in which Tertullian will countenance the Father's *persona* in that of the Son.

At the heart of all this, of course, we find the mission of the Son and the conversation which typifies the relationship of the Son, in this mission, to the Father. Even these (in *Adv Prax* 18, 21, 23, 31), with all their possibilities for evoking a pre-existent relationship, mainly function to signal a plurality to be found in the works *ad extra*, more particularly that of the redemptive mission.

By making *persona* also a 'name' in *Adv Prax* 26, Tertullian seems finally to bring the term into contact with the *gradus*, *forma* and *species* which are 'reckoned out in the name of Father, Son and Holy Spirit' (*Adv Prax* 2). Tertullian says, 'thrice we are baptised into each several Person at each several name'.

This way he passes beyond the mere notion of an unfolding of the one divine power in three presentations and gives each of these presentations a name, a *persona*, a concrete existence. It does not seem to strike him that, logically, they ought to become three separate powers, and this is probably because he has in reality left behind the power-nuanced distinctions of the beginning of the tract and turned his attention to a different kind of distinction evident in the same economy and works *ad extra*.

Although, then, *persona* moves in the same sphere as *gradus*, *forma* and *species*, something more distinct, concrete and personal attaches to it, and in some measure it stands a little further away from the power-defined cast of Tertullian's Trinitarian scheme explored earlier.[141] It is not that *persona* bears no relation to *substantia*, though no mutual Stoic key binds them. Rather *persona* carries such a ring of distinctness that the power theme, emphasised by the unifying *substantia*, cannot contain it. In the context of Father–Son language it offers the glimmer of a different approach, one which will assume ascendancy later but was left at a raw unexploited stage by Tertullian himself. For him, whilst the *personae* are so much more distinct and clear, and to some degree personal, than the

[141]Cf. Ibid. 565.

distinctions in *Adv Prax* 2, yet they still emerge mainly in the functional realm. The conjunction of the two persons in *Adv Prax* 24 is through 'works and words.' A juridical tone (*proximas personas officiales*) already occurs in *Adv Prax* 3:[142] So, although the term *persona* does not look as natural to the power-scheme of distinctions as the other three terms, yet it fits. It forms a monument to the memory of the Monarchian tradition inherited by Tertullian, guarded by him to the best of his powers, but ultimately doomed to undergo radical changes at the hands of the later tradition. Tertullian marks its peak as a Trinitarian theory, but through him the imperial model entered Latin theology and ultimately invaded its ecclesiology.

[142]Cf. G. Bray, *The Doctrine of God*, Leicester, IVP, 1993, where he holds that legal imagery in the term *persona* is fundamental to Western theology. Roman law was concerned with regulating and controlling the use of power which has its ultimate source in God. Theology, therefore, came to be understood as the dispensation of divine power: in the work of the persons of the Trinity, in the structure of the church, in the means of grace. The controversies which continue to divide the Western churches today concern questions posed in legal terms about matters of authority and jursdiction (39–40).

CHAPTER 9

Conclusions: Tertullian and the Western Doctrine of Divine and Human Power

Tertullian and the Rule of Faith

Today's controversies aside, it is clear that in Tertullian the concept of divine power pervaded the Rule of Faith. Indeed, omnipotence swamped his prolonged debate with Hermogenes and Marcion. Hermogenes wished for a god who could blame matter for the world's ills. Marcion wished for a god that had nothing to do with the world at all. These were tempting options and Tertullian only side-stepped them in favour of the conventional 'creation from nothing' because of strong, constructive reasons. These all sprang from a commitment to the Rule of Faith.

Concerning creation itself he was opposed to dualistic thinking which seemed to smear the physical world. Ascetic in temperament though he was, he endorsed the Christian apologetic tradition's affirmation of the goodness of creation, and of human fleshly existence in particular. This was not Stoic pantheism, or Roman utilitarianism, or even Jewish holism alone. It was peculiarly and powerfully Christian. Christians believed from the beginning that God had somehow assumed a human bodily existence, suffering even its death. They believed that he had also given his verdict on the virtue of bodily existence by reviving and transforming that body after crucifixion – a clear vote of confidence. But to underpin this, would it not be enough to say that God shaped previously existing chaos or matter into the present world? Hermogenes thought so, and believed that in this way he could clear God of blame for the world's disreputable features. Tertullian was prepared, however, to bind God to the world irrevocably whatever the risks. The 'creation from nothing' did just this. The free exercise of power and initiative involved in it placed God in a position of complete responsibility and commitment: to a personal relationship with human beings, to the natural world, to full recovery of the world's full potential for good. The incarnation spelt out the enormity of that commitment.

So, as sole originator of the tangible world, by unique power, God was solely responsible for it. He shouldered that responsibility in the most costly manner. Through incarnation he suffered solidarity with us in our ordinariness. At this point Tertullian did not permit even Greek immutability (and thereby impassibility) to obstruct incarnation belief. He was prepared to trade in the immutability of the Word, so long as he could secure the full physical humanness of Jesus, the Son of God. At the same time the word of Jesus was also the word of the creator. It replicated the power which created from nothing. It too created, or rather, renovated. One thing was sure: the world produced from nothing still had such intrinsic value that it merited a second wave of creative power. This was the beginning also of a new 'third race'.

The world, for Tertullian was in its essence good, because God produced it. The same power produced the Church and it, too, was to evidence the goodness of the creator. Holiness was to be its distinguishing mark. It would all flow from the divine power to re-create. The Spirit of power was the key to it, not human authority, in sanctification, discipline, sacraments and forgiveness. With the axis of 'creation and re-creation' the now familiar Western model for the work of the Spirit was emerging.

However, the Church was not the only response to evil that divine power could produce. The remaking of an essentially good but exploited cosmos required a more severe remedy. Here Tertullian strikes away from the tradition in Irenaeus and feels obliged to have God deploy the full force of creative power for the destruction of the world. So would come about the final removal of invasive evil. I criticised this move for being overkill in the fullest literal sense. It was particularly unnecessary as the best lines of solution already lay to hand in the Irenaean concept of a transformed cosmos. Moreover Tertullian's own eschatology took a different line with its model of resurrection-transformation and its millennial outlook. He is carried away by his own argument, and the result is a concept out of joint with his normally positive view of the world. Even here, however, the preoccupation is with re-creation not with destruction. The God who could create from nothing could, and would, do it again. In Tertullian's own perverse way it is a reaffirmation, at least, of the world's physical worthiness in principle.

The doctrine of the general resurrection is Tertullian's most typical stance on human destiny. By advocating it he had coolly positioned himself out on a limb. It was no place for an apologist in the Greek world to be. As we saw, for many Greek writers the body had no future, and even Hellenised Judaism was ambivalent. In its own way it was another major challenge to the dualism in Greek thought between material and non-material. Tertullian is underwriting a holism of body and 'soul'. He did this to a fault to our eyes today, since 'soul' seemed, in his thought, to be a kind of substance (*De carne* 11, *De res* 17). I do not see this conviction contradicted by his other preference for speaking of 'spirit' and body. The latter use is probably unconscious usage influenced by biblical texts and a preoccupation with the *Spiritus* of God. One thing which cannot be levelled at Tertullian is a dualism in which the substantial body is subordinated to the 'spirit'. Both aspects of human existence are real and substantial. It is not therefore a distasteful operation of power for God to resuscitate human flesh, to bring 'clean out of unclean'. In *De resurrectione* 9, Tertullian calls Christians to the love of their enemies. This extends to their total welfare, so the flesh too is the neighbour to be loved. It is called the 'sister of Christ'.

In Tertullian's work, the Rule of Faith culminated in the doctrine of the resurrection, which focused upon this very human flesh. The resurrection was the crowning glory and ultimate confession of faith. All Tertullian's elaboration of the divine power came to rest on this hope. And in this way the apologist burnt his boats and said farewell to the main contours of a Greek account of anthropology. It almost *was* the Rule of Faith.

The doctrine of the Trinity, strictly, lies outside of the Rule of Faith with its more simple and basic tenets. It is perhaps significant, then, that the Monarchian debate shows up the inadequacy of the model of power, even for Tertullian. It is in his favour that he saw that very thing himself and turned to the more personal language of sonship and of *persona*, whatever the limitations of the latter. The God described this way was usually present, I think, to his own mind but not everywhere in his writings. In this sense the imbalance of his work rightly serves as a warning to us today.

Tertullian's handling of the power-theme

It is not difficult to find logical flaws in Tertullian. He was not a leisured philosopher with time on his hands to redraft an argument and cover it from every angle. His works were mainly urgent polemic, and if they could stop his opponents in their tracks it was enough. The collected extant writings are not a systematic theology, and have not been massaged by the author to produce consistency. The most striking feature in some of the major flaws is the misuse of the power-theme. For instance, Tertullian's attempt to reconcile the justice and goodness of God relies upon one common, undergirding power as the key. This proves inadequate to the task. Similarly, his defence of God's freedom leaves him with a hypothetical preference for a God who actually creates evil from within himself rather than one who may not be able to dissolve evil. And even the dissolution of evil involves wasteful and negative use of power, so that the whole cosmos is destroyed to the extent that it needs a second creation from nothing, a rebirth. On occasion the divine Trinity is chiefly a triumvirate whose main hallmark is monarchy rather than sociality, though the handling of 'person' moves in another direction. There are dubious assumptions about the character of God in these theories, and they come back to haunt Tertullian in his handling of the Christian life and of discipline. However, more searching questions about Tertullian's use of the power-theme face us today.

Early writers like Tertullian (*especially* Tertullian) have fallen into disrepute because, it is sometimes argued, they were pioneers of a doctrine of God which betrayed Jesus. Whereas Jesus stood for a God who was vulnerable and open, early Latin thought opted for an unqualified creator, a concept which has in it all the seeds of religious triumphalism and legalism. Modern thought claims to rescue the Christian concept of God by modifying the creator theme, especially its note of omnipotence. It would have been gratifying to uncover, from a study of Tertullian, a straight verification or contradiction of this simple and elegant analysis. However, the evidence is more complex. It is certainly true that in his writing there is an exaggerated application of God's omnipotence. He fell back upon it as the easy response and credited it with more answers than on its own it could deliver. As is usual in such cases, there are historical explanations to hand. It would be helpful at least to note them and not project on to Tertullian's work a timeless quality. Some features are not of the essence of the Rule of Faith but originate, at least in part, from external pressures.

One obvious avenue of questioning concerns the religious setting of Tertullian's time. William C. Placher puts the early Christian writers nicely into context by reminding us that, in the Hellenistic world, although views on the divinity were varied, many did 'assume that God above all means power – sometimes power pure and simple, with a frankness that makes us cringe'.[1] The circumstances were not conducive to emphasising the vulnerable God. The doctrine of creation hardly, in and of itself, required the idea that God thereby put himself 'at risk', but the central theme of the cross 'does seem to point to a doctrine of divine

---

[1]W.C. Placher, 'Narratives of a Vulnerable God', *Princeton Seminary Bulletin*, NS 14 (1993) 134–151 (p. 135).

vulnerability... and this the Fathers, with their particular doctrine of divine impassibility, were scarcely able to countenance'.[2] The odds were stacked against Tertullian's being able acceptably to sound the note of God's genuine involvement in our vulnerable human world. In the light of this the results of his work were not so poor. In direct conflict with ideologies which were neither purely Christian nor purely philosophical in the classical sense, Tertullian really played the omnipotence card to fend off what he saw as a destructive and paralysing dualism. He wished to defend, not abandon, the very God of Jesus Christ. This was a God not ashamed of the world, nor of becoming one of its inhabitants, nor of renewing it. The birth of everything from God's own free operation, in which he alone took responsibility, boosted faith in such a God. However, the struggles with dualistic writers now fixed the texture of all Tertullian's work and gave it a permanent, if unbalanced quality. A device that had served so well at such a fundamental level became a tool for every key doctrine Tertullian tackled. He made it perform tasks for which it was not designed, but blended its various elements in most of the classical beliefs summarised in the Rule of Faith. For his time, the attempt met with surprising success.

Tertullian worked in a political setting as well as a religious and philosophical one, though admittedly political and metaphysical did not occupy separate intellectual territories. Obviously, the chief political element was imperial Rome. Tertullian worked in a reactionary climate where the emergence of new gods was associated with conspiracies against the monarchy.[3] According to Mark Burrows, Tertullian wished to root Christianity in antiquity, as did other apologists, but he also wished to detach it from the Jewish religion and the odium it had endured as a result of the Jewish Wars.[4] Hence 'Tertullian underscores the emergence of a new bond between the God of Moses and the Roman Empire.'[5] However, as we noted early on, the initially sympathetic tone of references to the emperor turn to censure. The emperor is really trying to substitute himself for the one God. The question is not how Christians are to live under Roman law, but how they and the emperor will fare under God's tribunal.[6] The claimed powers of the emperor could only be held by him or by God.

[2]P.R. Forster, 'Divine Passibility and the Early Christian Doctrine of God', in N.M. de S. Cameron, ed., *The Power and Weakness of God*, Edinburgh, Rutherford House, 1990, 23–51.

[3]M.S. Burrows, 'Christianity in the Roman Forum: Tertullian and the Apologetic Use of History', *Vigiliae Christianae* 42 (1988) 206–235 (p. 206).

[4]Ibid. 224–227.

[5]Ibid. 227.

[6]Ibid. 129.

As a result, persecution and the struggle with a sometimes hostile empire led straight to one disastrous result: the transfer of emperor language to God. It was one thing to oppose God's claims to the emperor's claims, as Jesus himself did. It was another to paint God in the emperor's colours. It was this more than anything else that distorted the God of Jesus Christ who had so clearly denounced human concepts of power. I want to suggest that this move, more than the well-established belief in God as creator (held by Jesus himself), bears blame for some of the developments in the West which cause so much heart-searching today. Along with it went a sense of unintelligent absoluteness and an alternative Christian oath binding the believer to God in impersonal subjection. The soldier's amoral and unthinking obedience to a despot at this point replaced the image of disciples gathered round their personal and self-revealing Lord. The rejection of military service had contained both an element of pacifism and a resistance to the imperial cult. Walter Wink argues that the note of coercive domination and the repugnance of the cult hang together. It was a sacralised military existence wholly at the service of Roman imperialism.[7] Wink is interested mainly in what he regards as a confrontation between the reign of God and the 'Domination System'. Whatever one's judgement on that, Tertullian's challenge was not carried out without fatal assimilation into his thought of the very imperial way of talking which he opposed. A new, though different, *potestas* stood in opposition to the imperial *potestas*.

In Tertullian's case, a Roman sense of civil authority, a rhetorical training, always legal in tone, and a highly developed sense of moral judgement sometimes made the change of pitch emphatic. I say emphatic rather than complete, because often enough the failure lay in what was unsaid rather than said. Reference to God's universal love, patience and magnanimity sometimes came in muted tones. Do we have here a distorting influence upon every aspect of Tertullian's handling of the Rule of Faith? The answer has to be in the negative because, as we have been able to show, he still upheld the doctrinal outlook present in the earlier apologetic tradition. This alone calls into question the claim that, at least in Tertullian, the imperial taint has decisively influenced early Christology. According to this view, Christ's lordship originally took an 'eschatological' meaning contrasted with the transient time-bound lordships of human kingdoms. It was the dogma of the incarnation which brought it forward into this age.[8] However, Tertullian's doctrine of the incarnation shows no sign of such a

---

[7]W. Wink, *Engaging the Powers: Discernment and Resistance in a World of Domination*, Minneapolis, Fortress Press, 1992, 210–211.

[8]Don Cupitt, cited in P.S. Fiddes, *The Creative Suffering of God*, Oxford, Clarendon Press, 1988, 89.

colouring even though it is quite advanced as a Christological definition (and is sometimes called a 'theological miracle'). Paul Fiddes is certainly correct to reply that describing Christ as a political guarantor does not exhaust all the possibilities for unravelling the incarnation dogma. In his words, God has chosen 'to identify himself in a dead man; he has chosen to define his deity in weakness'.[9] So Tertullian himself spoke of God 'reigning from the tree'.

All the same, the imperial terminology penetrated Tertullian's conception of the Church's holiness and discipline. Baptism, we saw, became an oath of allegiance echoing the military oaths sworn to the emperor and offering a similar kind of obedience. The Church was a shadow-empire in which Christians gave themselves over to the one Spirit of power and renewal. The distinctive Latin spirit of Tertullian's theology focused his thoughts further on the Church as a political society and on order and discipline. Tertullian's criticism of contemporary philosophy was not just theological. He judged that it was impotent to inspire its devotees to what he regarded as righteous living.[10] A moral imperialism was born. The conception of a rival empire, albeit without sword, was irresistible. In succeeding centuries, the idea of *potestas* in Christian thought took its lead not from the usage in Tertullian that focused on the potentiality and mighty acts of God, but from the usage that moved in this imperial Latin sphere where *potestas* pointed to an all-pervading legal jurisdiction. Modern writers have complained at the corruption of this up to the present. J. Blank complains that according to the classical tradition the *potestas* as an area of competence and authority should have been kept quite distinct from spiritual authority (*auctoritas*).[11] A similar distinction is made by Walter Wink between the visible and invisible poles of power. The former is the outer aspect of systems, organisation, and officials, the latter the inner spirit or driving force.[12] By introducing the imperial political terminology for the Church's discipline, and by aggravating this move by a strong legalistic and penitential emphasis, Tertullian laid the foundations for an oppressive juridical framework for Church life and the confusion of spiritual and legal authority. It is easy to condemn imperial vocabulary in traditional institutional Catholicism. It may be necessary, however, to

---

[9]Ibid.

[10]A.J. Guerra, 'Polemical Christianity; Tertullian's Search for Certitude', *Second Century* 8 (1991) 109–123 (p. 114).

[11]J. Blank, 'The Concept of "Power" in the Church: New Testament Perspectives', J. Provost and K. Walf, eds, *Power in the Church. Concilium* 197 (1988) 3–10 (pp. 3–4).

[12]W. Wink, *Naming the Powers. The Language of the New Testament (The Powers*, Vol. 1) Philadelphia, Fortress Press, 1984, 9.

explore whether it has penetrated non-Catholic terminology. We could ask, for instance, why it is that Calvin chooses the word 'decree' to describe the electing purpose of God, and whether it has not led some of his critics to jump to conclusions concerning the nature of 'causation' in the will of God.

Tertullian on trial today

It is time to address more directly some of the concerns contained in modern critiques of the Christian handling of power-theology and to see how far a guilty plea is appropriate from Tertullian. Four concerns in particular warrant mention: the role of a 'domination' view of divine power, the debate about God's immutability, the role of authority in the Church and the perceived effects on women in the Church.

The order given above is not one of priority but of logic. Power as domination seems the broadest and most fundamental question. It would be unwise for Christian thinking, however conservative, to ignore modern insights here by dismissive appeal to the claim that they only arise from the modern democratic ideals of western society, not from the logic of the Christian sources. For one thing, perhaps past Christian communities could have justly claimed to be participants in the rise of the modern form of democracy. For another, it is often the empirical situation which drives Christian theologians back to their sources for a review of conventional interpretation. Undoubtedly, theological reflection on the nature of power today owes its existence in some measure to external stimuli: the holocaust, a century of war, mass media coverage of dictatorships, systems such as Marxism and apartheid, empowerment for women, etc. Today's Christian communities could therefore gain from listening to what early sources might say to us in the light of these new concerns.

It is now commonplace to point to the servanthood and cross of Jesus as an indicator of the kind of God facing us in Jesus Christ. He is not a God falling upon human beings with crushing might but the one who suffers in solidarity with human sufferers. Jurgen Moltmann is well known for taking the cross as the determinative revelation of God. The observation that this is to 'undercut the history and record of God's revelation to and dealings with his people' and to 'reduce the significance of who and what Jesus is in his total ministry'[13] is just one example of criticisms heard on Moltmann at this point.

---

[13]E.D. Cook, 'Weak Church – Weak God', N.M. de S. Cameron, ed., *The Power and Weakness of God*, 69–92 (p. 80). A quite different kind of writer has written starkly: 'the Crucified One is virtually the real definition of what is

Process theology, too, has had a major impact in questioning the power-theology of traditional theism. Ray Griffin, for instance, is typical of a view which wishes to exonerate God for evil in the world (just as Hermogenes did) by jettisoning any relationship between God and the world that seems to give God a semblance of 'control' over it.[14] Griffin works with the dubious axiom that only an analogue taken from our direct experience can make talk about God's influence meaningful. He does not seem to consider the indirect analogue which serves as no more than a clue to divine agency. The only analogue acceptable to him, as a starting point, is 'the relations of influence between persons' where the relationship is 'never one of complete determination, but always one of persuasion, where the influenced subjects necessarily make a partially free response'.[15] Statements like this have drawn the criticism that they prove too much. The theology behind them cannot guarantee that the final end will be good. Semantic refinement which redefines omnipotence as 'omnipotent love' or 'infinite patience', does not go far enough to reassure many traditional theists on this score. If it is argued that at least the new approach reforms the *mode* or *definition* of power, then this is a way open also to traditional theism. It too could clarify its description of how omnipotence is exercised without surrender of the concept itself.

Griffin damns by association Luther's view of the divine power over creation by introducing prejudicial terms such as 'coercive', 'deterministic', 'monopolistic'. However, these are not descriptions of omnipotence itself, but of the ways that it might be exercised. But Griffin repeatedly attaches the labels of 'causal necessity' and 'determinism' to a variety of traditional theologies, allowing no acquittal for the plea that the *way* God affects things is not completely open to scrutiny. If the end is sure and known then, according to Griffin, necessity rules and freedom is a fiction. However, once process theology invests the love-influence of God with a sure optimism it is caught in the same net. One answer which Griffin ought to consider is the acceptance of a conundrum of human freedom in tandem with divine certainty

meant with the word "God"' (E. Jungel, *God as the Mystery of the World*, 17, quoted in W.C. Placher, 'Narratives of a Vulnerable God', 148).

[14]R. Griffin, *God, Power and Evil: A Process Theodicy*, Philadelphia, Westminster Press, 1976, 230.

[15]Ibid. A slightly different process concept is presented by L. Ford in 'The Rhetoric of Divine Power', *Perspectives in Religious Studies* 14 (1987) 233–238. Less emphasis falls upon the idea of persuasion and a broader idea of 'shared power' governs the conception of God's relation to the natural world. Significantly, however, the problem of grounds for optimism is ignored except that God is credited with being the cause that holds back the total collapse of things into disorder through conflict. The *creatio ex nihilo* receives short shrift from Ford (p. 238).

(after all, reductionists are forced to accept a conundrum of freewill in tandem with material determinism). Then one may gather together whatever human analogues throw light on the modes of divine influence. This would have to be done whilst recognising the limits of all analogues to disclose the full nature of divine agency. If this suggestion is followed, the idea of omnipotence might still be a respectable term.

Process theology has not flourished in Britain as it has in the United States, but it has its advocates and has made a serious impact. As a result of its influence, some analogues have little charm. Paul Fiddes tells us what they are: the God moving events around as on a chessboard, the 'power of an absolute monarch multiplied to infinity'[16] and the world as a machine.[17] What all these protests have to say to us is simply that we should be choosy with our analogues. But what does it have to say about the performance of Tertullian?

The second-century fathers spoke with one voice about the omnipotence of God, and all included the doctrine of creation by God alone in their Rule of Faith (though Justin Martyr is ambivalent). Griffin is right at least about this, that it is a first-order term in traditional Christian theism. Although modern philosophical subtleties were unknown to Tertullian and his predecessors, the chief concern of process theology today was well known to him through Marcion and Hermogenes. However, Tertullian did not abolish the principle of omnipotence and put his faith in an analogue of human relations and persuasion (it was a feature open to him in his treatment of 'persona'). Nor did he give up the ideal of authentic human free agency. He simply refused to attach the term 'necessity' to the events of the world, even though his Stoic background would have made it a tempting option. In addition, Tertullian's vision of God's omnipotence as potency, and not just act, added an air of restraint. The power was controlled and harnessed to reason and wisdom. More important still, he made the cross central to his understanding of how God's power did operate: God reigned from the tree. Like other writers, he saw God's character revealed in his sending good to the just and the unjust alike. The central element in God's love is the love of one's enemy,[18] and 'for the politically powerless it was the most radical revolutionary act, supported by open criticism of injustice and cruelty'.[19]

Unfortunately, as we have seen, this was not an unblemished record. Tertullian yielded to the temptation to clothe the principle of

[16]P.S. Fiddes, op. cit. 32.
[17]Ibid. 38–39.
[18]E. Osborn, 'The Love Command in Second-Century Christian Writing', *Second Century* 1 (1981) 223–243 (p. 241).
[19]Ibid.

omnipotence in a dangerous analogue, that of absolute monarchy, borrowed from the imperial context. Although this does not prove that principle and analogue are inseparable, it does throw attention on the staying-power of that analogue in the history of the western Church. Even if the attribute of omnipotence has won for itself a stay of execution it must live on under searching scrutiny. The word 'power' need not be regarded as some kind of contagion. D.L. Migliore reminds us that power simply means the ability to do something. Every human being, even living creature, possesses and exercises power to some degree, so that there 'is no life where there is no power', and in all religions God is experienced as awesome power.[20] It is necessary, however, to avoid distorted images of God as coercive power, brute force and compulsion, images often associated with God as Father.[21] The Gospel, according to Migliore, redefines power: 'not mere almightiness, but creative power, not impassive but compassionate power, not immutable but steadfast, life-giving power that liberates and transforms the world'.[22] On this scale of reckoning, Tertullian, for all his flaws, does not come out too badly much of the time.

The second critical area concerns divine immutability. This discussion will be briefer, since much has been said already. Tertullian did not introduce novelty to the prevailing doctrine of God. The Platonising elements in Hellenistic thought ensured that God was protected from the inferiority implied by change. How far was Tertullian's thought on immutability prepared to go with this rule? The apologist asserts divine immutability over against Hermogenes. His main concern here, however, is not to develop a theory of the One and the Many, but to uphold God's uniqueness. In the scheme of Hermogenes, matter threatens to compete with God. But if God alone is eternal and cannot be diminished or improved, his rank is established. It all comes back to the Rule of Faith and the guarantee that God's supremacy gives of the restoration of the good. Tertullian can make surprising capital out of this supremacy. Immutability does not serve the interests of distancing God from the world and setting him apart in motionless bliss. On the contrary, it supports God's goodness. God must be eternally and consistently good; his goodness must be natural and rational, as well as perfect.[23] Marcion's God was imperturbable and listless, unable to

---

[20]D.K. McKim, in a review of J.M. Mulder, ed., *The Power of God* (Philadelphia, Westminster Press, 1983), *Princeton Seminary Bulletin*, NS 6 (1985) 148–149.

[21]Ibid.

[22]Ibid.

[23]J.M. Hallmann, 'The Mutability of God: Tertullian to Lactantius', *Theological Studies* 42 (1981) 373–393 (pp. 376–377).

condemn, a goodness inappropriate to God because it is unresponsive to the changing situations of human beings.[24] As Joseph Hallmann points out, Tertullian seems here to view God as mutable and passible, as someone who does indeed have personal feelings (*Adv Marc* I 25), open to both sensations (*sensibus*) and affections (*adfectibus*).[25] To be fully God and good, God must experience some form of hatred against evil.[26]

Whatever else Tertullian intends by his doctrine of immutability, it does not aim to support God's remoteness and non-involvement in the world, though Hallmann must surely be correct in arguing that Tertullian does not satisfactorily and critically work out his position, nor always recall the positions he has adopted previous to any particular polemic.[27] Here, then, the way is prepared for the negotiation of immutability apparent in Tertullian's incarnation doctrine. We have already seen how Tertullian was not prepared to exclude God's saving involvement in the world. Perhaps by paradox, perhaps by the omnipotence of God, God can remain totally consistent and yet take on a full fleshly and vulnerable humanity. Whatever the philosophical inadequacies of the apologist's approach, it is clear that divine omnipotence does not entail, for him, divine distance. This rules out a common complaint represented well by the statement, 'It is the most powerful ruler who is safe and secure from external threat. Impassibility guarantees omnipotence.'[28] For Tertullian, the opposite was the case. Omnipotence guaranteed the possibility of vulnerability.

The third major area of modern unease concerns the ecclesiastical aspects of Tertullian's treatment of power. Exaggerated ecclesiastical power, it is often felt, springs from exaggerated theological power. Where the Church opts for a legal basis to ecclesial authority, it 'is framed according to a monarchical understanding of Church authority. Many Catholics question the primatial claims of unelected officials and advocate a greater role for the clergy and laity in the selection of bishops.'[29] Reformed churches may enjoy more democracy in the way of elections and non-professional representation in their centres of decision-making, yet often a mystique surrounds its clergy, with the well-cultivated suspicion that clericalism is really God's way of sharing power. According to one theory, where a ruling group cannot command authority on the basis of recognition and support, techniques of power

[24]Ibid. 377.
[25]Ibid.
[26]Ibid. 377–378.
[27]Ibid. 379.
[28]W.C. Placher, op. cit. 136.
[29]P. Granfield, 'Legitimation and Bureaucratisation of Ecclesial Power', J. Provost and K. Walf, eds, *Power in the Church*, 86–93, 88.

come into play.[30] These do not need the doctrine of apostolic succession to support them and can operate to a greater or lesser degree in most denominations. These, and other ways of exercising influence over people, are many and varied.[31] However, it has to be agreed that the abuse or imbalance of power is likely to draw strength from any doctrinal justification, and centuries of static teaching on the *potestas* of any individual and group will have taken their toll. How far has the ecclesial concentration and centralisation of power taken its legitimation from the second-century Church, and does Tertullian represent an example of this?

So far as the second century is concerned, there are conflicting views but some probabilities emerge. Even a Catholic authority is ready to say that with the writings of the early second-century Ignatius, the 'monarchical bishop is not necessarily in place'.[32] Ignatius is still arguing the case for it. Monarchical authority arose not from a standard first-century pattern, but from the threat of heresies such as Gnosticism.[33] An episcopalian writer agrees with this and believes that in the late first century work of Clement of Rome the 'monepiscopacy' only points to an elected chairman of the college of presbyters and a presbyterial pattern of ordination, 'with the consent of the Church.'[34] Even later, Irenaeus espouses a monepiscopacy, but a presbyterial succession.[35] John E. Lynch maintains that this philosophy prevailed as far as the fifth century.[36] Moreover, throughout the second century apostolicity had more to do with the Rule of Faith and the teaching office than with administrative authority. The apostolic faith was the original faith, not one sustained by a direct successor to the apostles.

---

[30]This is the theory most associated with the well-known M. Foucault, as summarised by K. Gabriel, 'Power in the Contemporary Church in the light of sociological theories: Max Weber, Michel Foucault and Hannah Arendt', J. Provost and K. Walf, *Power in the Church*, 29–38 (p. 37). There is considerable interest amongst ecclesiologists in Foucault.

[31]W. Siebel singles out sexual attraction and money amongst the more common ways: 'The Exercise of Power in Today's Church', J. Provost and K. Walf , eds, *Power in the Church*, 39–49 (p. 27).

[32]R. Eno, *Teaching Authority in the Early Church*, Wilmington, Michael Glazier, 1984, 25.

[33]Ibid.

[34]E.G. Jay, 'From Presbyter-bishop to Bishops and Presbyters. Christian Ministry in the Second Century: A Survey', *Second Century* 1 (1981) 125–162 (pp. 132–136).

[35]Ibid. 152–153. For texts illustrative of Irenaeus on episcopacy and apostolicity, see Eno, op. cit. 42–50.

[36]J.E. Lynch, 'Power in the Church: An Historico-Critical Survey', J. Provost and K. Walf, eds, *Power in the Church*, (pp. 13–22).

We have seen that this was the standpoint of Tertullian too. True, we have observed that imperial language crept into his description of God's power and that legalistic descriptions of sin and forgiveness dog his work. These are generally believed to lay the basis for the western penitential system and, consequently, for the exercise of expansive powers by the clergy. But what about the doctrinal, legal, spiritual and administrative powers (the Roman *potestas*) that came to have such a determinative role in the later western Church? Did Tertullian himself fashion the office itself in terms of power and authority as a kind of 'imperium'?

A typically modern response has come from H. von Campenhausen. He judges that Irenaeus does not 'contemplate a special sacramental "character" of the episcopate, nor does he ever stress the authority of the bishops' and that Tertullian's approach is not essentially different.[37] True, Tertullian was himself a layman, but he had a high, rigorous view of the discipline of the Church. From *De fuga* 11 and *De praes* 41 in particular, von Campenhausen notes that Tertullian ascribed no dogmatic privileges to the episcopate.[38] In addition, teachers who hold no office act with a spiritual authority of their own.[39] The main function of the episcopate is to guard the apostolic truth encapsulated in the Rule of Faith. Tertullian too, a layman, is a teacher and inflexible on the orthodox truth. It has priority over office, even though he in fact respects, in principle, the governing and teaching authorities.[40] The granting of the '*Pax*' in Tertullian's penitential thought is a matter for decision for the whole church.[41] We have already commented upon the subversion of the rights of the bishops which occur in Tertullian's Montanist phase.[42] In brief, Tertullian does not appeal to naked authority, being a rational debater, and does not convert his imperial-sounding terminology into an argument for an office which is itself some kind of *imperium*.

What Tertullian did not do, other factors were to do in the later development of the Church. It was Cyprian who introduced the sacral

---

[37]H. von Campenhausen, *Ecclesiastical Authority and Spiritual Power in the Church of the First Three Centuries*, London, A. & C. Black, 1969, 72 and 75. See also D.J. Rankin, 'Tertullian's Consistency of Thought on Ministry', E.A. Livingstone, ed., *Studia Patristica*, Vol. XXI, Leuven, Peeters Press, 1989 (pp. 270–276).

[38]Ibid. 174–175.

[39]Ibid. 175, 228. The latter gives the support texts.

[40]Ibid. 211–212.

[41]Ibid. 217. The textual authority is *De paen* 9, *De pudic* 22.

[42]Handled by von Campenhausen, op. cit. 228.

powers to the officer's powers,[43] and it was the securing of 'forgiveness for a Church that had known sin' that finally came to strengthen the status of the bishop.[44] It has also been suggested that the rise of the see of Constantinople, near the centre of privilege and patronage, finally introduced a juridical freight for ecclesiastical positions of pre-eminence.[45] The development of more cordial Church-State relations after the accession of Constantine and the need to negotiate with a world-wide empire brought on 'the development of a universal ecclesiastical power', a style of episcopacy concerned with global issues, and a loss of the autonomy and lay-consent in appointments.[46] The dangers of converting the authority of Church leaders from that of pastoring and teaching into that of sacral *potestas* or of the interdict[47] have been well taken by modern writers. That step can be the result of centralisation where the Church is numerous and wealthy, or it can be from conceiving power as vicarious from the Lord of the Church.[48] These developments were not altogether unconnected with Tertullian's thought. His part, however, was to exalt penance, discipline and legal rigorism to such a degree that the character of Church leadership later came to be stated in defensive, juristic and sacramentalist terms. This lent strength to the increasing need for the authority amongst the clergy in later times to carry out such a task. It is an interesting illustration of the influence exercised by soteriology over ecclesiology. All the same, the development of ministry was not a necessary extension of Tertullian's use of the power-theme but was brought on by other external factors. It is not irrelevant that '*potestas* in the sense of official authority is never used by Tertullian with reference to the official ecclesiastical positions of the clergy, especially of the episcopate'.[49] The point is that there is no evidence of a necessary logical progression from Tertullian's doctrine of divine power to the development of an authoritarian power-driven structure of ministry in the Church.

The final modern issue arising from Tertullian's theology of power concerns its impact upon the role of women in the Church. The main concern centres upon the doctrine of creation. It is commonly argued

[43]Von Campenhausen, op. cit. 270.

[44]Ibid. 236.

[45]B.E. Daley, 'Position and Patronage in the Early Church: The Original Meaning of "Primacy of Honour"', *Journal of Theological Studies* NS, 44 (1993) 527–553.

[46]Lynch, op. cit. 15.

[47]J. Provost and K. Walf, eds, *Power in the Church*, xvii–xix.

[48]Ibid. The writers also, it should be said, believe that the same conviction can be a protection against abuse of power.

[49]A. Beck, op. cit. 63ff., and cited by von Campenhausen, op. cit. 233.

that the doctrine of almighty *creatio ex nihilo* has emphasised the dualism of spirit and nature and, more particularly, of spirit and flesh. Male-dominated theology has associated the male with the superior 'spirit', the female with the inferior 'flesh', and has then vilified the 'flesh' as the source of so many evils. An abuse of the environment has fitted in comfortably with this dualistic and unsympathetic treatment of the physical world.[50] From here one can blame Christian doctrinal orthodoxy for the whole inglorious history of the treatment of women by men in the Church, and perhaps in society in general. And who was more orthodox than Tertullian?

It is tempting to develop a counter-thesis that where such dualistic connections have been made we are looking not at a cause of male oppressiveness, but at a result and disreputable rationalisation of it. But we are more concerned to ask if the theological connections are logically necessary and to exploit Tertullian as an obvious yardstick. At the outset it looks promising. He was an early exponent of 'creation from nothing', and he stressed the power factor. He opposed the appointment of women to the episcopacy. He is famous for alleged misogyny, and in particular for berating women for their adverse effect on male welfare. In his hands marriage was damned with faint praise. Tertullian, if anyone, will provide a control instance of the analysis outlined above.

Another circumstance is in our favour. Tertullian's views on women have attracted the attention of researchers and particularly of some women scholars. A number of conclusions are emerging. F. Forrester Church was one of the first to challenge the claim that in Tertullian is found a dualism of flesh and spirit issuing in a dualism of woman and man. Tertullian calls the flesh the 'hinge of salvation' (*De res* 8). For him, the flesh that lives in Christ is already a new substance (*De pudic* 6).[51] Of course, flesh and spirit are sometimes contrasted, as in martyrdom. But this does not show that weakness and strength are the respective attributes of women and men, for women also have strength in the glorious field of martyrdom.[52] The notorious 'devil's gateway' passage

---

[50]The feminist case for this diagnostic reconstruction has been well summarised by G. Jantzen, 'Who Needs Feminism?'. Jantzen names Origen and Augustine as guilty parties (p. 340), but not any writer earlier than this even though the *creatio ex nihilo* considerably pre-dates Origen. For one of many examples of the influence of this type of diagnosis upon even Catholic theologians, see W.M. Thompson, *The Jesus Debate. A Survey and Synthesis*, New York, Paulist Press, 1985, 414–424.

[51]F. Forrester Church, 'Sex and Salvation in Tertullian', *Harvard Theological Review* 68 (1975) 83–101 (pp. 88–89). See also a useful summary of Tertullian's vindication of the 'flesh' in E. Osborn, *The Emergence of Christian Theology*, Cambridge University Press, 1993, 234–235.

[52]Ibid. 97.

(*De cult fem* I 1, enjoining modesty of dress upon women because otherwise they become the gateway to sin for men) is balanced by others which either place the blame for sin upon man and woman equally, or on Adam as the sole source of human evil.[53] The perception that Tertullian sees the image of God only in the male can be cleared up by reference to the Irenaean distinction between 'image' and 'likeness'. The former is external and peripheral. The latter is internal, spiritual, central and the possession of all, male and female alike, when they come to Christ.[54] And although Tertullian opposed the appointment of women to episcopal office, he held that women may have the same 'advancement to the dignity of judging as men.'[55] So, the famous 'gateway' passage can mislead us. The misogyny looks like a 'mythogyny'! All the same, we should hardly today call Tertullian's attitude towards relations between the sexes healthy. His millennial outlook and expectation of an early end to the world greatly sobered his view of life producing a sympathy for celibacy.[56] This was probably aggravated by his obsession with the *disciplina*. It is not misogyny which underlies his attitudes on sex but moral rigorism. This meant that in his Montanist phase Tertullian could accept the prophecy (of a woman!) that sexual abstinence increases a person's receptivity to the revelatory activity of the Holy Spirit (*De exhort* 10, 11). He quite failed to appreciate the new freedoms and dignity that the New Testament implied for women. However, he was not a misogynist and did not feel threatened by the prominence of such women as Prisca in the Montanist movement. It is perhaps significant that his overzealous protection of office concerned the order responsible, in his mind, mainly for teaching and orthodoxy. But prophesying ranked high in his thinking and, in his Montanist phase, was sometimes even raised above the episcopate. He never closed prophecy to women.

All the same, if Tertullian is not a woman-hater, yet it would be a flattering understatement to say that he did nothing for their

---

[53]Ibid. 83–88. See *De cult fem* I 1; *De jejunio* 3; *Adv Marc* II 8; *De pat* (*passim*); *De test* 3. However, we cannot afford to forget the discreditable impact of even one discussion like that of the 'Devil's gateway' passage. Its unworthy motivation has been well exposed and summarised by M.R. Miles, 'Patriarchy as Political Theology: The Establishment of North African Christianity', L. Rouner, ed., *Civil Religion and Political Theology*, Boston University Press, 1986, 169–186. She has some fine and timely observations. However, the article does not put key texts sufficiently into context nor take account of the work, for example, of F. Forrester Church (n. 51 above) as well as other writers. It is significant that, apart from Timothy Barnes, the only modern writer appearing in the footnotes is Elizabeth S. Fiorenza.

[54]Ibid. 90–91.

[55]Ibid. 99. See *Adv Val* 32.

[56]E. Carnelly, 'Tertullian and Feminism', *Theology* 92, 1989 (31–35).

advancement in the ranks of the clergy. We have seen no evidence that a theological dualism underlies this position. It would be enough to say that it was simply the legacy from earlier writings and practice which accounts for his stance here. Other influences have been blamed. Feminist writers have claimed that a major pull in thinking about Church order in the second century was the public patriarchal structure of the Roman empire, but this has been found not to be so in Irenaeus, for instance.[57] It has also been suggested that the household model of the Church's life, inherited from the New Testament, was giving way to a more political model betrayed in Tertullian's legal terminology. This view rests on Tertullian's reference to the rights of clergy (*ordo ecclesiasticus*) to baptise, teach, offer eucharist and restore to fellowship after penance.[58] We have seen, however, that in Tertullian these are also the privileges of the Church as a whole and of all believers as priests.[59] Certainly, we know that Tertullian was very interested in good order, though we are far from sure that he regarded the Roman empire as a model of it.[60] Another pressure was the prevailing concern for orthodoxy and the burden laid on the clergy to give attention to teaching the Rule of Faith. In an atmosphere where apostolicity meant doctrinal continuity, the preservation of Christian truth was considered their most important role.[61] At the same time, the Church was becoming a public body and needed credible officials to speak for it. The attitude of non-Christians to the Church's public agents worked against the appointment of women since the public civil scene was closed to them.[62] The Church, it has been said, had missed an opportunity to exploit the

---

[57]V. Burrus, 'Hierarchalization and Genderization of Leadership in the Writings of Irenaeus', E.A. Livingstone, ed., *Studia Patristica*, Vol. XXI, Leuven, Peeters Press, 1989, 42–48 (especially 42, 48 but also *passim*). The writer believes that a different model of student and teacher prevailed in Irenaeus, rather than a political model. It, therefore, did not involve monopoly of power but empowerment and was open to women.

[58]K.J. Torjesen, 'Tertullian's "political ecclesiology" and women's leadership' in E.A. Livingstone ed., *Studia Patristica*, Vol. XXI, Leuven, Peeters Press, 1989, 277–282 (pp. 278–279). The refinement that the clergy constitute a rank similar to the *ordo senatorius* (cited from E. Herrmann) does not seem to have any support in the texts studied above in connection with Tertullian's view of authority.

[59]See Rankin, op. cit. and even Torjesen herself, op. cit. 280.

[60]Torjesen, op. cit. 278, citing Tertullian's advice that the clergy must not use their rank 'as if they were part of an imperium', though this hardly shows, as she claims, that ministries had already become legal rights and privileges.

[61]Jay, op. cit. 152.

[62]Torjesen, op. cit. 279–281.

freedoms it could have brought to women.[63] More light is needed on Tertullian's motives and impulses to settle the full story. What is clear is that his negative statements towards women do not signal a theological deduction from various dualisms. They are not, therefore, to be blamed on the *creatio ex nihilo*. For that reason, although lamentable, their effects are not irreversible. Their appearance is not legitimised from the Rule of Faith nor from traditional Christian theism. Other historical factors, strengthened by male complacency and prejudice, can account for them. In an ideal world, Tertullian's own theology could have conditioned him differently. His was a long battle to defend the dignity of the flesh on the grounds of God's good and powerful willing it into being. In his better moments he glimpsed the equality and affirmation of gender that this implied.

Tertullian's teaching: a verdict

In answer to modern criticisms, then, the data before us warn against treating the ancient Christian doctrine of creation as the scapegoat for wrongs at last receiving attention. The historical setting exercised a powerful pull, understandably or not, on Christian attitudes. It was not the essentially Christian elements which created these wrongs but the failure of its best exponents fully to shake off the more injurious contemporary influences: Greek dualism, male vested interest, the Roman obsession with empire, exaggerated asceticism and other such movers of human history. The doctrine of creation can be detached from the abuses of power and allowed to stand on its own without those ill effects.

In conclusion, the basis for Tertullian's approach to the world, and God's power over it, lay in great measure in the Bible itself, not excluding the New Testament. We cannot take beliefs thought by many to be unacceptable today and bury them in Tertullian's backyard. Israel had long thought of God as originator of everything and dependent on nothing. The belief in law, judgement and a kingdom of God came to a new uncompromising sharpness in the New Testament account of Jesus' own teaching. Equally, loyalty and service to Jahweh very quickly in the New Testament took the form of loyalty and service to Jesus. This discipleship came with an undiluted and unconditioned character. It fed the martyrs. No Latin theology invented these themes, and they already enjoyed prominence in the Greek apologists. However, other factors aggravated the undue emphasis evolving in Tertullian's treatment of the doctrine of God. The inadequacy of the power-key for wider theological questions finally came to exposure in Tertullian's handling of the

[63]Miles, op. cit.

doctrine of the Trinity. Yet, his claim to be in a sense the last of the Greek apologists also remains intact, and, insofar as the early apologists lead back to New Testament Christianity, Tertullian is still a force to be reckoned with. Laying the axe to his work may be laying it to some of the roots of the tree and so destroying the very virtues which those who wield the axe are anxious to recover.

Bibliography

Primary Sources

For the Latin text of Tertullian use was made of the edition in the series *Corpus Christianorum, Series Latina*, Turnholt, Brepols, 1954. However, I have mainly followed the translations offered by E. Evans and T.R. Glover, sometimes departing from their rendering where I thought this was justified. Occasionally, I have modified the translations in the series, Ante-Nicene Fathers, republished over a number of years by W. Eerdmans, simply because many readers have access to it. Other texts have been consulted and in some cases, use made of accompanying introduction or commentary.

Arbesmann, R., Daley, E.J., & Quain, E.A., *Tertullian: Disciplinary Moral and Ascetical Works*, New York, Catholic University of America Press, 1959

Evans, E., *Tertullian Adversus Marcionem*, Oxford, Clarendon Press, 1972

Tertullian's Homily on Baptism. The Text edited, with an Introduction, Translation and Commentary, London, SPCK, 1964

Tertullian's Treatise on the Incarnation. The Text edited with an Introduction, Translation and Commentary, London, SPCK, 1956

Tertullian's Treatise Against Praxeas. The Text edited, with an Introduction, Translation and Commentary, 1948, London SPCK

Tertullian's Treatise on the Resurrection. The Text edited with an Introduction, Translation and Commentary, London, SPCK, 1970

Fredouille, J.-C., *Contre les Valentiniens*, Tome II, *Commentaire et Index*, Paris, Centre National de la Recherche Scientifique, 1975

Glover, T.R., *Tertullian, Apology, De Spectaculis*, London, Heinemann, 1960

Grant, R.M., *Theophilus of Antioch. Ad Autolycum, Text and Translation*, Oxford, Clarendon Press, 1970

Keble, J., *Five Books of St Irenaeus Against Heresies*, London, J. Parker & Co., 1872

Mahé, J.-P., *Tertullien: La chair du Christ, Introduction, Texte Critique, Traduction et Commentaire*, Paris, Centre National de la Recherche Scientifique, 1975

Nielsen, J.T., *Irenaeus of Lyons Versus Contemporary Gnosticism – A Selection From Books I and II of Adversus Haereses*, Leiden, E.J. Brill, 1977

Refoulé, R.F., *Tertullien. Traité de la prescription contre les hérétiques. Introduction, texte critique, et notes*, Paris, Les Éditions du Cerf, 1957

Robertson, A. & Donaldson, J., *The Writings of the Fathers Down to AD 325*, Vol. 1, *The Apostolic Fathers, Justin Martyr, Irenaeus* (in the series, *Ante-Nicene Library*, Edinburgh, 1867. Republished as *Ante-Nicene Fathers*, Grand Rapids, Michigan, W.B. Eerdmans, 1979)

Saint, W.P. Le, *Tertullian, Treatises on Marriage and Remarriage*, London, Longmans, Green & Co., 1951

   Treatises on Penance. On Penitence and On Purity. Translated and Annotated, London, Longmans Green & Co., 1959

Smith, J.P., *St Irenaeus. Proof of the Apostolic Preaching, Translated and Annotated*, London, Longmans, Green & Co., 1952

Waszink, J.H., *De Anima, Edited with Commentary*, Amsterdam, J.M. Meulenhoff, 1947

   Tertullian, The Treatise Against Hermogenes, Translated and Annotated, London, Longmans Green & Co., 1956

Secondary Sources

Aeby, P.G., *Les missions divines de Saint Justin à Origène, Paradosis 12, Études de littérature et de théologie anciennes*, Fribourg, University Press, 1958

Alès, A. d', *La Théologie de Tertullien*, Paris, G. Beauchesne, 190

Armstrong, A.H., Review of E.P. Meijering, *Tertullian contra Marcion. Gotteslehre in der Polemik Adversus Marcionem I-III*, Leiden, E.J. Brill, 1977, in *Journal of Theological Studies*, NS 29 (1978) 556–557

Armstrong, G.T., *Genesis in Die Alten Kirche, Beitrage zur Geschichte der Biblischen Hermeneutik 4*, Tübingen, J.C.B. Mohr (Paul Siebeck) 1962

Arnold, E.V., *Roman Stoicism*, Cambridge University Press, 1911 (re-issued, London, Routledge & Kegan Paul, 1958)

Ayers, R.H., *Language, Logic and Reason in the Church Fathers. A Study of Tertullian, Augustine and Aquinas*, New York, Lubrecht & Cramer, 1979

'Tertullian's "Paradox" and "Contempt For Reason" Reconsidered', *Expository Times* 87 (1976) 308–311

Aziza, C., *Tertullien et le Judaisme*, Paris, Faculté des Lettres et des Sciences Humaines de Nice, 1977

Balfour, I.L.S., *The Relationship of Man to God. From Conception to Conversion in the Writings of Tertullian*, PhD thesis, Edinburgh, 1980

Barnes, T.D., 'Tertullian the Antiquarian', E.A. Livingstone, ed., *Studia Patristica*, Vol. XIV, Berlin, Akademie-Verlag, 1976, 3–20

Tertullian, A Historical and Literary Study, Oxford, Clarendon Press, 1971

Bauer, W., *Orthodoxy and Heresy in Earliest Christianity*, Philadelphia, Fortress Press, 1964

Beck, A., *Römisches Recht bei Tertullien und Cyprian. Eine Studie zur Frühen Kirchenrechtsgeschichte*, Halle, Max Niemeyer, 1930

Bender, W., *Die Lehre über den Heiligen Geist bei Tertullian*, München, M. Heuber, 1961

Bentivegna, J., 'A Christianity without Christ by Theophilus of Antioch', E.A. Livingstone, ed., *Studia Patristica*, Vol. XIII, Berlin, Akademie-Verlag, 1975, 107–30

Bissels, P., 'Die frühchristliche Lehre vom Gottesreich auf Erden', *Trierer Theologische Zeitschrift* 84 (1975) 44–47

Blackman, E.C., *Marcion and His Influence*, London, SPCK, 1948

Blank, J., 'The Concept of "Power" in the Church: New Testament Perspectives', J. Provost and K. Walf, eds, *Power in the Church. Concilium* 197 (1988) 3–10

Botte, B., 'Oikonomia: Quelques emplois spécifiquement chrétiens', *Corona Gratiarum, Miscellenea Patristica, Historica, et Liturgica* (for E. Dekkers), Bruges, M. Nijhoff, 1975

Boyle, O'Rourke, 'Irenaeus' Millennial Hope: A Polemical Weapon', *Recherches de Théologie Ancienne et Médiévale* 36 (1969) 5–16

Braun, R., *Deus Christianorum. Recherches sur le vocabulaire doctrinal de Tertullien*, Paris, Publications de la Faculté des Lettres et Sciences Humaines d'Alger XLI, 1962

Review of G.L. Bray, 'The Legal Concept of *Ratio* in Tertullian', *Vigiliae Christianae* 31 (1977) 94–116, 'Chronica Tertullianea', (1977), *Revue des Études Augustiniennes* 24 (1978) 323–324

Review of C. Moreschini's 'Tradizione e innovazione nella
  pneumatologie di Tertulliano', in 'Chronica Tertullianea', *Revue
  des Études Augustiniennes* 27 (1981) 329
Review of C.A.B. Stegman, 'The Development of Tertullian's
  Doctrine *Spiritus Sanctus*', (A Dissertation: Southern Methodist
  University 1979) 'Chronica Tertullianea', *Revue des Études
  Augustiniennes* 27, (1981) 328–329
Bray, G.L., 'The Filioque Clause in History and Theology', *Tyndale
  Bulletin* 34 (1983) 91–114
The Doctrine of God, Leicester, IVP, 1993
Holiness and the Will of God. Perspectives on the Theology of Tertullian,
  London, Marshall, Morgan & Scott, 1979
'The Legal Concept of *Ratio* in Tertullian', *Vigiliae Christianae* 31
  (1977) 94–116
'The Patristic Dogma', P. Toon and D. Spiceland, eds, *One God in
  Trinity*, London, Marshall Morgan & Scott, 1980
Burkill, T.A., *The Evolution of Christian Thought*, Ithaca, Cornell
  University Press, 1971
Burrows, M.S., 'Christianity in the Roman forum: Tertullian and the
  apologetic use of history', *Vigiliae Christianae* 42 (1988) 206–235
Burrus, V., 'Hierarchalization and Genderization of Leadership in the
  Writings of Irenaeus', E.A. Livingstone, ed., *Studia Patristica*, Vol.
  XXI, Leuven, Peeters Press, 1989, 42–48.
Cantalamessa, R., 'The Development of the Concept of a Personal God
  in Christian Spirituality', *Concilium* 103 (1977) 57–66
'Tertullien et la formule christologique de Chalcédoine', F.L. Cross,
  ed., *Studia Patristica*, Vol. IX, Berlin, Akademie-Verlag, 1966,
  139–50
Campenhausen, H. Von, *Ecclesiastical Authority and Spiritual Power in
  the Church of the First Three Centuries*, London, A. & C. Black,
  1969
The Fathers of the Latin Church, London, A. & C. Black, 1964
Cardman, F.J., *Tertullian on the Resurrection* (Dissertation, Yale
  University), New Haven, Connecticut, 1974 (microfilm)
Carnelly, E., 'Tertullian and Feminism', *Theology* 92 (1989) 31–35
Carpenter H.J., 'Popular Christianity and the Theologians in the Early
  Centuries', *Journal of Theological Studies*, NS 14 (1963) 294–310
Chadwick, H., *Early Christian Thought and the Classical Tradition*,
  Oxford, Clarendon Press, 1966
'Freedom and Necessity in Early Christian Thought about God',
  Concilium 166 (1983) 8–13
Church, F. Forrester, 'Sex and Salvation in Tertullian', *Harvard
  Theological Review* 68 (1975) 83–101.

Claesson, G., *Index Tertullianeus* (3 vols), Paris, Études Augustiniennes, 1974–1975

Clercq, V.C. De, 'The Expectation of the Second Coming of Christ in Tertullian', F.L. Cross, ed., *Studia Patristica* Vol. XI, Berlin, Akademie-Verlag, 1972, 146–151

Cochrane, C.N., *Christianity and the Classical Tradition, A Study of Thought and Action from Augustus to Augustine*, Oxford University Press, 1957

Colish, M.L., *The Stoic Tradition From Antiquity To The Early Middle Ages*, II: *Stoicism in Christian Latin Thought Through the Sixth Century*, Leiden, E.J. Brill, 1985

Congar, Y., 'Classical Political Monotheism and the Trinity', *Concilium* 143. *Religion in the Eighties*, Edinburgh, T. & T. Clark, 1981, 31–36

Cook, E.D., 'Weak Church – Weak God', N.M. de S. Cameron, ed., *The Power and Weakness of God*, Edinburgh, Rutherford House, 1990, 69–92

Cooper, C., 'Chiliasm and the Chiliasts', *Reformed Theological Review*, 1970, 11–21

Daley, B.E., 'Position and Patronage in the Early Church: The Original Meaning of "Primacy of Honour"', *Journal of Theological Studies*, NS 44 (1993) 527–553

Daniélou, J., *A History of Early Christian Doctrine*, Vol. III: *The Origins of Latin Christianity*, London, Darton Longman & Todd, 1977. 'La typologie millenariste de la Semaine dans le Christianisme primitif', *Vigiliae Christianae* 2 (1948) 1–16

Davies, J.G., 'Tertullian, *De Resurrectione Carnis* LXIII: A Note on the Origins of Montanism', *Journal of Theological Studies*, NS 6 (1955) 90–94.

Decarie, V., 'Le Paradoxe de Tertullien', *Vigiliae Christianae* 15 (1961) 23–31

Demougeot, H., 'Paganus, Mithra et Tertullien', F.L. Cross, ed., *Studia Patristica*, Vol. III, Berlin, Akademie-Verlag, 1961, 354–365

Dillon, J., *The Middle Platonists. A Study of Platonism 80 BC to AD 220*, London, Duckworth, 1977

Dörrie, H., 'Der Johannesprolog in der frühchristlichen Apologetik', *Kerygma und Logos. Beiträge zu den geistesgeschichtlichen Beziehungen zwischen Antike und Christentum. Festschrift fur C. Andresen*, Göttingen, Vandenhoeck/Ruprecht, 1979

Drexler, H., 'Maiestas', *Aevum* 30 (1956) 195–212

Eno, R., *Teaching Authority in the Early Church*, Wilmington, Michael Glazier, 1984

Evans, E., 'Tertullian's Theological Terminology', *Church Quarterly Review* 139 (1944) 56–77

Evans, R.F., *One and Holy. The Church in Latin Patristic Thought*, London, SPCK, 1972

'On the Problem of Church and Empire in Tertullian's Apologeticum', E.A. Livingstone, ed., *Studia Patristica* Vol. XIV, Berlin, Akademie-Verlag, 1976, 21–36

Ferguson, E., 'Canon Muratori, Date and Provenance', E.A. Livingstone, ed., *Studia Patristica*, Vol. XVII/II, Oxford, Pergamon Press, 1982, 677–683

'The Terminology of Kingdom in the Second Century', E.A. Livingstone, ed., *Studia Patristica*, Vol. XVII/II, Oxford, Pergamon Press, 1982, 669–676

Fiddes, P.S., *The Creative Suffering of God*, Oxford, Clarendon Press, 1988

Finé, H., *Die Terminologie der Jenseitsvorstellungen bei Tertullian. Ein Semasiologischer Beitrag zur Dogmengeschichte des Zwischenzustandes*, Bonn, Hanstein, 1958

Florovsky, G., 'Eschatology in the Patristic Age: An Introduction', K. Aland & F.L. Cross, eds, *Studia Patristica*, Vol. II/II, Berlin, Akademie-Verlag, 1957, 235–250

Ford, L., 'The Rhetoric of Divine Power', *Perspectives in Religious Studies* 14 (1987) 233–238

Forster, P.R., 'Divine Passibility and the Early Christian Doctrine of God', N.M. de S. Cameron, ed., *The Power and Weakness of God*, Edinburgh, Rutherford House, 1990, 23–51

Fortman, E.J., *The Triune God: A Historical Study of the Doctrine of the Trinity*, London, Hutchinson, 1972

Fredouille, J.-C., *Tertullien et la conversion de la culture antique*, Paris, Etudes Augustiniennes, 1972

Frend, W.H.C., 'Church and State. Perspective and Problems in the Patristic Era', E.A. Livingstone, ed., *Studia Patristica*, Vol. XVII/II, Oxford, Pergamon Press, 1982, 38–54

'Open Questions Concerning the Christians and the Roman Empire in the Age of the Severi', *Journal of Theological Studies*, NS 30 (1979) 318–320

Review of J.-C. Fredouille's *Tertullien et la conversion de la culture antique*, in *Journal of Theological Studies*, NS 24 (1973) 249–251

Gabriel, K., 'Power in the Contemporary Church in the light of sociological theories: Max Weber, Michel Foucault and Hannah Arendt', J. Provost and K. Walf, eds, *Power in the Church*, *Concilium* 197 (1988) 29–38

Gager, John G., 'Marcion and Philosophy', *Vigiliae Christianae* 26 (1972) 53–59

Gerlitz, P., *Ausserchristliche Einflüsse auf die Entwicklung des Christlichen Trinitätsdogmas, zugleich ein Religions– und Dogmengeschichtlicher*

Versuch zur Erklärung der Herkunft der Homousie, Leiden, E.J. Brill, 1963

Gilson, E., *History of Christian Philosophy in the Middle Ages*, New York, Random House, 1955

Glover, T.R., *The Conflict of Religions in the Early Roman Empire*, London, Methuen, 1909

Gonzalez, J.L., 'Athens and Jerusalem Revisited: Reason and Authority in Tertullian', *Church History* 43 (1974) 17–25

Granfield, P., 'Legitimation and Bureaucratisation of Ecclesial Power', J. Provost and K. Walf, eds, *Power in the Church, Concilium* 197 (1988) 86–93

Grant, R.M., 'The Chronology of the Greek Apologists', *Vigiliae Christianae* 9 (1959) 25–33

Miracle and Natural Law in Graeco-Roman and Early Christian Thought, Amsterdam, North-Holland Publishing Co., 1952

'Review of Carl Becker's "Apologeticum"', *Vigiliae Christianae* 9 (1959) 254–256.

'Theophilus of Antioch to Autolycus', *Harvard Theological Review* 40 (1947) 227–256

Griffin, R., *God, Power and Evil: A Process Theodicy*, Westminster Press, Philadelphia, 1976

Grillmeier, E., *Christ in Christian Tradition*, Vol. 1 *From the Apostolic Age to Chalcedon (451)*, London, Mowbrays, 1975

Groh, D.E., 'Upper-Class Christians in Tertullian's Africa', E.A. Livingstone, ed., *Studia Patristica*, Vol. XIV, Berlin, Akademie-Verlag, 1976, 41–47

Guerra, A.J., 'Polemical Christianity; Tertullian's Search for Certitude', *Second Century* 8 (1991) 109–123

Hall, S.G., 'The Christology of Melito, A Misrepresentation Exposed', E.A. Livingstone ed., *Studia Patristica*, Vol. XIII, Berlin, Akademie-Verlag, 1975, 154–168

'Praxeas and Irenaeus', E.A. Livingstone, ed., *Studia Patristica*, Vol. XIV, Berlin, Akademie-Verlag, 1976, 145–147

Hallmann, Joseph M., 'The Mutability of God: Tertullian to Lactantius', *Theological Studies* 42 (1981) 373–393

Hamman, A., 'Resurrection du Christ dans l'antiquité chrétienne (II)', *Revue des Sciences Religieuses* 40 (1975) 292–318, and 50 (1976) 1–24

Hanson, R.P.C., *The Attractiveness of God. The Doctrine of God in the Early Church*, London, SPCK, 1973

'The Doctrine of the Trinity Achieved in AD 381', *Scottish Journal of Theology* 36 (1983) 41–57

Hatch, E., *The Influence of Greek Ideas and Usages upon the Christian Church*, London, Williams & Norgate, 1901

Heron, A., '"Logos, Image, Son": Some Models and Paradigms in Early Christology', R.W.A. McKinney, ed., *Creation, Christ and Culture: Studies in Honour of T.F. Torrance*, Edinburgh, T. & T. Clark, 1976, 43–62

Higgins, A.J.B., 'The Latin Text of Luke in Marcion and Tertullian', *Vigiliae Christianae* 5 (1951) 1–42

Hinchliff, P., review of Daniélou's *Origins of Latin Christianity*, in *Journal of Theological Studies*, NS 29 (1978) 222–224

Holland, D.L., 'Some Issues in Orthodox-Gnostic Christian Polemic', E.A. Livingstone, ed., *Studia Patristica*, Vol. XVII/I, Oxford, Pergamon Press, 1982, 214–222

'The Third Article of the Creed', E.A. Livingstone, ed., *Studia Patristica*, Vol. XIII, Berlin, Akademie-Verlag, 1975, 189–197

Hornus, J.-M., 'Etude sur la pensée politique de Tertullien', *Revue d'Histoire et de Philosophie Religieuses* 38 (1958) 1–38

Jacobs, J.W., 'The Western Roots of the Christology of St Hilary of Poitiers: A Heritage of Textual Interpretation', E.A. Livingstone, ed., *Studia Patristica*, Vol. XIII, Berlin, Akademie-Verlag, 1975, 198–203

Jantzen, G., 'Who Needs Feminism?', *Theology* 93 (1990) 339–343.

Jay, E.G., 'From Presbyter-bishop to Bishops and Presbyters. Christian Ministry in the Second Century: A Survey', *Second Century* 1 (1981) 125–162

Karpp, H., *Schrift und Geist bei Tertullian*, Gütersloh, C. Bertelsmann Verlag, 1955

Kelly, J.N.D., *Early Christian Doctrines*, London, A. & C. Black, 1973

Kenny, A., *The God of the Philosophers*, Oxford, Clarendon Press, 1979

Kereszetes, P., 'Tertullian's *Apologeticum*: A Historical and Literary Study', *Latomus: Revue des Études Latines* 25 (1966) 124–133

Kim, D.S., 'Irenaeus of Lyons and Teilhard de Chardin: A Comparative Study of "Recapitulation" and "Omega"', *Journal of Ecumenical Studies* 13 (1976) 69–94

Klein, R., *Tertullian und das römische Reich*, Heidelberg, Carl Winter, 1968

Kretschmar, G., *Studien zur frühchristlichen Trinitätstheologie. Beiträge zur Historischen Theologie*, Tübingen, Paul Siebeck, 1956

Kropatscheck, F., Review of Schlossmann's '*Persona* und *prosopon* im Recht und im christlichen Dogma', in *Zeitschrift für Kirchengeschichte* 27 (1906) 363–364

Labriolle, P. de, *La Crise Montaniste*, Paris, Leroux, 1913

Lampe, G.W.H., 'Early Patristic Eschatology', *Scottish Journal of Theology, Occasional Papers*, No. 2, London, Oliver & Boyd, 1957, 1–35

Langlois, P., 'La théologie de Tertullien', *Bibliothèque de l'école des Chartes* 125 (1967) 438–444

Langstadt, E., 'Tertullian's Doctrine of Sin and the Power of Absolution in "de pudicitia"', K. Aland & F.L. Cross, eds, *Studia Patristica*, Vol. II, Berlin, Akademie-Verlag, 1957, 251–257

Lawson, J., *The Biblical Theology of St Irenaeus*, London, Epworth, 1948

Leeming, B., *Principles of Sacramental Theology*, London, Longmans, 1963

Lewis, C.T. & Short, C., *A Latin Dictionary*, Oxford, Clarendon Press, 1962

Lohse, B., *A Short History of Christian Doctrine*, Philadelphia, Fortress Press, 1966

Lonergan, B., *The Way to Nicea: the Dialectical Development of Trinitarian Theology*, London, Darton Longman & Todd, 1976

McGiffert, A.C., *The God of the Early Christians*, Edinburgh, T. & T. Clark, 1924

   A History of Christian Thought, Vol. 1: *The West from Tertullian to Erasmus*, London, Scribner, 1933

Mackey, J.P., *The Christian Experience of God as Trinity*, London, SCM, 1983

MacMullen, R., 'Tertullian and the "National" Gods', *Journal of Theological Studies*, NS 26 (1975) 405–410.

Mahé, J.-P., 'Elements de doctrine hérétiques dans le De carne Christi de Tertullien', E.A. Livingstone, ed., *Studia Patristica*, Vol. XIV, Berlin, Akademie-Verlag, 1976

Mansfeld, J., *Studies in Later Greek Philosophy and Gnosticism*, I.1, London, Variorum Reprints, 1989,

Margerie, B. de, *La Trinité Chrétienne dans L'Histoire*, Paris, Beauchesne, 1975

Markus, R.A., 'Trinitarian Theology and the Economy', *Journal of Theological Studies*, NS 9 (1958) 101–116

Marsh, T., 'The Holy Spirit in Early Christian Teaching', *Irish Theological Quarterly* 45 (1978) 101–116

Meijering, E.P., 'Bermerkungen zu Tertullians Polemik gegen Marcion (*Adversus Marcionem* 1.1–25)', *Vigiliae Christianae* 30 (1976) 81–108

   'God, Cosmos, History. Christian and Neo-Platonic Views on Divine Revelation', *Vigiliae Christianae* 28 (1974) 248–276

   Tertullian contra Marcion. Gotteslehre in der Polemik Adversus Marcionem I-III, Leiden, E.J. Brill, 1977

   'Wie Platonisierten Christen? Zur Grenzziehung zwischen Platonismus, Kirchlichem Credo und Patristischer Theologie', *Vigiliae Christianae* 28 (1974) 15–28

Moingt, J., 'Le Problème du Dieu Unique chez Tertullien', *Revue des Sciences Religieuses* (1970) 337–362

Théologie Trinitaire de Tertullien, Vol. 1: *Histoire, Doctrine, Méthodes*, Paris, Aubier, 1966

Théologie Trinitaire de Tertullien, Vol. 2: *Substantialité et individualité. Étude du vocabulaire philosophique*, Paris, Aubier, 1966

Théologie Trinitaire de Tertullien, Vol. 3: *Problématiques de l'unité et des processions*, Paris, Aubier, 1966

Théologie Trinitaire de Tertullien, Vol. 4: *Répertoire Lexicographique et Tables*, Paris, Aubier, 1969

Miles, M.R., 'Patriarchy as Political Theology: The Establishment of North African Christianity', L. Rouner, ed., *Civil Religion and Political Theology*, Boston University Press, 1986, 169–186

Moltmann, J., 'The Motherly Father. Is Trinitarian Patripassianism Replacing Theological Patriarchalism?', *Concilium* 143 (1981) 51–56.

Morgan, J., *The Importance of Tertullian in the Development of Christian Dogma*, London, Kegan Paul, 1928

Muller, M., and Halder, A., 'Person', in *Sacramentum Mundi: An Encyclopedia of Theology*, London, Burns & Oates, 1969

Nedoncelle, M., 'Prosopon et Persona dans l'antiquité classique. Essai de billan linguistique', *Revue des Sciences Religieuses* 22 (1948) 277–299

Niebuhr, H.R., *Christ and Culture*, New York, Harper & Row, 1956

Oeyen, C., 'Die Lehre der göttlichen Krafte bei Justin', F.L. Cross, ed., *Studia Patristica*, Vol. XI, Berlin, Akademie-Verlag, 1972, 215–221

O'Hagan, A.P., *Material Re-Creation in the Apostolic Fathers*, Berlin, Akademie-Verlag, 1968

O'Malley, T.P., 'The Opposition *caelestia-terrena* in Tertullian', F.L. Cross, ed., *Studia Patristica*, Vol. X, Berlin, Akademie-Verlag, 1970, 190–194

Tertullian and the Bible. Language–Imagery–Exegesis, Utrecht, Van de Vegt N.V., 1967

Osborn, E., *The Beginning of Christian Philosophy*, Cambridge University Press, 1981

The Emergence of Christian Theology, Cambridge University Press, 1993, 234–235

'The Love Command in Second-Century Christian Writing', *Second Century* 1 (1981) 223–243

Otto, S., 'Der Mensch als Bild Gottes bei Tertullian', *Münchener Theologische Zeitschrift* 10 (1959) 276–282

Pannenberg, W., 'Person', F.H. Kettler, ed., *Die Religion in Geschichte und Gegenwart*, Tübingen, J.C.B. Mohr (Paul Siebeck) 1962

Pederson, O., 'The God of Space and Time', *Concilium* 166 (1983) 14–20

Pelikan, J., *The Christian Tradition, A History of the Development of Doctrine*, Vol. 1. *The Emergence of the Catholic Tradition (100–600)*, Chicago University Press, 1971

Pelland, G., 'Dans l'attente de la résurrection: un thème central de l' évangelisation dans l'Église ancienne', *Science et Esprit* 28 (1976) 125–146

Perkins, P., 'On the Origin of the World (CG II 5): A Gnostic Physics', *Vigiliae Christianae* 34 (1980) 36–46

Piault, B., 'Tertulllien a-t-il été subordinatien?', *Revue des Sciences Philosophiques et Théologiques* 47 (1963) 181–204

Placher, W.C., 'Narratives of a Vulnerable God', *Princeton Seminary Bulletin*, NS 14 (1993) 134–151

Pollard, T.E., *Johannine Christology and the Early Church*, Cambridge University Press, 1970

Prestige, G.L., *God in Patristic Thought*, London, SPCK, 1975

Patterson, L.G., *God and History in Early Christian Thought. A Study of Themes from Justin Martyr to Gregory the Great*, London, A. & C. Black, 1967

Rankin, D.J., 'Tertullian's Consistency of Thought on Ministry', E.A. Livingstone, ed., *Studia Patristica*, Vol. XXI, Leuven, Peeters Press, 1989, 270–276

Ring, T.G., *Auctoritas bei Tertullien, Cyprian und Ambrosius*, Cassiciacum, Band XXIX, Würzburg, Augustinus, 1975

Roberts, R.E., *The Theology of Tertullian*, London, J.A. Sharp, 1924

Saint, W.P. Le, '*Traditio* and *Exomologesis* in Tertullian', F.L. Cross, ed., *Studia Patristica*, Vol. VIII, Berlin, Akademie-Verlag, 1966, 414–419

Schoedel, W.R., 'A Neglected Motive for Second Century Trinitarianism', *Journal of Theological Studies*, NS 31 (1980) 356–367

Schlossmann, S., 'Tertullian im Lichte Der Jurisprudenz', *Zeitschrift für Kirchengeschichte* 27 (1906) 251–275

Sider, R.D., *Ancient Rhetoric and the Art of Tertullian*, Oxford University Press, 1971

   'On Symmetrical Composition in Tertullian', *Journal of Theological Studies*, NS 24 (1973) 405–423

   'Tertullian on the Shows', *Journal of Theological Studies*, NS 29 (1978) 339–365

Siebel, W., 'The Exercise of Power in Today's Church', J. Provost and K. Walf, eds, *Power in the Church*, *Concilium* 197 (1988) 39–49

Spanneut, M., *Le Stoïcisme des Pères de L'Église de Clément de Rome à Clément d'Alexandrie*, Paris, Éditions Du Seuil, 1957

Stead, G.C., 'The Concept of Divine Substance', *Vigiliae Christianae* 29 (1975) 1–14

Divine Substance, Oxford, Clarendon Press, 1977

'Divine Substance in Tertullian', *Journal of Theological Studies*, NS 14 (1963) 46–63

Steinmann, J., *Tertullien*, Paris, Chalet, 1967

Stockmeier, P., 'Gottesverständnis und Saturnkult bei Tertullian', E.A. Livingstone, ed., *Studia Patristica*, Vol. XVII/I, Oxford, Pergamon Press, 1982, 829–835

'Zum Verhältnis von Glaube und Religion bei Tertullian', F.L. Cross, ed., *Studia Patristica*, Vol. XI, Berlin, Akademie-Verlag, 1972, 242–246

Telfer, W., *The Office of A Bishop*, London, Darton Longman & Todd, 1962

Timothy, H.B., *The Early Christian Apologists and Greek Philosophy*, Assen, Van Gorcum and Co., 1973

Torjesen, K.J., 'Tertullian's "political ecclesiology" and women's leadership' in E.A. Livingstone ed., *Studia Patristica*, Vol. XXI, Leuven, Peeters Press, 1989, 277–282

Van den Brink, J., 'Reconciliation in the Early Fathers', E.A. Livingstone, ed., *Studia Patristica*, Vol. XIII, Berlin, Akademie-Verlag, 1975, 90–106

Van der Geest, J.E.L., *Le Christ et l'Ancien Testament chez Tertullien. Recherche terminologique*, Nijmegen, Dekker, Van de Vegt, 1972

Van der Nat, P.G., 'Tertullianea', Part I, *Vigiliae Christianae* 18 (1964), 14–31

Van Unnik, W.C., 'Der Ausdruck, "In den Letzten Zeiten" bei Irenaeus', *Neo-Testamentica et Patristica (Festschrift to O. Cullmann)*, Leiden, E.J. Brill, 1962, 292–304

'Two Notes on Irenaeus', *Vigiliae Christianae* 30 (1976) 201–213

Verhoeven, T., '*Monarchia* Dans Tertullien, *Adversus Praxean*', *Vigiliae Christianae* 5 (1951) 43–48

Visser, A.J., 'A Bird's Eye View of Ancient Christian Eschatology', *Numen, International Review For the History of Religions* 14 (1967), 4–22

Vokes, F.E., 'Penitential Discipline in Montanism', E.A. Livingstone, ed., *Studia Patristica*, Vol. XIV, Berlin, Akademie-Verlag (1976) 62–76

Wallace-Hadrill, D.S., *Christian Antioch. A Study of Early Christian Thought in the East*, Cambridge University Press, 1982

Warfield, B.B., *Studies in Tertullian and Augustine*, Oxford University Press, 1930

'Tertullian and the Beginnings of the Doctrine of the Trinity', *Princeton Theological Review* 4 (1906) 1–36

Waszink, J.H., 'Observations on Tertullian's Treatise Against Hermogenes', *Vigiliae Christianae* 9 (1955) 129–147

Webb, C.C.J., *God and Personality*, London, Allen & Unwin, 1918

Wiles, M.F., *The Making of Christian Doctrine. A Study in the Principles of Early Doctrinal Development*, Cambridge University Press, 1967

Wingren, G., *Man and the Incarnation: A Study in the Biblical Theology of Irenaeus*, Edinburgh/London, Oliver & Boyd, 1959

Wink, W., *Engaging the Powers: Discernment and Resistance in a World of Domination*, Minneapolis, Fortress Press, 1992

Naming the Powers. The Language of the New Testament (*The Powers*, Vol. 1), Philadelphia, Fortress Press, 1984

Wolfson, H.A., *The Philosophy of the Church Fathers*, Vol. 1: *Faith, Trinity, Incarnation*, Cambridge, Mass., Harvard University Press, 1964

Wood, S., 'The Eschatology of Irenaeus', *Evangelical Quarterly* 41 (1969) 30–41

Young, F.M., 'Atonement and Theodicy: Some Explorations', E.A. Livingstone, ed., *Studia Patristica*, Vol. XIII, Berlin, Akademie-Verlag, 1975, 330–333

Zeegers-Vander Vorst, Nicole, 'La création de l'homme (Gn 1.26) chez Théophile d'Antioch', *Vigiliae Christianae* 30 (1976) 258–267

Indexes

Selected Index to Tertullian's Works

Selected Subject Index

Rutherford Studies in Historical Theology
(Uniform with this Volume)

Religious Radicalism in England 1535–1565
C.J. Clement

The author here provides a kaleidoscopic analysis of the radical reforming spirits of the key generation of the English Reformation. Those hitherto lumped together as Anabaptists are here carefully characterized in their own individuality. This comprehensive study ends with an account of the theology of the English Radicals in their relationship to Lollardy, Anabaptism and Anglicanism.

1997 / 0-946068-44-5 / 448pp

'Rigide Calvinisme in a Softer Dresse'
The Moderate Presbyterianism of John Howe (1630–1705)
David Field

This attractive presentation of the thought of John Howe depicts him as treading a middle path between the rationalizing moralism of Anglicanism and the unflinching high Calvinism of the Westminster divines. Howe restated Calvinism in the face of searching criticisms. This study compares Howe with the Cambridge Platonists, with John Wilkins and with Richard Baxter, and throws light on the theological decline of English Presbyterianism before and after 1700. An important contribution to understanding of early nonconformity.

2000 / 0-946068-75-5

The Erosion of Calvinist Orthodoxy
Seceders and Subscription in Scottish Presbyterianism
Ian Hamilton
1990 / 0-946068-34-8 / 212pp

Tertullian's Theology of Divine Power
Roy Kearsley

This book traces Tertullian's handling of key doctrines and draws implications for some of today's crucial issues: Trinitarian faith, the status of the creation, gender, authority and power abuse. It takes the agenda of early Christian thought seriously and finds it profoundly relevant for today.

1999 / 0-946068-61-5 / 190pp

The Federal Theology of Thomas Boston
A.T.B. McGowan

In this volume, the author seeks to demonstrate that Thomas Boston was a consistent federal Calvinist, true to the *Westminster Confession of Faith*. The volume interacts with the discussions of the day, in relation to the nature and development of federal theology, but also with current debates in the Calvin/Calvinism argument.

1997 / 0-946068-59-3 / 248pp

An Ecclesiastical Republic
Church Government in the Writings of George Gillespie
W.D.J. McKay

This work is the first full-length study of George Gillespie, a key figure in the Westminster Assembly. It considers the nature of the kingship of Christ, the place of the Old Testament in ecclesiology and the structures and leadership of the Church, all issues of contemporary concern.

0-946068-60-7 / 340pp

The Doctrine of Holy Scripture in the Free Church Fathers
Nicholas Needham
1991 / 0-946068-39-9 / 157pp

Thomas Erskine of Linlathen
His Life and Theology 1788–1837
Nicholas Needham
1990 / 0-946068-29-1 / 543pp

Church and Creed in Scotland
The Free Church Case 1900–1904 and its Origins
Kenneth Ross
1988 / 0-946068-30-5 / 412pp

Thomas Chalmers: Enthusiast for Mission
The Christian Good of Scotland and the Rise of the Missionary Movement
John Roxborogh

Enthusiast for Mission tells afresh the inspiring story of Scottish church leader Thomas Chalmers, his conversion, parish experiments, support for overseas mission and struggle for spiritual autonomy up to and beyond the Disruption of the Church of Scotland in 1843.

1999 / 0-946068-49-6 / 338pp

Thomas Boston as Preacher of the Fourfold State
Philip Graham Ryken

Thomas Boston, the Presbyterian pastor-theologian, was the most widely published Scottish author of the eighteenth-century. *Thomas Boston as Preacher of the Fourfold State* is a historical, practical, and theological study of his preaching ministry, understood against the background of patristic, medieval, Reformation and Puritan theology.

1999 / 0-946068-72-0 / 372pp

Revelation of the Triune God
In the Theologies of John Calvin and Karl Barth
Sang-Hwan Lee

This study grapples in depth with the structure of two of the most influential works in Western theology – Calvin's *Institutes* and Karl Barth's *Church Dogmatics*. It concentrates on the Trinitarian revelation of God as the critical source of Calvin's *summa*, while also clarifying his hold on the oneness of God. In both Calvin and Barth Dr Lee highlights the indispensability of faith for theology. He insists on Barth's freedom from philosophical structural principles such as Hegel's idealism. A comparison of Calvin and Barth argues that differences are a matter of emphasis, particularly in their distinctive nuancing of the threeness and oneness of God. This is a powerful exposition of Reformed revelational theologies.

2000 / 0-946068-74-7

Rutherford Studies in Contemporary Theology
(Uniform with this Volume)

Transcendence and Immanence in the Philosophy of Michael Polanyi and Christian Theism
R.T. Allen
1992 / 0-7734-1635-8 / 196pp

The Problem of Polarization
An Approach Based on the Writings of G.C. Berkouwer
Charles Cameron
1992 / 0-7734-1633-1 / 597pp

Actuality and Provisionality
Eternity and Election in the Theology of Karl Barth
John Colwell
1989 / 0-946068-41-0 / 323pp

God Does Heal Today
Pastoral Principles and Practice of Faith Healing
Robert Dickinson
1995 / 0-946068-56-9 / 343pp

**A Study in the Concept of Transcendence
in Contemporary German Theology**
Loránt Hegedüs
1991 / 0-946068-40-2 / 112pp

The God Who Fights
The War Tradition in Holy Scripture
Charles Sherlock
1993 / 0-7734-1653-6 / 445pp

The Sacrament of the Word Made Flesh
The Eucharistic Theology of Thomas F. Torrance
Robert Stamps

Professor Tom Torrance is arguably the greatest living British theologian. Dr. Stamps' focus on the Eucharist in his prolific and wide-ranging corpus demonstrates the unity of academy and church, of scholarship and worship, in his theology. This work takes us to the very heart of Torrance's theology. Since Christ is the primal sacrament of all God's reality and truth to the church, the Eucharist for Torrance is essentially 'the sacrament of the Word made flesh'. Because Eucharist interacts with other dominant concerns in his thought, this study is a fine introduction to the structural articulation of Torrance's powerful theology.

2000 / 0-946068-76-3

Rutherford House
P O Box 300
Carlisle Cumbria
CA3 0QS UK

Web: www.paternoster-publishing.com